Advance praise for *Design Works*

"There's little doubt that business design, the great mash-up of design thinking and business strategy, is the next-generation innovation tool. This book handily demystifies design thinking, and deftly weaves it into the best thinking on creating superior strategy by offering a step-by-step how-to guide. *Design Works* is indispensable."
— **Stephen Dull** *Vice President Strategy and Innovation, VF Corporation*

"Leave it to Heather Fraser to distill the power of Business Design into a DIY playbook accessible to anyone charged with driving innovation! The same tools included in this book have helped my team double-down to begin creating innovation aimed at satisfying the needs of our consumers and shoppers, helping us to look beyond just those products we bring to market today."
— **Ann Mukherjee** *Senior Vice President and Chief Marketing Officer, Frito-Lay*

"Business Design teaches leaders how to engage these principles in tackling chronic problems and initiating change in the public or private sector. This is an eminently useful book that teaches the 'how-to,' and, more importantly, discusses why these methods are important."
— **Dr Robert S. Bell** *President and Chief Executive Officer, University Health Network*

"In the hands of the forward-thinking CEO, leadership team, or corporate strategist, this book brings to life the insights, principles, and practice of Business Design for competitive advantage. It comes at the perfect time as enterprises are forced to rethink, recreate, and redesign their futures. Winning is not a chance outcome — it is by design!"
— **Danny Naidoo** *IT Global Head of Innovation, Old Mutual Group*

DESIGN WORKS

How to Tackle Your Toughest Innovation
Challenges through Business Design

Heather M.A. Fraser

DESIGN WORKS

HOW TO TACKLE YOUR TOUGHEST
INNOVATION CHALLENGES THROUGH
BUSINESS DESIGN

UNIVERSITY OF TORONTO PRESS
TORONTO BUFFALO LONDON

© Heather M.A. Fraser 2012
Rotman-UTP Publishing
University of Toronto Press
Toronto Buffalo London
www.utppublishing.com
Printed in Canada

ISBN 978-1-4426-1390-4

Printed on acid-free, 100% post-consumer recycled paper with vegetable-based inks.

Library and Archives Canada Cataloguing in Publication

Fraser, Heather M.A., 1957–
Design works : how to tackle your toughest innovation challenges through business
design / Heather M.A. Fraser ; foreword by Roger L. Martin

Includes bibliographical references and index.
ISBN 978-1-4426-1390-4

1. Organizational change. 2. Business planning. I. Title.

HD58.8.F73 2012   658.4'06   C2012-900208-9

University of Toronto Press acknowledges the financial assistance to its publishing
program of the Canada Council for the Arts and the Ontario Arts Council.

Canada Council **Conseil des Arts**
for the Arts **du Canada**

ONTARIO ARTS COUNCIL
CONSEIL DES ARTS DE L'ONTARIO

University of Toronto Press acknowledges the financial support of the Government
of Canada through the Canada Book Fund for its publishing activities.

Dedicated to the memory of my parents,
Elizabeth and Herbert

PART 1

THE PRACTICE OF BUSINESS DESIGN

PART 2

TOOLS & TIPS FOR THE PRACTICE OF BUSINESS DESIGN

FOREWORD

Roger L. Martin

Dean, Rotman School of Management

It is pretty clear that in the twenty-first century many organizations are moving beyond analytics. These companies have come to realize that more analysis generally means more of the same — at a time when they are longing for something different. Often "something different" means being more like the companies that are the very best in their industries — the ones that are defining what is new and better in their realm — whether that is Apple, Jet Blue, or GE.

This has led many such organizations to look more closely at the world of design. As distinct from analysis, design holds an alluring promise. It puts forward fresh new techniques like ethnographic research, brainstorming, and rapid prototyping. For business people, these are exciting new techniques that provide hope for new insights and fresh ideas.

The challenge for those who embrace the tools of design is to graft all of this newfound creative output onto established organizational processes — processes that are generally not geared to include new creative ideas. Existing processes tend to ensure that the organization keeps doing the same thing that it has being doing all along. This is not a bad thing: exploitation of what currently exists is what pays for the exploration of what might be. Yet the organizational processes that defend the status quo are what cause so many design initiatives to hit the proverbial wall. As with most things in life, possession is nine-tenths of the law, and the existing processes have possession of the organization.

So, the new Business Design tools need to be made plug compatible with the existing infrastructure and strategy formulation processes. If the focus is entirely on creative discovery without consideration of how it converts to a winning strategy, creativity is practically useless. As Heather Fraser says in this book: "If a big idea isn't translated into a clear strategy to guide your efforts and investments, it may never be realized." Conversely, if the focus is entirely on traditional processes — on what is currently doable and provable — then nothing creative will influence the business strategy. A balance is required.

That is where Business Design comes in. Its origin lies in the challenge that Procter & Gamble faced in 2005. In 2001, newly appointed CEO A.G. Lafley — who saw huge potential for design to transform P&G's business — appointed Claudia Kotchka to be P&G's first Vice-president of Design Innovation and Strategy. Under her leadership, the company started investing heavily in design initiatives. But several years into the effort, it was clear that in order for the fruits of all of that great design work to be realized in winning marketplace initiatives, design needed to be utilized throughout the organization. In 2005, Claudia asked me to help her with that challenge. Together with Heather Fraser, we took the very best thinking on design — from our colleagues on the effort, David Kelley (who would go on to found Stanford's d.school) and Patrick Whitney (Dean of Illinois Institute of Technology's Institute of Design) — and figured out how to seamlessly integrate it with strategy development at P&G, something with which I was intimately familiar.

The framework we created for bringing about that integration was the 3 Gears of Business Design: Empathy & Deep Human Understanding, Concept Visualization, and Strategic Business Design. It worked so well at P&G that we brought it back to the Rotman School and established Rotman DesignWorks, headed up by Heather.

In the subsequent years, Heather has honed and refined the methodologies, and Rotman DesignWorks has grown the capability of students and executives to practice Business Design. This has become an important and distinctive part of the Rotman School experience, an experience that enhances the lives and careers of our students. In addition, it has helped business leaders around the world tackle their toughest challenges and design new strategies for success.

This book tells the story of the 3 Gears of Business Design, simply and practically. Its goal is to provide an easy-to-use guide for organizations that are eager to harness the power of Business Design. The good news is that any organization that is willing to try can learn the Business Design process. I hope you enjoy the read and benefit from the creative solutions the process so often generates.

INTRODUCTION
The Journey of DesignWorks
and the Intent of This Book

In the summer of 2004, a team gathered in the Dean's conference room at the Rotman School of Management to explore a game-changing opportunity for education and industry. In the room were: Roger Martin, visionary Dean of the Rotman School of Management at University of Toronto; David Kelley, co-founder of innovation consultancy IDEO, who later went on to establish Stanford's d.school; Patrick Whitney, now Dean of the Institute of Design at the Illinois Institute of Technology; and myself, Heather Fraser, a career-long business innovator who had just recently joined Roger in his quest to transform business education. Our goal, as stated at the time by Roger, was "to fuse together the complementary pieces of the puzzle provided by design education and business education in order to create the discipline of Business Design. Together and independently, these academic institutions would become partners with leading companies to enhance and transform the ways in which they compete."[1]

The idea behind Business Design was to integrate the best practices of business with design-inspired methods to help organizations tackle their innovation challenges. Our approach would focus on helping them identify new opportunities to better meet customer needs, generate more break-through solutions for their customers, and translate those big ideas into a focused and implementable business strategy that would increase their odds of innovation success. This was the inspiration for the 3 Gears of Business

Design: Empathy & Deep Human Understanding, Concept Visualization, and Strategic Business Design.

In 2005, Roger brought our group an exciting opportunity to put this thinking to work. One of the world's most admired companies believed that design thinking could play a key role in unlocking innovation, defining more competitive strategies, and ultimately delivering greater value to the market and the enterprise. That company was Procter & Gamble.

A.G. Lafley, Procter & Gamble's CEO at the time, wanted to propel P&G's level of innovation and growth into the future by pushing the value of design beyond its current application in products and packaging. To lead this quest, he appointed Claudia Kotchka, a P&G business leader with a strong track record for results and a passion for design, as the company's first Vice-president of Design Innovation and Strategy. Claudia called on Roger, a long-time strategic advisor to P&G, to bring together a team capable of creating a scalable program that would infuse design thinking into the strategic planning and innovation process of the enterprise. Our integrated framework was first put to the test with a Global Hair Care Team in December 2005. This initial program prototype was refined and our work continued under the guidance of Cindy Tripp, now Director of Design Thinking in P&G's Global Design Function. Design Thinking Workshops were scaled and ultimately rolled out to the enterprise globally to fortify P&G's reputation as one of the most innovative companies in the world.

Concurrent with scaling the P&G program, we launched a full-scale Rotman DesignWorks initiative to advance and expand the practice of Business Design. Our ambition was to turn this design-inspired approach into a methodology that could be applied in a more rigorous manner to full-scale innovation projects. To that end, we initiated another pilot in 2006 – a Summer Fellowship Program at Rotman DesignWorks. In collaboration with the Ontario College of Art and Design, we brought together teams of business and industrial design students to work on real-life projects. This allowed us to begin to deepen the practice and validate the usability of a variety of new Business Design frameworks and tools. That readied us to take on our next challenge – to translate this program into an MBA degree course at Rotman through a pilot of the Business Design Practicum. That gave us more opportunities to test drive our methodology on a wide range of projects and hone our teaching tools, leading to our first full-scale research project for Princess Margaret Hospital, featured in this book. By 2007, we were convinced that we had something that brought a fresh, practical, and strategic approach to innovation.

For the next five years, we provided a combination of teaching, research, and practice activities across a variety of business sectors (private sector, social initiatives, associations, and public sector organizations, locally and internationally) and to an increasing number of students and executives. We have had the honor of working with many blue-chip companies including P&G, Nestlé, Pfizer, Medtronic, Whirlpool, Frito-Lay, and SAP, as well as public institutions and government teams. We've also conducted projects that span many sectors and countries. More recently, we have expanded our educational initiatives into one of the more innovative and forward-thinking countries in the world — Singapore. Our program there entails an ongoing broad-scale program for Singaporean business executives, commissioned by the Singapore government agency SPRING, and a comprehensive "teach the teachers" Certification Program to transfer Business Design knowledge and skills to that country's first polytechnic, Singapore Polytechnic. Their ambition is to play an important role in Singapore's national innovation agenda, which calls for embedding design thinking broadly into their workforce.[2]

All of these activities enabled us to build out our methodologies and test the value of Business Design with many different organizations and types of challenges. Over these seven years, we have applied Business Design to a wide range of projects, graduated five cohorts of graduate students, and trained almost 2,000 executives in this practice, from small entrepreneurial organizations to large multinational organizations, and in both public and private sectors. Through this journey, we have concluded the following:

- *Business Design is a learnable innovation discipline that can transform the way enterprise teams rise to a challenge, shape their strategies, and mobilize teams.*

- *Business Design brings out the creative side of everyone without compromising the rigor required to make a meaningful market impact in a responsible manner.*

- *This approach has proven to get to bigger ideas faster by engaging more minds in a common ambition, with the buy-in and traction required to make important things happen in a strategic and productive manner.*

- *The practice of Business Design brings a valuable balance to conventional planning and business development, and can make an important contribution to expanding opportunities and breakthrough business strategies.*

Common Enterprise Challenges

You might wonder what kinds of business and organizational challenges others have tackled through the practice of Business Design. Here are some that enterprise leaders cite as they have embarked upon their Business Design journey at Rotman DesignWorks:[3]

> "We are not different enough. The changes we are making are incremental and not innovative."

> "We are spending time and money on a lot of initiatives, but we wonder if we are investing in the right things — those that really matter to our customer."

> "We've been stumped by the same challenge for years. We can't seem to make any meaningful headway. We need a new approach."

> "We come from a volatile, saturated industry. It's hard to find ways to drive growth."

> "How can we maximize the impact of design in a risk-averse, data-driven organization?"

> "How can we create a stronger appetite to experiment, fail, and learn in market?"

> "We can't afford to always outsource the design process. How do we engage our enterprise to participate in this process to gain first-hand market insight?"

If any of these resonate with you, the practice of Business Design can give you some practical frameworks and tools to tackle these issues, from insights and ideation through to strategy and activation. This book reflects the insights, observations, questions, and feedback from a wide range of enterprises that have engaged in Business Design. It shares the key frameworks and tools that our pioneering partners and students have found most valuable in their ambitions to transform and advance businesses. It draws on the work we have done at Rotman DesignWorks — the Strategy Innovation Lab at University of Toronto's Rotman School of Management — over the past seven years to hone these practices into a learnable, repeatable methodology that can enhance the way enterprise teams work together to create new value.

How This Book Works

This book demonstrates how the practice of Business Design can help you tackle innovation challenges and realize breakthrough outcomes at every stage of development by harnessing the insights, imagination, and ingenuity that exist within your organization. You may already be intrigued by the potential for design thinking to drive enterprise innovation, growth, and competitive advantage, as presented in Roger Martin's book *The Design of Business: Why Design Thinking May Be the Next Competitive Advantage.*[4] If so, you may be keen to know what you can do to turn design thinking into actions that will help advance your business in a pragmatic fashion. This book is intended to turn design thinking into design doing and reveal how, as the title of this book asserts, *design works.*

Part one of this book is about Business Design as a practice — what it is, how it is done, and the outcomes it can yield. The practice of Business Design, as presented in this book, is anchored in the 3 Gears of Business Design, a framework for thinking about how to design new solutions and strategies. I begin with an Overview of Business Design, then move through three chapters on each of the Gears and a chapter on Preparing for Your Quest. I conclude with a chapter on Transformation, sharing learning on how to embed these practices broadly into your enterprise to enhance your innovation culture.

Most of the chapters of part one (after the Overview on Business Design) are set up as follows: A Story to illustrate the application of Business Design; a brief overview of the Goals and Activities for that phase of development; and highlights of Principles, Frameworks, and Key Mindsets to guide you through those activities. Each chapter ends with reference to the related Tools & Tips that are included in part two of the book.

Part two is a collection of Tools & Tips for applying Business Design, with some brief instructions and examples from a variety of projects. These tools can serve to enrich your discovery and development processes and, most importantly, unlock the inherent ingenuity of your enterprise teams. This collection is by no means exhaustive, but these are the Tools & Tips that others have found useful in working through Business Design as we teach and practice it at Rotman DesignWorks.

A Word on Words

Every discipline has its own nomenclature, which is often dismissed as jargon. There are a few words used frequently in this book that I have chosen for specific reasons. Here are some of these terms, and an explanation of why I use them and how you should think of them:

Value: The most important notion in Business Design, and intended in the broadest terms to mean anything of relative worth, merit, or importance — financial or otherwise.

Enterprise: Any organization that aims to create value — public, private, or not-for-profit. It reflects the spirit of any organization that is ready to undertake projects of importance or difficulty, or untried schemes. That's the spirit of Business Design, and of this book.

Stakeholders: Your end customers (consumers, customers, clients, or guests) as well as important enablers and influencers. In a comprehensive solution, many of these stakeholders will be "users" of your new solution.

Frameworks: Not to be confused with methods or tools, frameworks help anchor, prompt, or organize your thinking.

Methods: Used to refer to a methodology, a way of getting things done. This word is used interchangeably with "tools."

Outcomes: I have focused on "outcomes" rather than "results" because results, in business, are often thought of in financial terms and take time to realize. Outcomes, on the other hand, should be more immediate and tangible.

Other terms are defined as they appear, and can help foster a language of design that can signify new ways of doing, thinking, and communicating within enterprise teams.

This book should serve as an ongoing reference, not a one-time read. Its value will be determined by what you do with it and how you reflect on your outcomes and the progress you make. Here are some things you might do as you read this book, apply the principles and practices, and develop your capacity as a Business Designer.

Reflect on and assess your current state. What's your biggest challenge? Ask yourself questions like: How ahead of the game do I believe we are in terms of creating our future? What is our success rate with big, breakthrough ideas? What holds us back from getting big ideas through to the market? What factors — structural, operational, or cultural — are slowing us down?

Have a dream project in mind. Think about that challenge and define it more specifically. This may be an unfulfilled ambition or major challenge that you haven't been able to tackle for some reason — the one that seems either insurmountable or too complex to solve within your current way of working. With a real-world challenge in mind, this book will enable you to imagine how a Business Design approach can help you tackle it. Even if you don't actually work through the methodologies at this point, you might imagine how they would work in the context of your challenge as you read through this book the first time to capture the gestalt of Business Design

Limber up with workshops and experiments, and reflect. Pick a topic and organize a workshop with a willing team. Don't be afraid to experiment with methods. It is best to work through the principles of all of the 3 Gears of Business Design that are described in this book to get the most complete outcome. If you discover that one method brings a particularly fresh perspective to your development efforts, inject it into ongoing projects. This is the best way to see immediate value in your newly discovered skills. Every time you put Business Design into practice, reflect on your experience and ask yourself what was different from what you normally do and how it helped reveal new opportunities and enhance your capacity to innovate.

Take the time to do it right, and commit to action. Taking on a full project is not a quick hit; it requires time, commitment, and perseverance to realize the ultimate impact. As you work through the development process, you will discover new insights, ideas, and "quick wins" that will allow you to activate your new learning. Business Design is not only about one big "Aha!" that comes out the other end of the process; it is about generating outcomes along the way that have both immediate and longer-term impact. At every step, you should ask yourself, "What value have we brought so far, and what can we do to act on it *now*?"

Teach, Propagate, and Celebrate. Success inspires success. If you like where the practice of Business Design takes you, you can move toward expanding the practice more broadly. With some evidence of value in discoveries, breakthroughs, team dynamics, and productivity, you can begin to strategically roll out Business Design in a systematic way, and boost your own expertise in the process.

Business Design is a journey of discovery and learning that can transform the way we work. I hope you will gain inspiration from the stories in this book, as well as practical ideas on how to begin this journey within your enterprise.

Additional support and reference materials can be found at fraserdesignworks.com.

PART 1

THE PRACTICE *of* BUSINESS DESIGN

OVERVIEW *of* BUSINESS DESIGN
Creating, Delivering, and Sustaining Value

The principles of great Business Design are evident in many successful business ventures. Here is one such example that sets up some important principles and brings to life the essence of the 3 Gears of Business Design.

In 1992, I was in Vevey, Switzerland, at Nestlé's global training center on Lake Geneva. I went to help myself to a cup of coffee and discovered a coffee machine that made an incredible cup of espresso by popping one small, easy-to-use coffee capsule into the machine.

Fast-forward sixteen years. It's 2008, and I come upon a magnificent Nespresso Boutique on the Champs Elysées in Paris. I thought to myself, "How remarkable. That's the same coffee system I coveted in Vevey sixteen years ago. Have they ever come a long way." That piqued my interest in the company and compelled me not only to become a customer but to investigate what was behind the Nespresso phenomenon from a business innovation standpoint, asking: *What had they done over the years to build such momentum and distinct market success?*

Coffee is one of the most popular beverages worldwide, with a yearly consumption of more than 400 billion cups and a steady upward trend in daily coffee consumption since 1993. The growth in specialty coffees and out-of-home consumption has also risen, fueled by the proliferation of cafés, franchises, and products that compete for that special coffee moment in people's everyday lives.[5]

To a coffee connoisseur, having your own stylish espresso bar in your home and being able to make a perfect cup of coffee at the touch of a button with no fuss or cleanup is the ultimate indulgence. To have instant access to a company that caters to you as a special member of an exclusive coffee club and delivers your customized order directly to you with one phone call or a quick online order makes the relationship that much more satisfying. That's the Nespresso brand experience.

This experience begins with the moment of discovery. Entering a Nespresso Boutique for the first time is a delight to anyone with an appreciation for coffee and stylish design. Beautifully designed and inviting, it might first make you wonder if you are entering a café, a design exhibit, or a store. There is a display of brightly colored high-tech pre-filled coffee capsules, an array of well-designed machines that are part of the unique brewing system, a selection of stylish accessories, a knowledgeable Coffee Ambassador to assist you with coffee selection, and an espresso bar to let you taste for yourself.

The purchase of a Nespresso system marks the beginning of a new everyday coffee ritual and membership in the Nespresso Club. Members have access to special offers and a customer service center that fulfills requests for coffee capsules or new accessories with one phone call or through their elegant online Boutique. Members can also be reassured that the company is committed to minimizing its environmental footprint in every way, including a capsule-recycling program. Nespresso offers a delightful customer experience, from the moment of discovery and enjoying your first perfect cup of Nespresso to an ongoing relationship with a company in which the customer comes first.

Nespresso's vision to create the ultimate coffee experience for coffee lovers worldwide is delivered through a new-to-the world experience that is built around a unique and proprietary coffee system. Importantly, the company did not simply expand the technology I discovered years ago in Vevey; it enhanced the core product and built a rich, holistic customer experience around that technology. The in-house R&D team has been able to deliver a stylish and high-quality system, through collaboration with the best design companies — for example, Alessi — and manufacturing experts such as Krups and Magimix. The company has built strong brand momentum through a distinct and focused route-to-market strategy that combines sophisticated retailing, merchandising, customer relations, and a well-choreographed fulfillment center. It has shown commitment to environmental and social responsibility through the Ecolaboration initiative, which includes a capsule-recycling program and a program that helps farmers who grow and supply Nespresso coffee by teaching them best growing practices. All of that adds up to a distinct business strategy.

Since 2000, Nespresso has grown 30 percent per annum on average to sales of over $3 billion today, selling more than 20 billion coffee capsules and 12 million machines since 1986. With presence in over fifty countries, Nespresso has opened more than 200 Boutiques since 2000, with flagship stores in cities all over the world. The Nespresso Club has more than 10 million members, and growing.[6]

Nespresso's remarkable success adds them to the roster of other companies that have enjoyed long-run success in the market, including iconic companies such as Apple, Disney, Procter & Gamble, Kaiser Permanente, Nike, IKEA, Four Seasons, Nintendo, Virgin, and many others. In studying these companies, one can appreciate that there are many things these companies do well. One can also see that there are three things they *all* do exceptionally well:

1. demonstrate a deep, holistic understanding of their customers and their needs;

2. deliver distinct offerings and experiences that uniquely meet those needs;

3. engage in a distinct combination of activities that leverage their enterprise capabilities in a way that is difficult for others to replicate.

This third factor is paramount to sustained success and is what gives these enterprises a sustainable advantage over competitors. This is the essence of strategy — defined by a distinct system of enterprise activities and capabilities that allow an enterprise to win in the market, give it an edge over competition, and deliver a better return on its investment. Clear strategies and activation plans are often the missing link in innovation and likely one of the reasons that the failure rate of new product introductions and new business ventures is alarmingly high. By one measure, from innovation consultant Doblin Inc., nearly 96 percent of all innovation attempts fail to beat targets for return on investment. No wonder innovation frustration is the talk of corner offices.[7] As Roger Martin points out in his Foreword, *"If the focus is entirely on creative discovery without consideration of how it converts to a winning strategy, creativity is practically useless."* Moreover, all of these three factors must work in concert; an effective strategy calls for a relentless devotion to serving the customer, continually expanding possibilities to do so, and activating a stream of experiments and expansion initiatives with a sense of purpose and perseverance in staying the course strategically.

This is the inspiration for the core framework: the 3 Gears of Business Design. Within this framework, the discipline is aimed at helping enterprises to increase their odds of success by cultivating a deeper and more holistic customer understanding, creating more breakthrough solutions, and designing enterprise strategies to succeed.

The 3 Gears of Business Design

This is the framework we developed in 2005 to help P&G and that we have since found to be an important anchor in our enterprise programs and projects at Rotman DesignWorks. This framework helps to ensure that development pursuits are always devoted to gaining a deeper understanding of needs, creating valuable new experiences for customers, and designing more competitive strategies with a clear activation plan. Practicing the 3 Gears as a multidisciplinary collaboration has not only led to more robust solutions, it has also helped build greater organizational momentum and has fostered a more innovative culture over the longer term, as was the vision for P&G's design quest set out in the introduction. Others who have adopted the 3 Gears have found it to be a useful ongoing framework for tackling challenges, no matter how small and tactical or how big and complex they may be (see figure 1).

FIG. 1 THE 3 GEARS OF BUSINESS DESIGN

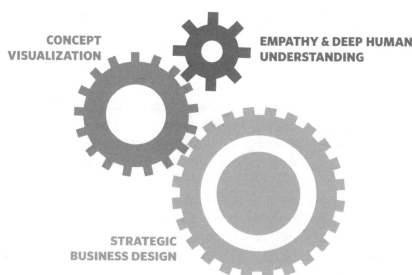

CONCEPT VISUALIZATION

EMPATHY & DEEP HUMAN UNDERSTANDING

STRATEGIC BUSINESS DESIGN

An overview of the 3 Gears of Business Design[8] follows, as well as an outline of the design-inspired methods and mindsets that can help you get the most out of the 3 Gears.

Gear 1: Empathy & Deep Human Understanding — *What's the opportunity?*

Business Design starts with empathy for others and a meaningful under-standing of people and what matters to them deeply and holistically. A deeper and more holistic understanding reveals gaps between what people need to be fully satisfied and what is currently available to them; those gaps present opportunities for adding new value to people's lives. While market reports and quantitative market research will give you a good measure of the customer characteristics, habits, and values that you believe to be important, it most often does not build empathy or contribute to a deeper understanding of the underlying motivations and unmet needs of your key stakeholders, most importantly the customer. Understanding them more holistically entails understanding them more *completely* as individuals, *apart from* the direct consumption or use of your current product or service. Con-sidering the wider activity surrounding your products and services expands your perspective on opportunities to create value in new ways.

It is also useful to understand the roles and relationships among peo-ple within the broader stakeholder system, not only the customer but also important enablers and key influencers in the equation. These important relationships will factor into your success, enabling your solution to get trac-tion and realize its full potential. This broader contextualization together with a deeper need-finding exploration helps to focus efforts on seizing untapped opportunities that will create meaningful new value for *all* stakeholders.

As a result, working through Gear 1 with methodologies that complement your current repertoire helps shed light on new opportunities and most often leads to a reframing of the problem or challenge at hand. Through this pro-cess, one often discovers that either the problem was not accurately defined or was too narrowly viewed at the outset. The process also helps inspire and motivate teams; as we have heard through our work at DesignWorks, *"Connecting with people at a deeper and more authentic level gives meaning and purpose to our work."*[9]

The outcome of this effort is a *reframing* of the opportunity before you, giving you a strong foundation for innovation and value creation as you move into Gear 2.

Gear 2: Concept Visualization — *What's the breakthrough idea?*

Generating truly breakthrough ideas that contribute to a better experience demands that you give yourself the license to openly explore new possibilities, including those that are outside your current operational paradigm. By limiting explorations to what is familiar and easily doable, organizations will limit their new ideas to those that may merely represent incremental moves, sometimes with diminishing returns. By focusing on what they need to produce or deliver as a product or service offering, they may leave gaps in the customer experience. A richer, more breakthrough experience that pushes out into novel, human-centered solutions considers the experience holistically and has greater potential to create meaningful new value.

Gear 2 leverages your renewed empathy and the need-based innovation criteria defined by Gear 1. Concept Visualization entails creating a new and more holistic, multidimensional experience through the process of imagining new possibilities. Bigger, more ambitious ideas require insight, vision, and courage — and there can be risk associated with that. By employing design-inspired principles and methodologies to explore bigger ideas early on, you can expand your vision of possibilities, gain further insight into what creates meaningful value, and refine ideas to create a distinctive vision that users value *before* you make significant investments.

The outcome of this effort is a *refreshing* of your vision with new possibilities that are dedicated to fulfilling unmet needs through a new and concretely defined experience aimed at creating more breakthrough, human-centered value.

Gear 3: Strategic Business Design — *What's the strategy to deliver the vision?*

An essential extension of the innovation process, Strategic Business Design helps you to clearly define how you will focus your enterprise's efforts and effectively activate a new vision by applying the same ingenuity and rigor you used to find a breakthrough solution to develop a strategy for implementing the solution. Many organizations have told us at DesignWorks that they have lots of ideas, but they don't know what to do with them, and how they fit with other ideas in the hopper. That's the reason that Gear 3 is the critical step toward early activation and future success.

Gear 3 entails translating a new vision into a novel business strategy, defining how you will focus your energies and build the capabilities required to make the big idea viable and valuable. If a big idea isn't translated into a clear strategy to guide your efforts and investments, it may never be realized. In Business Design, a winning strategy is defined by the unique combination of enterprise activities that comes together as a distinct system. That system is your source of competitive advantage, as you will see in the chapter on Gear 3. Once a strategy is defined, development priorities will become clearer, allowing you to focus on what you need to do to activate your strategy to deliver your breakthrough vision.

This vital gear leads to a *refocusing* of your enterprise resources on a strategy that will begin to create value early on and set you on a path for long-term, market-inspired value-creation.

While each of the 3 Gears has value on its own, the greatest return, as noted earlier, will be realized through a commitment to all 3 Gears at all times, as demonstrated by others' success. To maximize outcomes, Business Design is best practiced collaboratively across disciplines. Value comes from having many sharp minds on the project and working openly and iteratively through every gear, using the most appropriate frameworks and tools along the way to get the most out of each of the 3 Gears.

Subsequent chapters go deeper into each of the 3 Gears, with stories to illustrate what activities are involved and how the practice of Business Design plays out. Throughout this book, I also include a selection of interviews for insight and inspiration on the important ingredients of good Business Design, practiced both intuitively and explicitly.

Business Design:
Methods and Mindsets

In order to tackle these 3 Gears, you can turn to a variety of design-inspired methods and mindsets to help you increase your odds of innovation success. Through education and practice, designers develop ways of doing their work and relating to the world that have not been traditionally taught in business schools or broadly built into the best practices of an enterprise. That is not to say that many successful business people do not think like a designer; many innovative business people do so intuitively. That's often an important part of why they're successful, as is demonstrated by Nespresso and other successful enterprises. The key is to do so more mindfully and intentionally.

The practice of Business Design can help unlock innovation in any kind of business. At Rotman DesignWorks, we've applied the discipline of Business

Design to innovation challenges on food products and services, medical devices, enterprise knowledge management, marine engineering, hospital experiences, business services, healthcare systems, economic models for artisan clusters, chocolate bars, and cell phones, to name a few.

You may be asking: What are some of these design-inspired methods that can help you work through the 3 Gears? The list below outlines some of the methods demonstrated in this book that can help you design original and tangible outcomes that create new-to-the-world value across all 3 Gears:

Need finding: developing a deeper understanding of the people who matter as the focus of Gear 1, complementing quantitative analysis with more ethnographic methods like observation and listening to user stories;

Visualizing: helping others to "see" relationships, new concepts, and even new strategies in visual ways instead of relying on documents and verbal descriptions;

Iterative prototyping: translating abstract concepts into concrete prototypes — tangible representations of solutions and business models in rough form early on (before the big bucks get spent) — as a catalyst for thinking, dialogue, learning, and accelerated development;

Systems mapping: making connections, visualizing relationships, and synthesizing the way people, solutions, and enterprise systems all connect;

Collaboration: capitalizing on diverse perspectives and types of expertise within cross-disciplinary teams to create richer, more robust, and more viable outcomes;

Co-creation: inviting users and other stakeholders into the development process to gain valuable feedback and advance solutions and strategic models;

Storytelling: capturing the richness and complexities of big ideas through compelling stories so others can not only see but *feel* the impact of the vision in a holistic and human manner;

Experimentation: trying new things and testing uncertainties with the intent to learn and advance development.

I have worked on many projects over my career, including my ten years at P&G and fifteen years in the brand communications business, where these methods were put into practice in a more intuitive manner. I have observed that those who go about their work in this way often make progress faster, with earlier and broader buy-in, and ultimately with better results. Business Design is about applying these methods more broadly, deliberately, and consistently across an enterprise.

Innovation also entails having the right mindset in tackling the task at hand. Sometimes considered as the "softer" side of business, these mindsets bring important value to the innovation process across all of the 3 Gears:

Empathy: being able to see and feel what others see and feel, leading to a deeper understanding of the opportunity to better serve needs;

Openness: being receptive to new ideas, new people, and new ways of doing things, often characterized by curiosity, an active imagination, and an ability to suspend judgment;

Mindfulness: being aware of people, places, and things in order to develop deeper understanding and an expanded repertoire of reference points and position yourself to capitalize on serendipity in seizing unexpected design opportunities;

Intrinsic Motivation: being fueled by purpose and passion that come from a genuine interest, excitement, and engagement in your work;

Embracing constraints: seeing constraints as a source of creativity, to avoid trade-offs and compromises in the pursuit of the ideal solution and the most distinct enterprise strategy;

Courage and Vulnerability: putting new ideas on the table without being worried about whether the ideas are wrong or right; knowing that bad ideas in the exploration phase often lead to good ones later on in development;

Positivity and Optimism: believing in possibilities with a hopeful and even naive view of what could be, not trapped by what is today, allowing for an intuitive "leap of logic" in making the case for a new future reality;

Resilience: driving forward toward creative and productive resolutions, even in the face of minor setbacks or failures along the way.

The discipline of Business Design integrates all of these methods and mindsets into a logical and well-balanced way of doing business through the 3 Gears. As in other design disciplines, to ultimately excel in Business Design you must start with the right mindset, and apply the appropriate methods. These methods will unlock your best thinking and tap into your intuition, imagination, and ability to create original solutions (see figure 2). Experiencing a new way to think will reinforce your innovator mindset as you discover new ways to create value. Practiced on an ongoing basis, Business Design is an exercise in agility — emotionally, intellectually, and tactically.[10] Over time, these design methods will become an increasingly intuitive way to work.

FIG. 2 MINDSETS, METHODS, AND THINKING

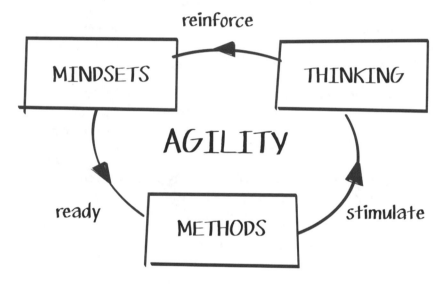

How Can Business Design Impact Strategies for Innovation and Growth?

Gear 3, Strategic Business Design, brings important value to the practice of Business Design, as it defines *how* you will deliver big ideas and enhance your competitive advantage. That's why we call our center at Rotman a *Strategy Innovation Lab.* In thinking about how Business Design helps drive innovation and growth strategies, I like to refer to a valuable strategy framework created by Roger Martin, Dean of Rotman and former Director at Monitor Company, a global strategy consulting firm. Roger Martin frames up enterprise strategy as a set of five key choices:[11]

Aspirations and Goals: What is your guiding purpose and what are your measurable goals?

Where to Play: In what market space will you play — in terms of customer segment, geography, channels, products, and services?

How to Win: What is the value proposition that will win the customer, and how will you deliver that through a distinct set of activities that will give you a sustainable competitive advantage?

Capabilities: What specific capabilities must be in place to deliver on that proposition and in what distinct combination?

Management Systems: What systems are needed to support and manage those capabilities?

When organizations come to Rotman DesignWorks to learn about Business Design, they have already set their *Aspirations and Goals* high. Business Design is for enterprises that are committed to creating and delivering increasing value to their customers and their enterprise. With high ambitions, these enterprises are looking for ways to elevate their performance by lifting them out of their current patterns and behaviors, unlocking their enterprise-wide ability to innovate and grow.

They tell us that it is often challenging for their organizations to think more openly about *Where to Play* because of a strong, deep focus on an internal product or service that can cause them to obsess within a narrow field of opportunity. This choice is often made without consideration of a broader set of possibilities. In Gear 1, a deliberate outward focus on customers to gain a deeper, more holistic understanding of their unmet needs provides a springboard for thinking more thoughtfully about the market opportunities before choosing precisely *Where to Play*. It will also give you customer insights on *How to Win*. Procter & Gamble has done this with Tide in expanding beyond the home laundry room to the segment of out-of-home fabric care through franchised Tide Dry Cleaners.

Inspired by an opportunity and the insights you gain from Gear 1, a truly breakthrough proposition calls for envisioning *How to Win* the customer through new-to-the-world solutions and holistic experiences, rather than limiting development to creating a better version of the products and services that already exist in the market. Gear 2 introduces methods to help enterprise teams push beyond what is familiar and more obviously doable, and think more intuitively and holistically about the customer experience, imagining elements beyond current enterprise capabilities.

To deliver on the proposition, Gear 3 uses visualization and prototyping methods to design a strategy on *How to Win* through a distinct combination of activities and the *Capabilities* required to carry them out. Translating a breakthrough proposition into an equally breakthrough enterprise strategy increases your odds of gaining competitive edge and enjoying better long-term returns. By contrast, organizations cite that by strictly reinforcing and perpetuating their tried-and-true model, they are running the risk of driving a less and less distinct strategy relative to that of competitors over time. To deliver the ultimate coffee experience, Nespresso's strategic advantage is defined by a distinct set of activities that entailed designing and delivering a unique coffee system, engaging a network of strategic partners, reinventing the marketing mix, and building a platform for environmental responsibility.

In managing execution and measuring results, enterprises often experience resistance to change and ideas that don't fit historically successful, deeply embedded management systems. As an extension of Gear 3, a new value-creating solution and enterprise strategy often calls for an evolution or even revolution over time in *Management Systems* to support what needs to get done and measure what matters.

The practice of Business Design can essentially help you achieve more ambitious growth goals by reframing opportunities on *Where to Play*, and refreshing your vision and strategy on *How to Win*. It has helped organizations realize the benefits of a deeper understanding of stakeholder needs (Gear 1), broader exploration of value-creating possibilities (Gear 2), and greater emphasis on creating more distinct strategies that will give them a distinct competitive advantage (Gear 3).

Business Design:
A Platform for Enterprise Transformation

As the nature of business continually changes, your competitive advantage will be determined by the strategy you design for future success, as well as the principles and practices that shape your innovation culture. An important aspect of any enterprise is its capacity to seize new opportunities and grow through every level of the enterprise. The practice of Business Design can help enhance your collective capacity to adapt and grow within an ever-shifting business and social context. Importantly, the application of design methodologies can also create immediate value within your enterprise just by introducing ways of *doing* things differently, as revisited in the final chapter of this book, on Transformation. Business Design can create value within the enterprise by:

- creating a stronger customer focus and sensitivity within the enterprise;

- giving license to explore bigger ideas in the planning process;

- stimulating collaboration, dialogue, and learning as part of development;

- creating greater alignment and productivity through clear and focused strategies.

The mindsets and skills of Business Design are also valuable at every level of your organization. As an individual, you will be better equipped to lead by harnessing the power of teams, envisioning new possibilities, and navigating the course of progress in an inspired and confident manner. As a Business Design team, you will have a greater sense of alignment and the ability to create and act on opportunities in a more productive and accelerated fashion. Business teams find they are more focused and purposeful in their pursuit of value creation because they collaborate and co-create more effectively around a common set of principles and practices. As an enterprise-wide platform, the practice of Business Design can help enhance your ability to continually seize new opportunities and gain competitive advantage (see figure 3). At the highest level, these principles and practices have the potential to fortify an innovation economy. That's what Singapore has in mind, as noted in the introduction.

FIG. 3 BUSINESS DESIGN: A PLATFORM FOR INNOVATION & GROWTH

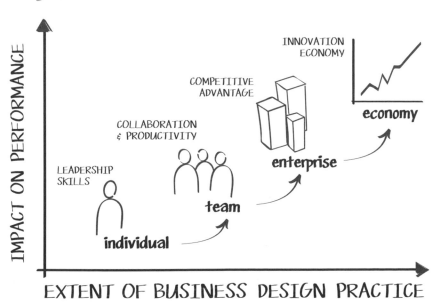

Activating the Practice of Business Design

As you move into the 3 Gears, here are some things to keep in mind:

- Business Design is, above all, a set of principles and practices revolving around the 3 Gears; it is not a rigid, linear process. At all times, a true business designer acts as an advocate for the user, a protector of the integrity and intent of the envisioned idea, and a disciplined strategist who pursues a clear path toward future success.

- At the same time, Business Design provides a framework with an expandable tool kit. You can integrate these methods into your own repertoire of methods and leverage them to boost your innovation and strategy practices. You can draw upon the methods at any stage in the discovery, development, and delivery process. Business Design is not a mechanical process, nor is it about filling in boxes or templates; it is about unlocking fresh thinking and new ideas and, in a sense, creating entirely new boxes.

- Ultimately, you will want to create your own methods for fortifying your application of Business Design, and design your own repeatable, scalable practices that fit the culture and structure of your organization.

- Business Design is an ongoing exercise in agility. Try the principles out on day-to-day projects or challenges, or use Business Design as a complete process in a long-term development project. The more you apply these principles and practices, the more intuitive they will become for you individually and collectively. The more you practice, the more you will rewire your way of thinking and working together and nurture a culture of innovation.

- You can either do a rapid run-through of the basics of Business Design in a matter of days, or stretch it out as a full-blown development process over months, or use it on an as-needed basis for big initiatives that you are working on over years.

Much of the philosophy outlined in this book is encapsulated in the following excerpt from an interview with Isadore Sharp, visionary founder of Four Seasons Hotels and Resorts, whose story is told in his book Four Seasons: The Story of a Business Philosophy.[12] *He shared his views with me on the more human side of building a business and the importance of empathy, imagination, courage, openness, and trust. It is an inspiring prelude to the practice of the 3 Gears of Business Design.*

At Four Seasons, the focus has always been and is still on the customer. And the customer is always changing. Give people what they need and are expecting, and always exceed those expectations.

For a lot of the first things that we put together, other people who had more experience would say, "You're crazy. That's going to cost you money. People don't really need it." There were a lot of naysayers. People need to have the courage to come up with something that they believe might work. *Because it also might not.* And that happened along the way. It took me five years to get the first small little motor hotel built. Five years of naysayers. People laughed me out of the room, and wouldn't give me the time of day. But it didn't deter me. I could see how it would work, even though they would point up all the reasons why it might not.

Being innovative calls on your ability to believe in yourself and in your own opinions, in spite of the fact that nobody else might agree with you. Because you do run up against a lot of very, very smart people. It takes courage to do the right thing and be prepared for the consequences.

We decided to position ourselves in the industry by establishing our advantage through service. Such a soft target — how do you describe it and say it in a way that's going to be different? In order to be the best, we would have to have a workforce that was able to give the customers that special experience, making our service different. That had to be through the efforts of the people who met the customer, dealt with the customer, and talked with them — whether it's the sales person, the doorman, or the housekeeper.

What makes our service special comes from a culture, and a culture can't be mandated. It has to grow from within. Could we create a competent, qualified workforce that would be better than our competitors based on an ethical credo? That, again, was laughed at. Some said, "This is foolishness. It's not a philosophy class we're running here." But we created a workforce based on an ethical credo — the Golden Rule. In practice over the many, many years, this credo became a part of our culture. Today we've got over 35,000 employees who believe in this. And, yes, it makes us better. Everybody.

My son, Greg, once said *"The mind is like a parachute. It only works when it's open."* That's exactly what it's about — keeping an open mind and listening before you decide what could be the case. When you create an environment that allows people to express themselves, they come up

ISADORE SHARP
FOUNDER,
FOUR SEASONS HOTELS AND RESORTS

with ideas. We encourage people to participate and speak up. If you think we're doing something that's not right, please speak up. And if you ask the question, "Why do we do this?" and we do not have a good answer, maybe we shouldn't be doing it. I think that's how people grow together — when you have that openness, and don't criticize people for having ideas and trying something that doesn't work. You give people the encouragement to use their common sense, and give them an opportunity to think about their job and how to make it better. You will get enormous amounts of input. When you encourage them, recognize them, and give credit, people continue to do a good job. We have many people who come up with the ideas. It could be anywhere. And they do. All we do is say, "Before you move on any idea, please make sure we just talk about it. Because maybe we've already thought about that, and maybe it's been discarded or maybe someone else has had a better way of dealing with it." So nobody's got the autonomy just to do what they think, they've got the autonomy to think and come up with ideas. This openness and transparency is the way the company grew.

People ask me "How can you rely upon all these people and give them complete authority to do what is needed to satisfy the customer?" I say that we're not giving them a blank sheet — we're getting people to use their common sense and be reasonable when they're thinking about something. They say, "Well how can you trust them for that?" I say that everybody who works usually has a much greater responsibility than their job, whatever their job might be. For example, when they're dealing with their family, those are major, major decisions that they have to deal with. They have to decide what is the right thing to do for my family? They have the ability to do that. Why wouldn't they have the ability to know how to react when a customer comes in and they're irate with something? Most people have an ability to use their common sense. If people know you trust them, they will go to great lengths not to disappoint you. If you say, "It's up to you. What do you think you should do?", people will, by nature, rise to that challenge.

This is what you [the author] are writing about. You're writing about empathy. You're writing about philosophy. You're writing about choices and the soft parts of business — about getting people to think about a more well-rounded way of running a business.[13]

GEAR 1: EMPATHY & DEEP HUMAN UNDERSTANDING
Reframing the Opportunity

In fully embracing the "human factor," it is often valuable to step back and look at the bigger picture to define the business opportunity more precisely. Here is a story about how a reframing of the opportunity and a deeper understanding of important stakeholders can raise the bar on ambitions and more precisely define Where to Play and How to Win. This story shows how one team tackled a challenge using the methods and mindsets of Gear 1 and what they discovered that led to a radical reframing of their opportunity.[14]

The Healthcare Company Story:
Seeing the Problem with Heart

The Challenge

A leading healthcare company came to DesignWorks with a challenging problem. About 40,000 Canadians die from sudden cardiac arrest every year.[15] The company had a solution for some of these Canadians — a heart rhythm device that monitors and, if necessary, resets a patient's heart rhythm following sudden cardiac arrest. While not all patients are indicated for such a device, for those who are eligible, it could save their life.

The company believed there was an opportunity to increase the conversion of device-qualified patients and thus save lives while expanding sales. To tackle this challenge, the company and a major teaching hospital in Canada enlisted Rotman DesignWorks to undertake a study to shed light on this important issue and explore North American practices in the management of conditions for which a device is indicated, with a focus on resolving the Canadian challenge. At the outset of the project, it was thought the business opportunity lay in improving the effectiveness of referrals to electrophysiologists (EPs), the specialists who perform the procedure to implant these life-saving devices, along with more effective patient education. At the completion of Gear 1, the scope was broadened to include consideration of the broader systemic challenge, which radically reframed the opportunity.

The Breakthrough

The first Gear 1 breakthrough was a reframing of the challenge that not only identified where the more significant problems lay but also magnified the business opportunity. Mapping the broader patient journey revealed a more accurate picture of the patient flow and the relationship among all of the key professionals involved along the way in managing patients' heart health. These other stakeholders included internal medicine, emergency room staff, general practitioners, and nurses at every point along the path. Often nurses in general practitioners' offices, emergency rooms, clinics, and specialists' offices have the most face time with patients. As a result, these nurses had valuable insights into the patient experience.

Understanding the context more broadly revealed that the patient journey begins long before the EP becomes involved, and even long before the patient's referring physician is brought into the picture. Visualizing the patient flow from one professional stakeholder to another, and from one site to another (i.e., GP's office, emergency room, hospital/clinic), revealed a rather complicated system of rework, with patients often returning to the same people and places or, in some cases, dropping out of the system altogether. This visualization became known as "the pinball machine" (as depicted in figure 4). The directional arrows show how patients bounced around from one person or place to another in the system, while the "exit" arrows indicate where they dropped out of the system.

As the arrows show, patients would land in Emergency and be referred to a cardiologist or perhaps back to their GP, who might or might not be equipped to educate, diagnose, or refer the patient. Patients who made it to a cardiologist might or might not have proceeded to an EP, depending on their test results. And, even if they were referred to an EP, they might have been sent back for repeated tests. These patients remained "active" in the system, but without timely or complete resolution. Even worse, some patients, for a variety of reasons, were dropping out of the system completely, as indicated by the red arrows. These patients were not being flagged for critical fast tracking and resolution of their potentially fatal condition. For the majority of patients, this experience led to higher anxiety, resignation, or ineffective resolution. For those at serious risk of a sudden cardiac arrest, not obtaining a device was particularly stressful.

FIG. 4 HEALTHCARE PINBALL MACHINE

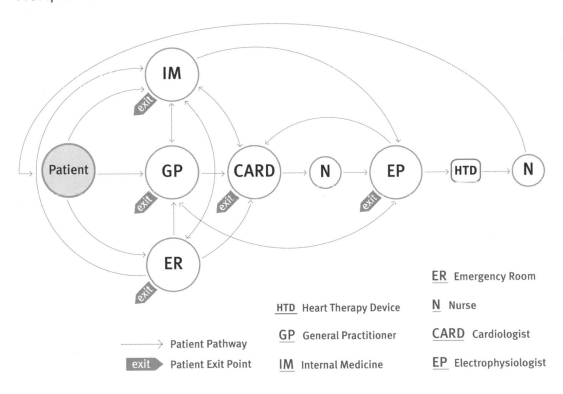

Through further analysis, it was estimated that only 5 percent of cardiac patients made it to an EP, and only an estimated 10 percent ever made it to a cardiologist, who often refers a patient to the EP.[16] That meant as many as 90 percent of one particular group of cardiac patients were bouncing around in the system, from their GP to other medical professionals. Many of these patients were ending up in Emergency and being discharged without any further referral or follow-up. That was putting lives at risk, eating up healthcare system dollars, and resulting in lost business for the company. *Given these facts, the original business challenge was then reframed to consider the entire patient journey and the broader referral system.*

The second breakthrough in Gear 1 came through a deeper understanding of all the stakeholders in the system. This helped identify the human factors behind the system challenges, and what stakeholder needs had to be considered in designing solutions to improve outcomes and the patient experience. Through patients' stories, we learned they were frustrated by the lack of information and lack of empowerment they experienced. The stories from healthcare professionals revealed that individual practitioners appeared to be technically competent but that they all had a different set of protocols to follow. They did not have a clear referral pathway and did not really know if others adhered to the same test standards and protocols. The issues were thus complex and systemic; there was a pronounced need for broad and consistent education for both patients and professionals, simplified and shared protocols, and a clear path for patient referrals. While the issues were complex, the specific areas of opportunity became clearer.

The Outcome

Key Where to Play and How to Win opportunities arose in the areas of targeted intervention, patient management education, and defining referral systems and protocols. While there were broader and longer-term solutions to be put into play, Gear 1 alone provided a new framework for focusing efforts and developing solutions. Some first steps included expanding a fast-track procedure for patients who presented specific red flags in terms of symptoms and test results, refocusing on Emergency Room reception procedures for identifying a specific patient profile, and creating marketing programs aimed at increasing general practitioner awareness. The learning was also shared broadly within the organization. One of the patient participants from this project was even invited to tell his story at a company event, and the company continued to support him in his patient advocacy initiatives. This patient, and the compelling story of the company's new patient experience vision, which was presented at the company's sales meeting, *humanized* the challenge for the broader company team. In the longer term, it was clear that there needed to be more extensive professional education, patient counseling aids, alignment on clearer and more consistent protocols, and a more clearly defined and effective referral network.

This invaluable reframing and sensitivity to stakeholder needs set the team up to better meet the challenge of addressing a bigger opportunity than had originally been envisioned. To address this challenge, the company's team drew on the success of others, both locally and globally. It created new and specific tactical solutions to bridge the gaps in the system and help all healthcare partners do their job in a way that facilitates moving patients through a more efficient process.

"THE OUTPUT OF THE PROJECT HAS HELPED US REFRAME THE ISSUE AND GET FOCUSED ON WHAT REALLY MATTERS, WHICH IS ULTIMATELY THE PATIENT. THIS HELPED DRIVE ALIGNMENT WITHIN OUR ORGANIZATION AND ULTIMATELY LED TO MORE FOCUSED EFFORTS AND IMPROVED LONG-TERM RESULTS."
— Company Team Leader

This story points to the value of stepping back to see the problem through a broader lens and listening to important human stories that reveal points of pain and deep unmet needs, as further revealed in this chapter. It also underscores the principle that if you do not fully understand the human system that underpins a challenge and address the needs of everyone in that system, you may be trying to solve the wrong problem. And when you do come up with a solution, you will not get the buy-in and traction you need to succeed because you have not built the solution to meet the needs of all stakeholders. This is often the case where there are multiple stakeholders who are critical to your success, as in business-to-business and healthcare. This process requires an open mind and empathy to see the picture through the eyes of others, backed by rigorous analysis and synthesis of data and a reframing of the business opportunity.

How many times do we fixate on a problem we are sure we can solve, and spend extensive time and resources on a singular point of tension, wondering, "Why can't we make more meaningful progress in our business?" That is when it is time to step back, consider the big picture, and dive into a deeper exploration of the underlying human systems and needs. This will help identify the issues that are holding back progress and, in this case, not fully delivering on the ability to save more lives. Selling more products and services often requires taking the time to understand and appreciate where the biggest opportunities lie.

People play a key role in every business. It is people who choose products and services, and people who facilitate and support the delivery of those products and services. The importance of people to your business is why Business Design, like other design practices, is human-centered. Better meeting the needs of your important stakeholders, especially the end user, is Job 1. By seeing the world through the eyes of others, you will develop a deeper understanding of the relationships, challenges, and needs of your important stakeholders. Gear 1 is the critical first step toward understanding both *who* matters in your broader human network and *what* matters to each of them. This undertaking almost always leads to a reframing of your challenge through a better understanding of those people and their needs.

You likely have an intuitive understanding of the dynamics at play and the needs of your stakeholders; that intuition plays a valuable role in getting a handle on the big picture early on. The activities of Gear 1 will help you to identify your stakeholders and define relationships more explicitly, bringing greater clarity to the challenge at hand. This will also help create a greater sense of empathy with your stakeholders and motivate you to generate ways to better meet their needs, which you will do in Gear 2. This first gear is always full of surprises and "Aha!" moments that reveal new opportunities to create value and tap into your problem-solving skills. Prepare to be surprised at how many people influence the course of actions, how their deeper needs are often not what they seem to be on the surface, and how this can not only reframe your opportunity but provide the inspiration and platform for solution innovation as you tackle Gear 2.

Your Goal in Gear 1

Your goal in Gear 1 is to clearly frame Where to Play and How to Win in two ways. First is contextualization of the opportunity and second is articulation of unmet needs. Contextualization often leads to a substantial reframing and can have quite radical implications for the magnitude of the opportunity. The articulation of unmet needs will serve as the springboard for innovation and the creation of new value.

The balance of this chapter, as in the others, will highlight the key activities and mindsets required to successfully implement Gear 1 using the methods in this book, followed by some principles and considerations for getting the most out of Gear 1. Tools & Tips related to Gear 1 are identified at the end of this chapter.

Important Activities and Mindsets

There are a number of activities that are helpful to undertake in Gear 1 (see figure 5). The first activity is "Broadening the Lens" through journey and stakeholder mapping. This mapping provides insights into your end users' current journey, and reveals all the other key stakeholders related to that journey and their relationships with each other. Once the map is complete, it is time for a "Deep Dive," using need-finding activities aimed at discovering insights, motivations, and underlying human needs as inspiration for innovation. To make sense of all the data you will collect through this process, you will need to conduct a rigorous analysis and synthesis. This "Sense Making" will help bring everything together into your "Inspiration" — the guiding Personas and unmet needs that will serve as an important springboard for solution development and innovation.

FIG. 5 GEAR 1 ACTIVITIES & OUTPUTS

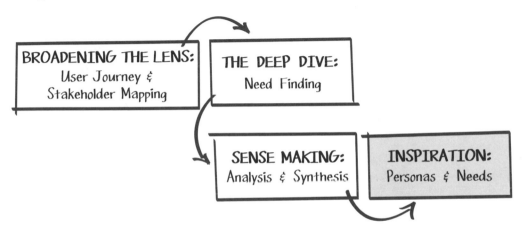

These activities call for an open heart and an open mind. Without both, you will limit your discoveries. A healthy dose of curiosity will lead you to new insights. We will revisit the importance of mindsets and possible traps at the end of this chapter, after you have had a chance to see what Gear 1 is all about.

Principles and Frameworks

The benefits of developing a richer understanding of people as the basis for creating new value are evident in so many successes. Here are some important principles behind the application of design methods that underscore the value of Gear 1.

Human systems are an essential component of success. Broadening the lens to understand the needs of *all* stakeholders and their interrelationships will form the basis of an important connection between human systems, solution systems, and business systems. Such understanding will be critical in making your business idea "stick" and succeed. This was demonstrated in the healthcare company case, where mapping the patient journey in the context of a broader stakeholder system revealed a more accurate picture of what mattered to whom, and how that translated into a bigger and clearer business opportunity.

In just about every case of working with clients at DesignWorks, considering the bigger picture has led to a more precise reframing of the opportunity. For example, you will increase the buy-in of your sales force or retail partners when you find ways to integrate their needs into a new marketing program that will benefit them. In creating new patient-management tools, it is critical to consider how this will help the doctor in his or her practice. Otherwise, the tools will just sit on a shelf and never be used. In designing new knowledge-management tools, it is important to recognize everyone who uses the system inside a company, as well as the human resource team that manages training and incentives related to the implementation of these management tools. Understanding the needs of everyone who is in a position to help influence or enable your vision and designing the experience to engage them in a meaningful manner that adds value to their lives will increase your likelihood of success.

As an exercise, list everyone who could possibly influence the success of your enterprise and ask yourself how deeply you understand each of them and their relationships with each other, and how well you are meeting each of their needs. I will bet that you will find you intuitively know who matters but that there are gaps in either your understanding of their deeper needs or how well you are integrating their needs into your development process.

Value is created when important unmet needs are served. Need finding is a source of fuel in the innovation process, and an essential catalyst in creating new value. We all know that intuitively, but often lose sight of it when we are focused on managing our operations and selling what we already have in the supply chain. At the root of many great brands and businesses is a deep understanding of human needs. For example, Four Seasons Hotels and Resorts is devoted to meeting the need for exceptional, personalized guest service on every level. Nespresso delivers on the coffee lover's need for an exclusive, premium coffee experience. Apple recognizes the need to allow customers to express individuality and creativity through a seamlessly integrated digital experience that has expanded from computing to an all-encompassing work and lifestyle system. Virgin strives to deliver a better experience in every category they enter, as evidenced by their service on Virgin Atlantic and as noted in the interview at the end of this chapter. IKEA satisfies the do-it-yourselfer's need for stylish and affordable furnishings for home and work. These companies have grown their businesses over time by expanding the ways in which they meet customer needs through new products, services, and communications that enrich their customer experience.

This is where a Deep Dive can yield new and timely insights. While a Deep Dive may entail a number of activities, the most revealing involve direct contact with people through observation and listening to their stories with empathy and an open mind, as opposed to just sifting through a stack of market research reports. While quantitative data will give you a good grasp of the numbers, it will likely not give you the insights into your stakeholder needs that will allow you to identify and seize emerging new opportunities. The Tools & Tips section of this book outlines a number of ways to explore and articulate these needs.

Listening to activity-based stories is a powerful way to discover new opportunities. Instead of asking, "What do you want in a shampoo?" say, "Tell me your stories about what you do to look and feel more beautiful." Inspired by the design research methodologies honed at IIT's Institute of Design,[17] that's what we did in our first workshop with Procter & Gamble, and it opened up a whole new perspective on product, service, and branding opportunities. After visiting a hair salon where P&G executives paid close attention to the products and accessories used in hairstyling, we invited consumers to come in the next day and share their stories about what they do to look and feel more beautiful. One woman said her visits to the salon provided an escape from her everyday worries, including her everyday stresses and an inattentive boyfriend. While she might not really *look* much different when she comes out of the salon, she revealed that she *feels* different because the hairdresser always makes her feel so special. A trip to the salon is like a fantasy moment for her, always lifting her spirits and confidence. Imagine if you could design for that!

While understanding how people choose and use your products and services will help you improve upon current offerings, it will tend to lead only to better versions of current solutions (e.g., an extension of an existing shampoo line). By expanding your understanding to the *activities* relating to your current products and services, you will also discover a broader array of untapped opportunities (see figure 6); for example, new services, appliances, and communication and relationship-building programs, as well as new types of outlets. By listening to *stories* with empathy and an open mind, and simply responding with "Tell me more," and wondering, "Why is that important to them?", you will glean fresher insights than you ever would by grilling people with hundreds of questions. It's guaranteed. These new discoveries will point you toward new opportunities. It will inspire broader solutions and lead to richer customer experiences.

FIG. 6 ACTIVITY-BASED NEED FINDING

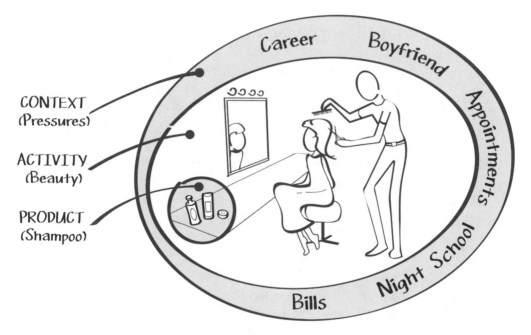

In the case of the healthcare company, in-depth interviews with both medical practitioners and patients revealed new insights. We didn't ask either group what they knew about heart conditions or devices, as that would only have led to their reciting what they knew technically. We spent most of our time listening to the practitioners recounting their best and worst stories about managing cardiac patients. These stories revealed the need for better patient management, more clearly defined referral networks, greater trust in colleagues and the system, a better grasp of protocols, and greater confidence in patient communications and counseling. These science-minded professionals revealed their more human side, which would not have been exposed had we asked about a heart condition or how a device might provide a solution.

We did the same with patients: we listened to their stories about living with their chronic heart condition. These patients were eager to understand what was happening to them and what they could do about it. They wanted the straight goods, without any confusing jargon. We heard stories about their experiences that went like this: "*The whole thing was scary. I didn't know what pills I had to take, where I had to go, who to see. Every doctor I saw wanted new tests done or wanted to know where I'd been ... I'm seventy-eight years old. I can't keep track of these things. My nurse really guided my wife and me. Without her I'd be lost.*" These patients felt like pinballs in the system, and they didn't like it.

There are a number of other examples from our work at DesignWorks showing how we gleaned new insights through similar activity-based research. For example, instead of researching "healthier food" (a product focus that would likely just lead to ways to create healthier food), we asked consumers to tell stories about how they manage their health. This revealed the ways in which people incorporate healthy living into their everyday lives — where they claim small victories and where they struggle. This inspired ways to make managing good health a richer and more holistic experience, leading not only to new and healthier food products but also to new support services and venues, or new streams of communication. In the case of a business-to-business printing company, instead of exploring the printing needs of their customers, we asked these customers to tell stories about getting their products into the market in a timely and efficient manner. This led to opportunities for the printing company to be a better business partner in logistics management as opposed to merely a supplier of one element of a bigger job. All of these open-ended, activity-based explorations have revealed unmet needs as well as opportunities to solve problems and create new value.

As a quick test of the power of stories, the next time you get the opportunity, ask customers to tell you a story about an activity central to their pursuits, and just let them talk. Take note of what you hear that opens your mind to new possibilities. Or try it out on a friend. You might be surprised at what you learn. People tell us this technique brings as much new value to their personal lives as to their business endeavors!

Humans are multidimensional and rich with SPICE. Focusing on the broader activity reveals more of a person's whole life. Recognizing their needs on many levels creates a richer understanding of the whole person. To make a solution not only relevant but also meaningful, it is important to consider all types of needs, not just the practical and rational. Humans have many kinds of needs — functional, informational, relational, emotional, and identity based. Addressing the functional needs is only a small part of the innovation process.

Many enterprises are well versed in the functional needs for products and services, particularly within their current domain. What can help broaden your scope of opportunity is thinking more holistically about human needs, in order to enhance the experience or better meet these needs. The following framework, referred to as SPICE (see figure 7), is based on analysis of interviews conducted on projects at DesignWorks.[18] It can help to stimulate a more holistic consideration of people's needs, and reveal other areas of opportunity beyond the design of a functionally better product or service. In articulating needs, you should consider the following factors:

> **Social:** What do people need from their relationships with others? In the case of the healthcare company, a doctor needs to have confidence and trust in his or her referral network. In other cases, a teenager might need to be acknowledged as a trendsetter among her peers; an employee might need recognition from his boss. As stakeholder mapping reveals, people are all interdependent to varying degrees.

> **Physical:** What do people need on a physical or functional level? In the case of the healthcare company, the referring physician needs to have a practical mechanism for handing off a patient. In other cases, a transit rider needs to be able to get to work and back in a convenient manner at a reasonable cost; IKEA shoppers need parking in order to be able to transport their furniture kits home. These functional needs are usually the easiest needs to spot.

> **Identity:** What do people need to enhance their sense of self-worth or reinforce their personal identity? In the case of the healthcare company, patients need to feel that their life matters, while practitioners need to be seen as professionals who are doing the best for their patients. In other cases, a mother needs to feel she is a caring parent; a young professional needs to be seen as being on top of his game. These are important needs to recognize and respect in the design of your solutions.

Communication: What kinds of information do people need, when do they need it, and how do they want to receive it? In the case of the healthcare company, everyone could benefit from some additional education. Patients needed to know what was happening to them and what to expect if they were to get a device; practitioners needed to know the latest in diagnosis and treatment protocols. In other cases, consumers want to know what is in the products they eat to conform with dietary requirements; FedEx customers need to know where their package is in the delivery system. People want access to information, on their terms.

Emotional: What do people need, psychologically and emotionally? In the case of the healthcare company, patients needed to feel more empowered, and the practitioners needed to feel confident in patient management. In other cases, a procurement officer needs to feel responsible in his purchases; an employee needs to feel empowered to do her job. These needs affect the overall design of the ideal experience, with the goal of helping people feel the way you would like them to feel as a result of your efforts.

FIG. 7 SPICE FRAMEWORK

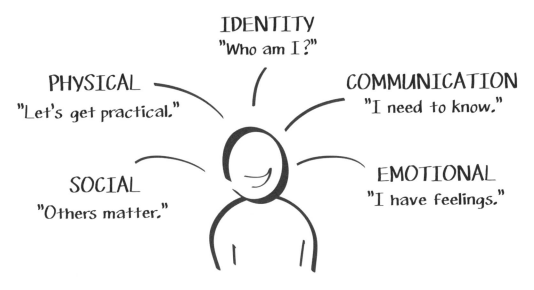

Figure 8 below lists some defining quotations from Gear 1 research on the healthcare company project that help identify needs to be met:

FIG. 8 THE SPICE IN HEALTHCARE

PATIENT	NEED	PROFESSIONAL
"I am not alone in this. I need support."	SOCIAL	"I need to know I can trust others in the network."
"I don't want to walk through life like a ticking time bomb."	PHYSICAL	"The latest technology helps prolong and improve lives."
"My life is worth living."	IDENTITY	"I do what's best for my patients."
"I just want to know what's happening to me."	COMMUNICATION	"I'm up to date on the latest knowledge and protocols."
"Why does it need to be so confusing and difficult?"	EMOTIONAL	"I want to feel confident about how I manage my patients."

With the stories you hear from your customers and friends, ask yourself what these stories reveal in terms of needs — where's the SPICE in their story? How deeply and holistically do you understand the needs of your important stakeholders?

Quantitative trend data can help to place these needs in context and give some dimension to broad opportunities, but they do not feed your sense of empathy or reveal the deeper insights that activity-based need finding will. For example, the rise in obesity in some countries is a major trend, but this, in and of itself, does not point to what to do or how to go about reversing the trend. Nor does studying people's demographic profiles and habits. Hearing people's stories about their efforts to stay fit and manage their weight will reveal much deeper insights and a richer, more multidimensional picture of their needs. All good research and opportunity framing involves a combination of qualitative need finding and quantitative analysis.

Key Considerations — *Who Matters?*

It is helpful in your initial stakeholder mapping and need-finding research to keep in perspective the role each stakeholder will play in your ultimate success. Organizations sometimes focus on a single archetypical user and neglect the others who are involved in enabling, delivering, or influencing whether or not and how a central idea goes into play. Stakeholders can generally be categorized into three groups: End Users, Enablers, and Influencers.

The end user is the central, ultimate benefactor of the solution. This is the person who makes the final call on whether there is value in the big idea. This could be a consumer or a business customer (in the case of a product or service that is purchased), a patient (who consumes products, information, and services to improve health and wellness), or an employee (if it is an internal program that seeks to help people do their work in a more productive and rewarding manner). In the case of the central stakeholder, there may not be a single, prototypical Persona, but rather a collection of individuals who have common, underlying, unmet needs that must be served by your new solution.

Enablers are critical to the success of delivering new solutions. They play a meaningful role in an end user's decision making and actions, or they act as gatekeepers in the decision-making process. An enabler could be a doctor in the case of patients, a mother in the case of children, a partner in the value chain, or a procurement manager in the case of business-to-business partnerships. In all of these cases, you not only want to understand enablers' insights into the end user, but also their own motivating needs. This is important if you are to enroll them in adopting a new idea. Here are some examples of how the success of a solution with end users is enhanced by understanding and meeting an enabler's needs:

> *A consumer:* If the consumer depends on advice about which product is best for her to buy in a store that you supply, understanding and considering retailers' needs in designing your solution will enhance their support in the purchase of your product.

> *A business customer:* If the key interface with the customer is a sales representative or another business partner (e.g., a distributor or other third party), he must see value in it for himself if he is to help complete the value equation.

A patient: If a solution is good for patient satisfaction and outcomes, it may not be realized if the needs of the relevant healthcare professionals or third-party payers (e.g., insurers) are not considered in the solution.

Employees: If the solution requires a rethink of training and incentives, understanding how employee needs align with the needs of senior management and HR will help design a way to integrate the best solution into enterprise practices.

Influencers shape users' and enablers' decisions and actions. Though they may not be directly involved in delivering a solution, their voice and wisdom may be very valuable. For example, in a food project, we brought in chefs and nutritionists who could see what was on the horizon; they could choose to either inspire thinking or be directly enrolled as part of the solution (e.g., sponsor a cooking show). Journalists are also key influencers — they can inspire you, support your quest, or, in the worst case, be your most exacting critic. In many cases, these influencers may be more in the know than you are. You need to decide if they are to be integrated into your scheme or not.

In the healthcare company case, the patient was the ultimate consumer of the solution. All of the medical professionals who served that patient, as well as the families and friends of the patient, were important enablers — they played a role in how solutions got activated. And the experts who validated the technology and defined clinical protocols were important influencers because they shaped the system and had an important voice in defining the practices of those within the system who cared directly for the patient. Thus, all of their needs were important to consider in devising an integrated solution.

"I HAVE BEEN DRIVEN TO USE MY KNOWLEDGE AND ENERGY TO HELP HUMANKIND."
— **Earl Bakken** *Co-founder of Medtronic Inc.*

In creating human value, a number of interrelated stakeholders will all play a role, to a greater or lesser extent, in creating and delivering solutions. It is important to understand the needs of all people in the system in the development of integrated solutions. As you move through Gear 1, you may discover other key influencers or potential enablers whom you should continue to integrate into your effort to understand the human factor and keep your enterprise relevant to everyone who matters to your success.

How Mindsets Matter in Gear 1

The healthcare company case and the other examples demonstrate the significance of the following important mindsets in Gear 1.

Empathy. This mindset will enable you to understand the human factor on a deep and authentic level. At this stage, your goal is to see things through the eyes of others, and feel what they feel, in order to appreciate their deepest underlying needs. Putting aside your own needs, opinions, and perspectives is critical. Too often, I have heard people watching consumers from behind a one-way mirror in focus groups make comments like, "She obviously doesn't know what she's talking about." That isn't empathy. Your aim should be to put yourself wholly in the shoes of that person.

Openness and mindfulness. It is important to remember to turn off your filter when observing others and listening to their stories. This Deep Dive is not about your own thoughts, judgments, and feelings. Open and unfiltered perception will allow you to discover new opportunities for creating value on a deeper and more meaningful level. Intuition, along with your natural curiosity and open-mindedness, will guide you through the need-finding process. Instead of interpreting what others say, ask yourself, "Why is that important to them?", with the goal of understanding their deeper motivations.

Intrinsic motivation. If you are motivated by a sense of purpose and find joy in your work, you will likely get a lot more out of the process and be motivated to solve the problem of an unmet need. Now is the time to set your extrinsic motivations aside (i.e., that next bonus or award). You are not collecting facts to support your case or preconceived notions; you are listening for new insights that will inspire you to create new solutions.

Finally, Gear 1 is most powerful when *everyone* on the team shares a deep understanding of and empathy for the end user and all of the others in the equation. Ideally, everyone on the team should have the opportunity for a meaningful, first-hand experience with those for whom they will design. At DesignWorks, we give everyone on the development team an opportunity to connect with the people who matter; that includes involving financial officers, operations experts, marketing folks, sales personnel, and product-development experts. This opportunity to connect on a human level brings *meaning* to your development pursuits. To repeat an important earlier quotation from a Singapore Polytechnic management workshop, "Connecting with people at a deeper and more authentic level gives meaning and purpose to our work."

Transforming Gear 1 learning into a clearly defined set of stakeholder needs will serve as the springboard for innovation in Gear 2. No one is more passionate about serving the customer and changing the rules of the game than Sir Richard Branson.

Here is an excerpt from an interview with this visionary entrepreneur that demonstrates how an enterprise that is customer-centered, that embraces new possibilities to extend the brand, and that acts on those ideas with agility and passion can deliver a non-stop stream of delightful surprises for customers. This excerpt sets the stage for an unbridled exploration of new possibilities in Gear 2.[19]

Virgin has made its name by breaking into new markets and offering great value, superior service, a fresh approach, and a bit of fun. When we assess new businesses, the first step is to submit every business idea to our "brand test." We are constantly presented with new and exciting opportunities that might make a lot of money, but if they fail the brand test, we move on. We also think that there is little point in entering a new market unless it provides the opportunity to really shake up an industry. Almost all our new ventures come about from our thinking up a product or service that we believe people really want. Looking back at the launches of Virgin Atlantic, Virgin Active, and Virgin Mobile, I'm reminded that we had a clear vision of what the customer wanted and how we would deliver it (with a sense of fun).

In the case of Virgin Atlantic, we offered great service, which meant that travelers received — among many other innovative services — extra touches such as onboard massages and seat-back TV screens. At Virgin Active, we focused on building large, family friendly health clubs with big gyms and swimming pools, and attentive staff. For Virgin Mobile, customers got a service that did not require signing up for onerous contracts and instead got flexible plans and a direct link to entertainment and music. This clarity of purpose and excellent customer care helped us to succeed. You'll notice that making a profit hasn't entered the picture yet. It's rare for me or the team to consider only the money that can be made. I feel it's pointless to approach investing with the question, "How can I make lots of money? We must bring in the numbers guys and work out some business plans." The consultants will say your idea will work, while the accountants will prove that it cannot. No one will ever agree on exactly how to make money.

This brings me to a secret to lasting success: securing your customers' trust, which should be part and parcel of your differentiation and marketing. At Virgin, we do this by relying on openness and simplicity when we communicate with our customers. Since we'd created companies everyone on staff was proud of, we were all deeply concerned about quality and customer service, and our marketing focused on why the businesses were different and special.

SIR RICHARD BRANSON
FOUNDER AND CEO, VIRGIN GROUP

TOOLS & TIPS
for Gear 1: Empathy & Deep Human Understanding

There are many ways to develop your empathy and human understanding.
The Tools & Tips referred to in this section can either get you started or add
to your current repertoire.

Observation: Absorbing context and human behaviors
(pages 150–152)

Empathy Exercise: Living the experience
(pages 153–154)

Stakeholder Mapping: Identifying and connecting people who matter
(pages 155–157)

Need-finding Research: Designing a deep dive
(pages 158–160)

User Journals: Understanding the current user journey
(pages 161–163)

Photo Elicitation: Discovering unmet needs through storytelling
(pages 164–166)

Listening and Recording: Getting the most out of interviews
(pages 167–169)

Mind Mapping: Making connections to understand the whole person
(pages 170–171)

Motivational Mapping: Searching for deeper meaning
(pages 172–173)

Subject Profiles: Synthesizing the interviews
(pages 174–175)

Discovery Exchange: Making intuitive connections and building
a framework for analysis
(pages 176–177)

Need Mining and Analysis: Turning soft data into hard data
(pages 178–181)

Need Articulation: Defining a platform for innovation
(pages 182–183)

Personas: Creating human archetypes
(pages 184–186)

The Current Journey: Contextualizing the opportunity through
empathic storytelling
(pages 187–189)

GEAR 2: CONCEPT VISUALIZATION
Refreshing Your Vision

Here is a story of a group of dedicated healthcare professionals who were given the license to dream big in Gear 2. Their collective vision planted the seeds of a comprehensive redesign of the patient experience in what was already a world-class hospital.[20] While this example, like that in Gear 1, focuses on the healthcare arena, one can imagine this as any service experience in which customer needs can be better met. No matter what business you are in, taking time to ask "What if?" and engaging others in envisioning new possibilities will draw your enterprise forward and begin to define How to Win from a customer standpoint.

The Princess Margaret Hospital Story: *Turning Lost Time into Found Time*

The Challenge

Living with and managing cancer is a physically and emotionally draining journey that too many people have to endure. When your life is at risk, you and all of those close to you are acutely aware of how every minute of every day passes. Faced with tough decisions and grueling treatments, the last thing you need as a patient is an experience that can heighten your anxiety, diminish your self-worth, and turn your journey into lost time. The desired experience — one of hopeful healing.

That was the inspiration in 2008, when Princess Margaret Hospital (PMH) in Toronto decided to dream big and create a better healing journey. The redesign of the physical space of its chemotherapy treatment department offered an important opportunity to better meet the needs of patients and enhance their experience when undergoing cancer treatment. Normally, within the financial constraints of a public healthcare system, envisioning a hospital as a Four Seasons Hotel would be a stretch, but that didn't constrain this team of visionaries. The challenge was threefold: *One,* create a better patient experience that would support better health outcomes. *Two,* do so with an eye to being operationally efficient and responsible in a public healthcare system. *Three,* engage a broad base of stakeholders who could contribute to a renewed vision for patient care and help advance the cause at Princess Margaret Hospital. Creating a better experience and value for the end user, living up to financial responsibilities, and enlisting stakeholder support are so often the challenges and, at the same time, the pillars of success for any meaningful undertaking.[21]

The Breakthrough

The breakthrough for PMH was a unified refreshing of the organization's vision for the patient experience, fueled by the medical staff's intrinsic motivation and devotion to world-class patient care. As with the healthcare company described in Gear 1, the process began with a broad scan of the patient experience. In this case, mapping the patient journey both inside and outside the hospital visit gave participants a holistic picture of patient needs in the context of day-to-day living. Research revealed unmet needs around reducing anxiety, empowering patients, and turning what was felt to be "lost time" into "found time" in their journey of hopeful healing.

The solution breakthrough came about by engaging a broad base of stakeholders who conceived and influenced a new vision for patient care. Building on the identified patient needs and Personas, and a deeper understanding of the patient journey, twenty staff at PMH, including oncologists, pharmacists, nurses, researchers, and administrators, underwent a group ideation session. We divided the participants into multidisciplinary groups and assigned each a patient Persona and journey framework. We asked them to think of solutions that would improve the treatment experience for their Persona. Participants had carte blanche to imagine new possibilities without constraints, in order to encourage the broadest possible pool of ideas. For instance, we asked them to consider metaphors and analogies to other industries (e.g., hospitality, travel, the arts, health and wellness, virtual/online services, etc.) as inspiration for the ideal patient experience

— turning the "lost time" patients feel waiting in a hospital into "found time" that could help them feel engaged and productive in their healing journey.

During the first ideation session and in a span of ninety minutes, staff generated more than 300 ideas, which included concierge services, cafés, first class "seating," Zen gardens, and relaxation pods. While many of the ideas seemed far-fetched, the groups realized that the intent behind them could potentially be preserved and translated into more feasible ideas. For example, one team drew analogies between patient treatments and flying on an airline. Some patients have "short-haul" treatments (e.g., less than sixty minutes) while others have long "transatlantic" treatments (e.g., more than four hours), like those of Virgin Atlantic. The team drew inspiration from this and envisioned ways to enhance comfort (e.g., adjustable seating), entertainment (e.g., in-flight activities), and productivity (e.g., web access, work stations). This led the team to develop a patient experience around comforting treatment pods, access to inspirations and activities to keep patients engaged, and visions for a never-before-seen, ideal chemotherapy chair that could one day be designed. Some groups focused on technology-based solutions (e.g., websites, personal devices) while another developed the concept of a service-oriented support system.

We also asked the teams to represent their ideas graphically in their brainstorming. Instead of words on paper, we encouraged participants to draw, sketch, or map out their concepts. This exercise made the ideas more tangible, allowing for more robust discussion and concrete idea development. The brainstorming session led to a number of new possibilities for the new treatment facility and patient experience. The solutions did not focus solely on the treatment space but also considered the purposeful delivery of patient-oriented services, activities, and information within the hospital, as well as services that could be accessed and delivered from home.

With so many exciting possibilities, the DesignWorks team pulled these together into rough, conceptual prototypes of the ideal patient experience and presented them back to hospital staff and patients in the form of visual storyboards. These storyboards were used to walk various stakeholders through an idealized yet realistic and improved patient experience. Staff at all levels and patients openly discussed the pros and cons of the prototypes and suggested improvements for each concept. Visualizing patient experiences in a rough, unfinished format made staff and patients more open to contributing feedback. The active solicitation of feedback by hospital staff and patients gave all stakeholders a greater sense of ownership in the final outcome. The prototypes were further refined and evaluated in an iterative fashion, until the ideal patient experience was fully formed (see figure 9).

FIG. 9 ENVISIONED PATIENT JOURNEY

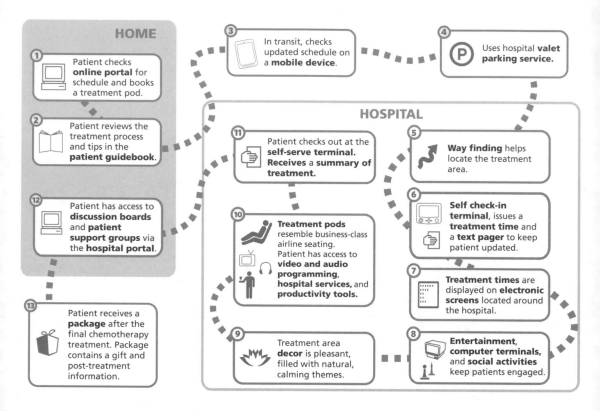

The Outcome

This case brings to life what open and imagination-rich collaboration can yield. Rather than simply representing *change,* this renewed vision signified meaningful and shared *progress.* This undertaking not only produced hundreds of inspired ideas, it engaged dozens of important stakeholders in the creation of a comprehensive new patient experience and an institution-wide commitment to progress with purpose. From a management perspective, it underscored what really matters to patients and what does not. That led to an important reprioritization of capital expenditures, a new vision for patient care, and operational efficiencies.

This new vision served as a lighthouse to guide future development, keep aspirations high, and motivate staff, donors, and patients. The research and vision for this project have also continued to serve as important references for decisions since the project began three years ago. Phase One of the new chemotherapy treatment center has now opened, with full completion in early 2012.

This story demonstrates how collaboration can lead to bigger ideas, how engaging a broad group of stakeholders instills a sense of ownership and pride, and how this engagement leads to traction in advancing big ideas. It also shows how giving yourself the license to dream can lead to better, smarter realities and a sense of where real value is created.

"THE PROJECT ALLOWED US TO BRING PEOPLE FROM ACROSS THE HOSPITAL TO DESIGN A NEW CHEMOTHERAPY SUITE WITH THE PATIENT IN MIND — AND WITH REAL PATIENT FEEDBACK ON THEIR EXPERIENCE OF CARE. DOCTORS, NURSES, RESEARCHERS, CLERICAL STAFF, VOLUNTEERS, MANAGEMENT — MANY OF WHOM HAVE NEVER WORKED TOGETHER BEFORE — WERE ABLE TO SHARE IDEAS, BUILD SOMETHING TANGIBLE, AND FEEL LIKE THEY HAD A STAKE IN THE FINAL OUTCOME."

— **Sarah Downey** *Vice-president, Princess Margaret Hospital*
University Health Network, Toronto, Canada

Once you have framed the opportunity to create new value through Gear 1, you are ready to refresh your vision for the future and imagine new possibilities. This is not the time to focus on incrementally fixing or extending what you have in hand; this is your opportunity to step out of your current paradigm and dream!

Gear 2 is about collaborating to generate fresh ideas and new ways to deliver a better, more satisfying experience for the end user. As you create your new vision, you will take your cue from the unmet needs articulated in Gear 1, with no preconceived notions of what will and will not work. Don't worry about *how* you will do it. Every enterprise needs to reconcile dreams with operational realities, but that can wait for Gear 3.

Your Goal in Gear 2

Your goal in Gear 2 is to refresh your vision for the future, seeing possibilities for How to Win by creating value through a new, high-value, and seamlessly integrated experience for the end user. After iterating through Gear 2, the development team should collectively feel excited and believe that "This is BIG! If we could deliver this, we would really change the game."

As in the chapter on Gear 1, this chapter will highlight key activities and mindsets, followed by some principles and considerations for getting the most out of Gear 2, and a list of related Tools & Tips.

Important Activities and Mindsets

Gear 2 is highly collaborative and iterative. It's fun. It can get messy. It's also most productive if you can put your imagination and team spirit ahead of your fears and ego. With the outcome of Gear 1 in hand as your Platform for Innovation (see figure 10), you may want to engage in some creative ice-breakers; being restrained and self-interested at this point will only limit your ability to contribute and realize a true breakthrough in your collective creativity. From there, you will move through Ideation and Concept Enrichment, pulling out the gems of your creative outputs. Then you will begin to knit them together in Experience Design — mapping out how all the pieces fit together into a seamless experience. Multiple Prototyping will keep you from getting stuck on perfecting one idea early on and will give you lots of options to explore through the Co-creation phase, when you seek feedback from users and other stakeholders. Through continuous iteration in low-cost, low-resolution prototypes and feedback sessions, you will gain more insight into what resonates with or repels your users. Both types of information are valuable and will help inform and shape your ultimate vision.

FIG. 10 GEAR 2 ACTIVITIES & OUTPUTS

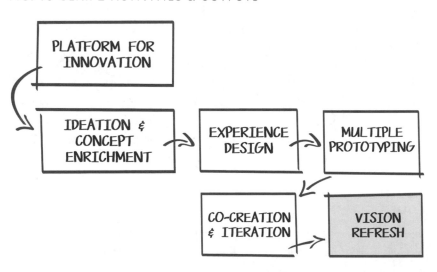

In order to get the most out of Gear 2, empathy, intrinsic motivation, openness, and positivity are important. Empathy keeps your user at the center of development. Intrinsic motivation fuels your sense of purpose and joy in the development process. Openness and positivity keep the team's juices flowing.

Principles and Frameworks

This is the time to suspend your current realities and focus entirely on creating the ultimate experience for your end user. Step away from the business you are currently in, how you operate today, or competition nipping at your heels. Give yourself the license to think big. The only element of your previous work that you will bring forward at this point is your collection of needs and Personas. It is time to dream!

Here are some principles to keep in mind as you move through this phase:

The end user reigns supreme. Through every step of Gear 2, it is important to keep a user-centered focus. There will be lots of time in Gear 3 to figure out what your ideas mean to the enterprise. In the case of PMH, the patient remained at the front and center of the development process throughout Gear 2. Even if you are part of a value chain, the ultimate end user is the shared customer. For example, you might make engines that go into the plane that gets sold to the airline that sells seats to the passenger. Everyone is an important stakeholder in that chain, but the end goal is to create a system that the end user (i.e., passenger) will appreciate. That's every stakeholder's common cause.

"DREAMS HAVE A WAY OF PREDICTING AND PRECEDING REALITY."
— Earl Bakken *Co-founder, Medtronic Inc.*

Dream! This is the time to think big without restraint. Even crazy ideas will reveal magical and surprisingly doable solutions. For all of the serious duties of their day-to-day work, the PMH team allowed themselves a few hours to dream — and dream big they did! Remembering that even the most far-fetched ideas have some inherent value will keep you from reconciling dreams with reality too early in the process. You can bet that visionaries like Steve Jobs of Apple, Sir Richard Branson of Virgin, Isadore Sharp of Four Seasons, and Earl Bakken of Medtronic allowed themselves to dream big. Everyone has the capacity to envision new possibilities, no matter what your position in the organization.

Design the solution as a seamless and multidimensional experience. In order to ensure that you create a comprehensive and breakthrough experience, it is important to consider how to meet needs better in many dimensions. Often, an enterprise will focus on new products or better services, but those are only part of a winning experience. It is also important to think about the needs defined more broadly by the activity and how those needs might be satisfied.[22] The following POEMS framework (see figure 11) essentially captures all the components of the solution that you could ultimately design:

FIG. 11 POEMS FRAMEWORK

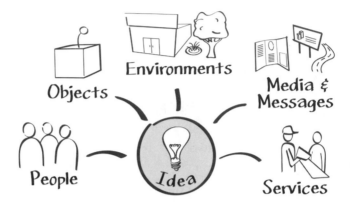

When applied to the Princess Margaret Hospital case, this framework helps stimulate considerations like these:

People: Who are the people that might help the end user? In the case of PMH, how could a nurse help counsel the patient?

Objects: Are there products or objects that could satisfy needs? In the case of PMH, could a device help people get the information they need more readily than by hanging around the nursing station with a crowd of other patients?

Environments: What kind of places might enable you to deliver the right experience? In the case of PMH, would more natural light and other elements of nature create a greater sense of calm?

Media/Messages: What information would be helpful, and how best could it be delivered? In the case of PMH, could scheduling information be accessed online, from home, rather than by calling the hospital and being put on hold?

Services: What kinds of support services would enhance the experience? In the case of PMH, could wireless access, computers, and movies fill the void of lost time and help patients feel more engaged and productive?

In the exploration phase of solution development, each one of the following dimensions is critical to designing a seamlessly integrated experience:

Explore in low resolution. Don't spend a lot of money on early prototypes. Instead, use your imagination to transform everyday items into rough-and-ready prototypes. You will be surprised at how this can stimulate thinking and dialogue. The Tools & Tips section of this book suggests a number of ways to represent your ideas without spending a lot of money. It is a better use of your money to explore lots of big ideas at a next-to-nothing cost than it is to spend a lot of money on expensive mock-ups early on in the development process. I touch on this again in the story about the Nestlé Confectionery team in the chapter on Preparing for Your Quest.

Resist early perfectionism. High achievers often want things to be right as soon as possible. Early perfectionism will slow you down and hold back breakthrough thinking. Making mistakes and learning from them is all part of the creative process.

Iterate. Iterate. Iterate. You'll never get the solution perfect out of the gate. You'll need to explore, experiment, recast, and refine as part of the ongoing process of creating and learning. This is the messy part, and can challenge those who want to complete the job too soon. The process of exploration and reconfiguring solutions in response to user feedback is all part of a productive development process — both in the "enterprise lab" and later on in the marketplace.

Engage end users and other stakeholders early and often. There is no place for boardroom thinking in this process. Design is about engaging others in the process and embracing feedback, even when it is not positive. Doing so will yield greater learning and more robust ideas. The most productive way to solicit candid feedback is to show users your ideas, ready yourself with pen and paper, and then ask with enthusiasm, *"Tell me what you like, but also everything that's wrong with this idea so I can fix it for you."* That's the true spirit of co-creation. In all of our work with low-resolution prototypes as a means of stimulating dialogue, I am always amazed to see how imaginative the users are with rough-and-ready prototypes and how willing they are to help you make the idea better, knowing you have their interests at heart.

Visualizing new possibilities and soliciting early feedback is critical to productivity and progress in the design process. Perhaps surprisingly, the process of engaging users early in the design process is not common practice. Feedback is often reserved until the time when a final and fully formed product is created (e.g., a refined product or marketing concept). The challenge with this approach is that significant changes will rarely be considered this far into the development process. Frequently, the request for feedback is really just a courtesy and formality, and any changes that result tend to be incremental. By engaging users and other important stakeholders in the feedback process early and often, you can glean important insights before committing any significant investments or resources. This allows for important early course corrections.

In the case of PMH, we presented the prototypes to patients and asked, "What works here?" "What doesn't?" "What could be better?" Sharing prototypes with patients not only provided valuable feedback on the concepts themselves, it also stimulated dialogue that revealed even more insights into their points of pain and ways to alleviate them. The fact that they felt their entire lives were put on hold while they focused on treatment and beating the disease, combined with the fact that long wait times in a Canadian hospital are a necessary evil, painted a fairly bleak picture for patients. While the hours spent in treatment or waiting for test results were never going to go away, the ability of patients to convert those seemingly wasted hours into something more meaningful would substantially improve their experience. For example, instead of staring at a blank wall or television screen, patients could have access to entertainment or work spaces that could help them feel more engaged and productive. They could support other patients in their journey through a "chemo buddy" program to give them a sense of purpose and self-worth. They could engage in other healing activities, such as light therapy or meditation, to supplement the essential clinical care. Drawing inspiration from patient stories and feedback, the team realized how the hospital patient experience could become an enabler of intellectual, mental, spiritual, and social support as well as of medical care. This led to subsequent concepts that would allow patients to continue, even enhance, their lives during their time in the hospital. Ideas included social and private recovery areas, work and education resources, engaging activities, inspirational cues, peaceful and natural designs, and new furniture.

Key Considerations

There are few rules in Gear 2, but here are a few things to keep in mind:

Everyone is creative. Everyone has ideas and can contribute to solutions. A healthy, open, and collaborative team dynamic will fuel creativity in every participant.

Quantity is important. The more ideas you generate and consider, the more you will get past the obvious solutions. That is why you need everyone on the team engaged in the creative process. If you keep users' needs front and center as an inspiration, you will see conceptual patterns in the volumes of ideas that will inform your grander idea.

There are no bad ideas. In fact, bad ideas are often the catalyst to brilliant breakthroughs.

Set your ego aside. In a shared quest, there is no room for personal agendas and egos. If you are willing to be wrong (or right!), you will be a more valuable contributor to success in the end.

This is a highly collaborative process. You will get the most robust solutions if you engage everyone who brings a unique perspective and expertise to the development table. Encourage participants to think outside the box, and let the creative juices flow!

How Mindsets Matter in Gear 2

As I mentioned at the beginning of this chapter, empathy, intrinsic motivation, openness, and positivity will help you get the most out of Gear 2.

> *Empathy* will help you see the world through the eyes of your end user, imagining, "If I were in their shoes, what would delight me?" An empathetic mindset will ensure that you always keep users' needs front and center throughout development. Empathy also fuels **intrinsic motivation** and infuses meaning into the project, giving a sense of purpose to your quest. If you are motivated by a sense of purpose, you will have more incentive to solve the problem of the unmet human need(s) you identified in Gear 1.

Openness and positivity create the best conditions for exploring new ideas. That means being open both to the ideas of others and to new ideas that are not within the scope of your current business. The show-stopper I hear most often is, "We're not in that business. We have no idea how to deliver that." If it builds on your current customer relationship and creates value for customers, maybe it is a business you *should* be in. There are a few things you must resist thinking or saying, because they will only minimize your outcomes. Here are some other classic idea-killing comments:

"That's totally absurd. If we do that, we'll all get fired."
"That's a lame idea, but I have a better one."
"Our sales people would shoot us if we ever suggested that."
"We did that three years ago, and it failed."

Courage and vulnerability are part of the creative process. That calls for overcoming the fear of exposing your imagination and putting bold ideas on the table.

By opening up the development process to a wide and diversified team, you can generate endless possibilities and share a broad sense of ownership in your future vision. That also means you won't need to sell the solution, as everyone will feel they have had an opportunity to put their own thumbprint on the future.

One man who has always believed that there are an endless number of new possibilities to improve human lives is Earl Bakken, a lifelong humanist and innovator, and co-founder and Chairman Emeritus of the world's leading medical device company, Medtronic Inc. Inspired in his childhood by the movie *Frankenstein* and the concept of using electricity to bring a being to whole life, he pursued his dreams and co-founded Medtronic in 1949, in a garage, where his first wearable pacemaker was eventually built. His innovation pursuits extend beyond Medtronic to include the Heart Brain Institute at the Cleveland Clinic, a holistic healing hospital in North Hawaii, and Earl's Garage, a program that inspires kids seven years' old and up with a sense of wonder, a passion for learning, and a capacity to create through minds-on, hands-on activities.

The following interview with Earl Bakken, on the pursuit of possibilities, reveals the importance of dreams, intuition, prototyping, and collaborating — essential ingredients in innovation. At age eighty-eight, he is still innovating and making important contributions to society and science.[23]

I'm a big dreamer, and many of my dreams have come true. I find that during the time at night between going to bed and actually falling asleep, when my "mind" is free from thinking about all of the daily stuff (and my mind is free from my brain), "pieces" start coming together to form whole pictures and ideas — similar to a puzzle. I may have talked with different people about different issues or problems and, during that state of "almost sleep," my mind has the ability to organize connections that help solve issues or needs or problems. I keep a notepad next to my bed, and an astronaut pen for writing upside down, and I often make scribbles of my ideas, which have to be deciphered in the morning.

I believe in a "Ready, Fire, Aim" mindset. In Hawaii we call it "listening to our na'au" or our gut. It is using your intuition to make decisions, solve problems, and create solutions. There are times when these kinds of decisions are the best. You get the facts and you make a decision without a lot of analyzing. There is the risk that you may not be exactly right at first, but you will see where you need to make adjustments in your aim as you advance toward your goal.

It's important to try new things. The act of doing provides leaders with experience, the ultimate teacher. I refer to the wearable pacemaker prototype that I designed and we built in four weeks. We didn't intend for it to be used on a human, so we didn't make it look fancy. When Dr Lillehei (heart surgeon and early collaborator) didn't want to risk losing another child's life, he attached it to a child. When I saw that, I had such mixed emotions. Had we made it well enough for a child? While it saved the child's life, we also learned valuable lessons, like recessing the knobs so the children couldn't change the settings.

In helping to put together a community health initiative here on Hawaii Island over the past twenty years, I have encouraged people to think out of the box. I try to connect the people I meet with each other so that assets can be combined and efforts can be supported.

EARL BAKKEN
CO-FOUNDER AND CHAIRMAN EMERITUS, MEDTRONIC INC.

The hospital that Earl Bakken refers to, the North Hawaii Community Hospital, a full-service acute-care hospital, opened in 1996 as the first hospital in the United States designed completely around the philosophy of "Integrative Medicine" and serves as an innovative prototype for a patient-centered, holistic, mind-body-spirit healing experience. Serving 30,000 patients in this community, NHCH has been rated number one in Medicare's Patient Satisfaction Survey.[24] Earl Bakken has earned a long list of awards in Innovation, Entrepreneurship, Leadership, Science, and Education. His story is recounted in his autobiography, *One Man's Full Life*.[25]

TOOLS & TIPS
for Gear 2: Concept Visualization

Part two of this book provides a selection of some basic Tools & Tips to help you explore, build out, and develop possibilities for creating new value:

Ideation: Generating new possibilities
(pages 192–194)

Metaphors: Using analogies to stimulate imagination
(pages 195–196)

Experience Mapping: Designing a new and ideal experience
(pages 197–198)

Iterative Prototyping: Making the abstract concrete
(pages 199–200)

Role-playing: Playing out the experience to close the gaps
(pages 201–202)

Storyboarding: Capturing the story in key frames
(pages 203–204)

Co-creation: Engaging others in the development process
(pages 205–207)

GEAR 3: STRATEGIC BUSINESS DESIGN

Refocusing and Activating Your Strategy

Translating big ideas into a strategy for realization isn't easy. The following story describes how a team in Singapore took trends, insights, and big ideas into Gear 3 to devise a complete transformation of their strategic model — defining How to Win through a breakthrough offering and a distinct system of activities to deliver their new vision.[26] It is an interesting application of Business Design, because it considers multiple businesses acting as an association for the collective good. In a corporate context, this would be comparable to getting business units across the enterprise to work together.

The Singapore WISH Story:
A Strategy of Passion and Pride

The Challenge

Confectionery and baked goods are an important sector of the economy in Singapore. The industry's association, the Singapore Bakery and Confectionery Trade Association (SBCTA), has long served as a body for sector advocacy, networking, and collaboration. The association recognized that while there were many individual players with the technology and skills to make unique Singaporean products, they did not have a common vision for creating economic gain across the industry.

A cross-disciplinary team at Singapore Polytechnic took on the challenge, using the Business Design framework. Their goal: to come up with a new Singaporean product to sell locally and internationally.

The Breakthrough

The development efforts of this team led to a significant reframing of the opportunity on Where to Play and How to Win for the SBCTA. They defined a compelling new proposition, created a unique new strategic model in which everyone would win, and defined a plan to activate quick wins and experiments to get early learning on the path to envisioned success.

As in all good Business Design stories, the project began with a broad scan of stakeholders and trends, leading to a focus on one particular stakeholder group — the ever-increasing number of people who travel to and through Singapore on business and pleasure. Their core need? To bring home something that is uniquely and authentically part of Singapore's culture and that captures the magic of this special country and evokes memories of their trip to Singapore.

The development team decided that instead of creating and testing a new product for the market, they would leverage their existing traditions and celebrate the already iconic treats of Singapore. Thus was born the Singapore WISH — a selection of Singapore's most loved traditional baked goods in a gift box.

The WISH experience was seamlessly integrated to create a special gift collection that could be accessed broadly across Singapore. Developed to be promoted in the future on airlines and in hotels and to be available at special flagship stores (where gift boxes could be customized) and in high-traffic shopping outlets, this uniquely branded treat is intended to captivate the traveler and delight those back home.

The team entered Gear 3 with an inspired vision, but knew that it would require a radical reframing of the association's strategy and a departure from the association's role and ways of operating in the past. To focus efforts, they translated the consumer experience into a system of activities that would benefit all association members. The Business Design process fundamentally shifted their concept of Where to Play and How to Win. They moved from a strategy that was internally focused on supporting the association network to one that was externally focused on creating a souvenir of authentic, iconic treats that no one would leave Singapore without. To achieve this, they defined a unique combination of network activities that centered on sourcing products, engaging promotional partners, and securing distribution channels. It turned the association from inward-looking networking activities to an outwardly focused promotion of their country. It transformed the role of a single-source provider into a collective pursuit, with commercial gain for all contributors. It went beyond manufacturing and distribution to market to promotion of a uniquely branded and iconic symbol of the country's confectionery traditions. It called for embedding the desire for this unique memento into the multiple points of access for visitors to Singapore. It reconfigured the association's activity system (shown later in this chapter) toward a radical new model, to meet higher ambitions and refocus the network's energies on a common cause — promotion of their country and shared prosperity for all association members.

The Outcome

With a new strategy to set them on a path toward this long-term ambition, the team identified several quick wins and experiments to activate their vision. In collaboration with SBCTA, the team conducted a poll on the items for the gift box and activated technical work on shelf-life quality, through Singapore Polytechnic's Food Science labs. Assembling prototypes of a fixed selection of Singapore's most iconic and popular sweets, the team conducted a small-scale marketing effort and sought consumer feedback. They also explored a potential pilot laboratory that would allow customers to make their own selections, while tasting the sweets and hearing the stories behind each one. There are plans to codify this pilot laboratory into a store-within-a-store offering made available to major retail department stores.

"WHAT THE BUSINESS DESIGN TEAM HAS DONE FOR US IS TAKEN OUR VISION AND SHOWED US THAT WE COULD EMBRACE NEW OPPORTUNITIES BY LOOKING AT THINGS DIFFERENTLY. THIS IS NOT ALWAYS EASY TO DO WHEN BUSINESS PEOPLE FACE A MULTITUDE OF CONSTRAINTS. WE ARE LEARNING THAT THE CONSTRAINTS CAN IN FACT BE THE BASIS FOR FRESH OPPORTUNITY."
— **Singapore Bakery and Confectionery Trade Association**

This story illustrates how collaboration, passion, imagination, and conviction can be harnessed through Business Design. Strategically, it demonstrates how an industry-focused association could reframe its shared purpose through a market-inspired opportunity. This was achieved by tapping into human insights and needs (both inside the network and with the ultimate target consumer) and visualizing a new dream that may have seemed out of reach at first but that became achievable with multiple prototypes of partnership and delivery models. The resulting reframing and refocusing of this association's strategy demonstrate the potential to create breakthrough new value for all stakeholders in the mix, starting with some quick wins and experiments to get out of the gate. By prototyping the strategic system before activation, they were able to focus their energies and move forward in a more intentional and productive way.

If a big idea can't be translated into a distinct enterprise strategy, focused activities, and a clearly focused action plan to drive toward success, it will never be realized. As Roger Martin points out in his Foreword: *"If the focus is entirely on creative discovery without consideration of how it converts to a winning strategy, creativity is practically useless."* That is the missing link in many innovation projects, and one of the reasons so many innovation initiatives fail to deliver a return on investment, as noted earlier. Gear 3 is about defining a strategy and designing a system of activities to win.

For many, Gear 3 is the most fun gear of all. It requires as much creativity and exploration as Gear 2, combined with a rigorous analysis of how alternative models will play out financially and competitively. It is the ultimate challenge for business-minded innovators. Gear 3 uses design-based methods like collaboration, systems mapping, visualization, and iterative prototyping to design a clear and distinct strategy. When you crack the strategy and see how it will work as a system, and activate your first Quick Win as a step toward How to Win, that is when your collective dream begins to take hold. That will position the enterprise on a new growth trajectory to add market value and advance your competitive advantage.

Gear 3 brings focus and momentum to your quest. The strategy you design will help channel your efforts in creating sustainable value for the end user, other significant stakeholders, and, most importantly, your enterprise. That is the all-round win. By configuring your system of activities so that all stakeholders win, you set the foundation for sustainable competitive advantage. This framework will help guide you from here on, including identifying and activating the early Quick Wins and Experiments that will set you on your new path. During this phase, it will be necessary to analyze financial sensitivities in order to pinpoint any risks associated with the unknown variables in your experience and business model. This analysis will inform both how you configure your model and what Experiments you will need to design in order to learn how to mitigate risk.

It is particularly valuable at this stage to engage a comprehensive mix of expertise, including operational, financial, human resources, and marketing people — because it will take all of these brains to construct an inventive and well-integrated system.

Your Goal in Gear 3

Your goal in Gear 3 is to define an enterprise strategy on How to Win – designing the distinct system of activities that will enable you to deliver your vision and create the basis for sustainable competitive advantage. This will enable you to refocus your collective energies on unique value-creating activities, with a plan to activate your learning and new vision through a thoughtfully sequenced plan for Quick Wins, Experiments, and expansion.

Important Activities and Mindsets

Gear 3 draws extensively on your capacity for systems thinking and visualization, and calls for a healthy dose of both creativity and analysis at appropriate points (see figure 12). Gear 3 begins with clearly defining the Value Proposition, then deconstructing your vision into concrete design components and the Capability Requirements to deliver them. All of these will culminate in a Strategy to configure your distinct system of activities. In assessing your Value Exchange, you will design the most efficient and competitive way to deliver value to your end user and ensure that every stakeholder benefits from a balanced exchange. Identifying and mitigating risk through multiple prototypes and analysis will lead you to Quick Wins and Experiments, and a clear road map to focus your efforts going forward – your overall Development Plan. Here's how your activities may unfold:

FIG. 12 GEAR 3 ACTIVITIES & OUTPUTS

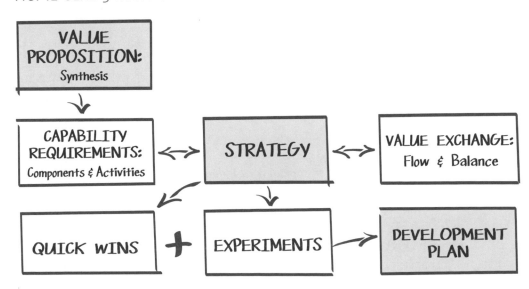

At this stage, it is important to be open to new ways of doing business and also willing to let go of old ways of working that can hold you back. If you can embrace with an open mind what appear to be constraints in your current business model, you are bound to find solutions that might otherwise have eluded you. Having courage to move forward and a sense of optimism and resilience as you encounter challenges along the way will help drive you forward toward achieving a successful outcome in Gear 3.

What makes this a "design" effort is the fact that you will use all your design methods and skills to create your enterprise strategy — visualization, ideation and multiple prototyping, systems mapping, iteration, co-creation, and storytelling. That's what makes the third gear both creatively and analytically robust.

I have broken Gear 3 into two sequential steps — Strategy first and Activation second.

Strategy — *Principles and Frameworks*

Designing the enterprise system is the ultimate act of creativity, because it translates a good idea into a well-thought-out and well-strategized action plan. This is the point at which dreams often get left on the table, because they have not been fully translated into what the enterprise has to do, uniquely and strategically, to make your refreshed vision succeed. Now is also the time to define the value to the enterprise and answer the inevitable questions: How are we going to win the market and, at the same time, make money by doing this, *and* how are we going to *keep* making money by doing this? How can we configure our system of activities so it is not easy for a competitor to replicate?

There are a number of important principles to keep in mind throughout this phase:

Strategy is anchored in a distinct value proposition. In the case of Singapore WISH, the overarching proposition was encapsulated as follows:

> *Singapore WISH*
> *Deliver an authentic cultural experience and a unique gift collection*
> *of carefully selected, locally produced Singaporean bakery items*
> *to delight travelers from abroad.*

The core proposition is delivered through an experience made up of concrete elements. This is the "big idea" defined in Gear 2. The first step in determining what has to be sourced, produced, promoted, and delivered through the system is to deconstruct the vision of the end user's experience. This will help you determine what you need to do well in order to realize your new vision and how it will get done. After that, the roles and contributions of all of the potential delivery stakeholders (including manufacturers, promoters, and partners) can be defined. In the case of WISH, requirements for product design, sourcing, branding, promotion, and distribution needed to be identified and explored.

Strategy is defined by a distinct system of activities aimed at delivering value. Designing a winning enterprise system calls for defining a unique and compelling market proposition and seamlessly delivering a high-value experience through a collection of concrete design components. Value is delivered, captured, and sustained by the enterprise through a unique system of interrelated activities. This is not a case of merely determining what it costs to make or do something and how much revenue can be generated. This is not driven by a spreadsheet exercise (though there is a place for that). Designing a winning strategy entails considering and knitting together the core activities in which you choose to invest time and money. For an enterprise strategy to be competitive, there must be something inherent in the design of the system that is uniquely deliverable by the enterprise and difficult for others to replicate. Otherwise, it will not justify the investment of effort and money. These factors are important when designing a sustainable system for any enterprise, whether public or private, as your model will need to be operationally sustainable and justifiable to those paying the bills.

Activity System modeling[27] is a valuable way to visualize your Strategy for How to Win. Let me first show how the Singapore WISH model was visualized. I will then describe how the Activity Systems of two other successful enterprises illustrate the way in which strategy is expressed as a distinct value-creating set of activities that support the enterprise's overarching value proposition and create a sustainable competitive advantage.

An Activity System is a visualization of strategy and is made up of:

Hubs: Core activities that together define how the enterprise uniquely creates value

Supporting Activities: Specific activities that fortify hubs

Linkages: How hubs and activities relate to and reinforce each other to create value

A powerful Activity System is one in which a unique system of activities synergistically creates value for the market and the enterprise.

A number of core activities (aka "hubs") will allow SBCTA to uniquely fulfill its vision. These include delivering *an authentic taste of Singapore's most iconic treats*, leveraging *Singapore's network of local producers*, building a *shared Singaporean branded experience,* and creating *visibility and access through strategic partnerships*. This system leverages strategic partnerships (with tourism, retail, and hospitality partners) to give visibility and access to this idea to travelers from abroad. The central hubs in the diagram below depict these core activity themes (see figure 13). Specific supporting activities feed and connect to these hubs. For example, co-marketing through selected airlines and hotels reinforces the brand and increases the visibility of and access to the product. Together, these activities represent a distinctive strategy for SBCTA.

FIG. 13 SINGAPORE WISH ACTIVITY SYSTEM

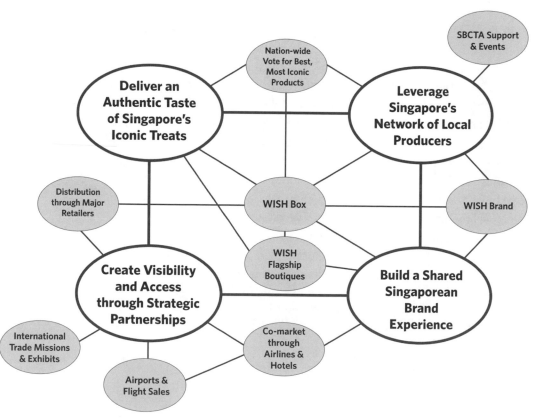

FIG. 14 NESPRESSO ACTIVITY SYSTEM

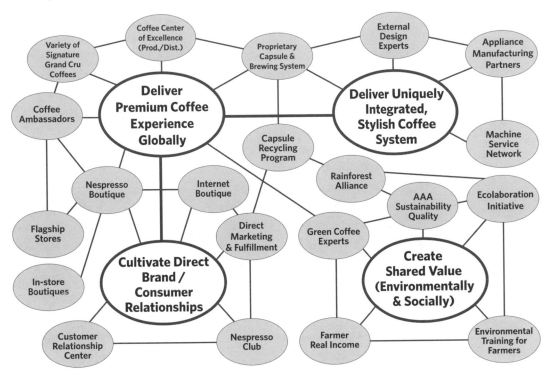

Nespresso is another excellent example of a game-changing strategy to bring moments of pleasure and indulgence to coffee lovers around the world by delivering a *premium coffee experience.* While the parent company, Nestlé, manufactures and sells consumer packaged foods largely through food retailers, Nespresso chose to create an entirely new category around a *uniquely integrated and stylish coffee system* (see figure 14). This unique coffee system leverages their ability to source and produce high-quality coffee, delivered in a convenient and proprietary capsule that is "brewed" through a special coffee machine. The company outsourced the machine's design to high-end designers (e.g., Alessi) and manufacturers (e.g., Krups and Magimix), and built a broad-based network of qualified service providers. They actively cultivate a *direct brand relationship with their consumer* through direct one-to-one marketing, an exclusive Nespresso Club membership of 10 million and growing, and direct on-request product fulfillment. They also designed their product supply chain to adhere to the parent company's commitment to *Shared Value* and high standards of social and environmental responsibility. They adhere to strong Rainforest Alliance standards to ensure the highest quality and sustainability practices in their sourcing, farmer relations, and accredited associations as part of their Ecolaboration initiative. These choices are reflected in a strategically distinct and well-integrated system. It is this strategy that has attracted more than 10 million coffee lovers to Nespresso and propelled revenues to over $3 billion in 10 years.[28]

Similarly, Four Seasons Hotels and Resorts have made some equally important strategic choices in their quest to deliver the highest level of service and a *unique luxury-hotel experience* to their guests. At the core of their success is their *superior staff service attitude*; people are carefully recruited and trained, and abide by an important ethos — the Golden Rule, as noted earlier by Isadore Sharp. There is no customer service department at Four Seasons because all employees are passionate and professional about their individual roles in making a guest's stay as personalized, luxurious, and delightful as possible. Four Seasons have chosen to manage their *medium-sized properties* and *focus on service and hotel management,* rather than own the real estate and manage financing and capital. As part of their hotel management practices, they adhere to high standards in *consistent global branding,* as reflected in their communications and in the location and design of properties. In more recent years, they have been able to extend this expertise into residences. Thus a set of well-integrated choices makes up the Four Seasons Activity System[29] (see figure 15), which has earned them recognition as the top-rated hotel and resort enterprise in the world.

When we go through this exercise in executive training, there is always an "Aha!" moment in which participants discover the power of the system: "Now I can see that it is not just the product — it is the entire system of activities. We should always be challenged to defend how our system is *different.*" That is the competitive advantage. Inspired by Roger Martin's strategy consulting work, here is a checklist of what to keep in mind when assessing the power of your system, and its ability to create a sustainable competitive advantage for you:

- Does it create *value* for every stakeholder in the ecosystem?

- Is it a *breakthrough* in that it is not just more of the same but something that will truly disrupt the market?

- Is it *distinct* in that it is different from your competitors' systems and gives you a competitive advantage?

- Does it *fit together* as an integrated system and support your enterprise vision and purpose?

- Is it *sustainable* in terms of both financial viability and competitiveness? Is it a system that competitors cannot easily replicate?

FIG. 15 FOUR SEASONS ACTIVITY SYSTEM

Money can be made, saved, and spent in many ways. Exploring a number of options for sources of revenue and determining how best to make and save money will lead to financial viability of your big idea. Often we believe that, in order to generate revenue, we need to sell more widgets or services. Such is the core revenue stream for many companies; yet there are many ways to make money that we often overlook. This is where your creativity and financial acumen will come into play. When looking at the whole end-user experience, imagine where you can *make money* through new sources of revenue. These sources include sales of your own product, selling others' products in your outlets (e.g., Apple selling peripherals such as speakers and accessories such as computer cases), service programs (e.g., extended warranties offered by retailers in electronic product sales), sponsorships or advertising revenue (at events or on-line), or user fees (as in the case of ATMs or mobile phones). In the case of Singapore WISH, the primary source of revenue was the Wish box, supporting producers and the association at large.

On the flip side, you will want to be creative about how you can *save money* in delivering solutions — through efficiencies in scale (e.g., high-volume production), off-shore product supply or production, long-term contracts with vendors, and many other means. In the case of Singapore WISH, partners could capitalize on existing capacity by sourcing from established producers and could leverage the existing access to travelers through airlines and hotels, avoiding heavy investment in new manufacturing or selling channels.

When you maximize how you can make and save money, you will be able to *spend money* and invest in your core strategic activities. Will you invest in your distribution network, as Frito-Lay does with its Direct-to-Store distribution system? In brand marketing, like Procter & Gamble or Nepresso? In recruiting, training, and retaining staff, like Four Seasons? In the case of Singapore WISH, one of the key strategies was investment in creating and promoting a compelling new brand.

Every stakeholder must win. Reciprocity in the ecosystem is an essential principle in balanced stakeholder exchange and sustainability. It is clearly important to create value for the end user and the enterprise, but for your model to be sustainable, it is equally important to create value for all key stakeholders. When designing the value exchange among stakeholders (i.e., who gives what and what they get in return), it is important to ensure a balanced exchange. While the exchange of money is what is most easily measured, value can also come in the form of credibility, brand image or reputation enhancement, distribution or access to the market, or knowledge and expertise. The key is to recognize and appreciate all forms of value in the exchange. Otherwise, the system will eventually unravel. For this reason, it is important to see the exchange through the eyes of others. Practice empathy and put yourself in the shoes of others.

For example, take the following simple case of a healthcare company that operates within an ecosystem in which value is exchanged among multiple partners (see figure 16). The healthcare company needs patient referrals to their new services, and it needs the endorsement of the patients' most trusted advisor, the doctor. The doctor wants information to help counsel her patients in a knowledgeable (and time-efficient) manner, and an opportunity to earn revenue through patient visits. The patients need advice and are willing to pay for it; and ultimately they need a solution (product or service) that will improve their health.

FIG. 16 HEALTHCARE VALUE EXCHANGE

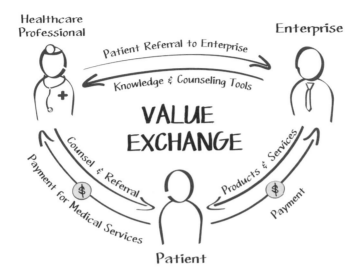

In this scenario, one would want to ensure that the enterprise was seen to be the best source of credible, usable information, or it could easily be substituted for another like-intentioned player and lose valuable access to the patient market.

Strategy – *Key Considerations*

This phase of design is as creative and iterative as the Concept Visualization of Gear 2. It requires the same degree of iteration and a conscious toggling back and forth between generative, optimistic thinking and critical, analytical thinking. Considerable thought is required to create new systems that can pave the path for your success. Here are some things to keep in mind:

Prototype multiple options. Consider a number of ways of strategically delivering your solution to the market. For example, you might build a new capability within the enterprise or outsource it through strategic partners (as in the case of Nespresso, which chose to work with outside designers and manufacturers).

Consider who is friend or foe. You are likely not the only player going down your envisioned strategic path. Consider the partners with whom you can have a reciprocal and sustained alliance. In the case of Nespresso, they chose to collaborate with machine designers, manufacturers, and service networks.

Draw on your enterprise strengths. As part of Preparing for Your Quest (next chapter), mapping your current Activity System will show that you have a well-entrenched system in place that can be leveraged to give you a head start, accelerate realization, and strengthen your competitive advantage. My interview with Isadore Sharp at the end of this chapter shows how Four Seasons have gone about doing that.

Prepare to evolve your strategy, and rethink how you manage and measure progress. Really big business ideas often call for the evolution of your strategy. Success will depend on how you manage that new system relative to your existing system and how, as Roger Martin puts it, you make your big ideas "plug compatible" with the existing infrastructure of business. You may also need to rethink how you manage and measure success in direct and indirect ways.

Strive for scalability and competitive advantage. Ultimately, your goal is to set your enterprise on a path to create more value for the market and more value for the enterprise, and to do so in a way that enables you to continue to expand the impact of your value-creation through a distinct strategy and a scalable system that gives you a sustainable advantage.

Ultimately, the design of a business is not unlike the design of any other object or experience concept. This is the phase in which all dimensions of thinking come together to create a breakthrough strategy: creativity, analysis, critical thinking, systems thinking, and synthesis. There is a lot of logic and a lot of creativity in this phase, which is activated with a sense of purpose and conviction.

   Long-run success comes from building from a base of customer devotion and knowing Where to Play and How to Win, combined with perseverance and enterprise agility.

The following interview with Sir Richard Branson brings to life how building competitive advantage is a long-haul effort that entails determination, agility, mitigating risk, and embracing failure along the path to success.

In 1984, when tiny Virgin Atlantic first picked a fight with the mighty British Airways, the odds certainly appeared stacked against us. In fact, my bankers were so unenthusiastic about my prospects that they called in their loans after our first flight, forcing me to switch banks! But our inexpensive arsenal was loaded with surprising and unconventional weapons. Perhaps the most effective of these was our agility, which was integral to our corporate culture, in part because of our size. British Airways was weighed down by bulky, hierarchical decision-making processes that made any change very difficult, whereas we were able to change direction or stop on a dime. When our customers or crew told us they didn't like something, we'd drop it and quickly move on to the next idea. Our small size — we had only a few planes — allowed us to give customers an experience the bigger players couldn't afford to match across their large fleets. For instance, our Upper Class passengers are provided with free door-to-door limousine service, both to and from the airport. Our competitors would have to offer this service on every global route, not just the few routes competing with Virgin — a much more expensive proposition for them.

Looking back on Virgin's history, our ability to adapt quickly to changes has helped mitigate reverses. You must be quick to accept that something is not going well and either change tack or close the business. Although I believe in taking risks, I also believe in "protecting the downside." This means working out all the things that could go wrong and making sure that all those eventualities are covered. We have come close to failure many times. Most entrepreneurs skirt close to it. I nearly failed when Virgin was in its infancy, I nearly failed in the early 1980s, and, of course, I have nearly died more than once trying to achieve world records for boating or ballooning. But through a combination of luck and planning, both Virgin and I are still here. As an entrepreneur, you learn quickly that there's no such thing as a failure.

SIR RICHARD BRANSON
FOUNDER AND CEO,
VIRGIN GROUP

Activation — *Principles*

Defining your strategy will help you focus your energies. Then it is time for activation — time to get some Quick Wins and Experiments underway in pursuit of your ultimate vision. The following principles are important to keep in mind as you develop your activation plan.

Big wins come through a series of successes and failures. No enterprise can wait for a complete re-engineering before getting some wins under its belt. Wins come in the form of customer and business wins, as well as through learning from things that do not go exactly as expected. Celebrate the small victories, and embrace learning from failures, as noted by Sir Richard Branson.

Quick Wins activate your strategy out of the gate and move you closer to where you want to go. These are the smaller and more readily doable initiatives that will start you down a new path. If they fit with your general enterprise purpose and address an unmet need of your customer, there is no reason not to activate a component of your new idea as a way of getting started. In the case of Singapore WISH, participants geared up for the future by developing a new product configuration to sell under a new brand to generate sales and valuable in-market learning. In the case of the healthcare company in the chapter on Gear 1, they expanded their fast-track system to keep at-risk patients on the healthcare radar while pursuing longer-term initiatives. In the case of Four Seasons, they continually add new guest services to their repertoire as a way of reinforcing their strategy and advancing their broader practices.

For bigger, more uncertain moves, Experimentation leads to valuable learning about next steps. Identify what you know, then learn and ascertain as much as possible about the elements you are less sure of. This will tell you what you need to know and give you greater confidence to go to the next level of investment. Nespresso has been experimenting with new ideas since the beginning, most recently with those related to their Ecolaboration platform. Experiments are an essential ongoing activity in carving out a new, longer-term path.

"A LOT OF EXPERIMENTS HAVE CONTRIBUTED OVER TIME TO THE SUCCESS OF NESPRESSO — FROM THE ORIGINAL IDEA, TO OUR SPECIFIC ROUTE-TO-MARKET AND DIRECT-TO-CONSUMER BUSINESS MODEL, BOUTIQUES, BRAND COMMUNICATION STRATEGIES, TO TRENDY AND DESIGNED MACHINES. MORE RECENTLY, THE WAY NESPRESSO HAS ENGAGED AND COMMITTED TO SUSTAINABILITY THROUGH OUR ECOLABORATION INITIATIVE, FROM RECYCLING TO SUSTAINABLE COFFEES, WILL ALSO CONTRIBUTE IN THE NEAR FUTURE. AS AN EXAMPLE, AAA COFFEE PROGRAM STARTED IN THE FIELD IN 2003 AS AN EXPERIMENT, AND AFTER 8 YEARS OF LEARNING WE STARTED TO BROADLY TELL OUR STORY IN 2011."[30]

— **Guillaume Le Cunff** *Nespresso Global Marketing*

Mapping your development path will bring all of this into focus — the elements to be activated or tested, key milestones and decisions along the way, and ways of measuring success, including both operational and customer-based learning. This will position you to drill down on execution and iterate on a finer level. As you move into execution of specific components, repeat the same design process on every element — the product, the delivery of the service, the space, and communication elements. Build prototypes, engage stakeholders, and iterate from the "development lab" right through to the marketplace.

Activation — *Key Considerations*

At this point, most high-performing teams have the skills and systems to activate the development and execution of their vision. It is a matter of having the right people on the right tasks at the right time. Here is what you will need to guide your efforts:

- a roadmap on Quick Wins, Experiments, and development efforts that includes activities, people, money, and timing;

- a disciplined project manager to engineer and navigate your course;

- milestones and measurements to tell you when and if you are on track;

- a good business case and a sequencing of activities and investments that make good business sense and help mitigate risk along the way.

How Mindsets Matter in Gear 3

As I mentioned at the beginning of this chapter, Gear 3 calls for a healthy dose of both creativity and analysis at appropriate points. The right mindset in Gear 3 is crucial.

Openness to the perspectives of others and new ways of doing business will allow you to design a viable strategy for migrating toward a new vision. That will be essential in exploring new activities, new partnerships, and new ways of managing and measuring success that may call for a departure from the past.

Embracing constraints will help you find new ways of overcoming barriers and avoiding undesirable trade-offs and compromises. It's hard work to find creative resolutions to seemingly insurmountable constraints, but collaboration and conviction can help you find clever solutions.

Courage is part and parcel of innovation. Anything new makes most business people nervous. Your role is to be clear on your vision, razor sharp on your strategy, and responsible in your activation plans to make small, measured moves toward a breakthrough idea. That takes courage.

Resiliency and optimism will help you through the minor setbacks that may result from experiments and keep you in a "learner mindset" as you embrace those failures and iterate in the progression toward your vision.

The following excerpt from my interview with Isadore Sharp illustrates how Four Seasons Hotels and Resorts have continued to stay close to their customers and evolve their strategic Activity System, looking for ways to expand their offerings to satisfy customer needs and leverage their brand, service, and hotel management strengths. At the same time, they apply a strategic and analytical eye to ensuring strategic fit and operational competitiveness.

We have looked at alternative businesses as a way of diversifying — retirement homes, cruise ships, and a lot of other things. People come up with ideas, and they may sound good at first. As you look into it, you discover either that it works or that it doesn't work. A lot of these things didn't work for us because we didn't have that expertise. You have to know what you can't do well much more than what you can do. Residences were part of what we could do well. They became a way to diversify. It's real estate, and a way of making the economics of building a hotel better. Whether it's a rental or a condominium, that part of the real estate was improved because of the brand name. The combined use of the real estate made the business model better.

It's about designing and building the right product, but it's also the services, whether it's the maintenance, the concierges, or the doormen. I asked one of the many people who were living there, "Why did you decide to live here when you could live in any place?" He said, "I'll tell you exactly why. My wife and I are a little older now. We have other homes and we want this to be our home when we're in town because I know that the service I get here will be reliable. If my wife needs anything, she can push one button on the telephone and there will be somebody at the door who's very competent." That's the reputation of the brand and knowing that the company doesn't just say it but we can live up to that promise.

So that's where the residential component fitted perfectly with the hotel, again relying upon our people to make a difference.

TOOLS & TIPS
for Gear 3: Strategic Business Design and Activation

The following Tools & Tips will give you a solid repertoire to combine with your tried-and-true tools for designing models, assessing risk, and moving big ideas forward in a series of successive wins.

The Proposition: Synthesizing the opportunity
(pages 210–211)

Capability Requirements: Delivering the breakthrough
(pages 212–214)

Activity Systems (Future): Designing a strategy to win
(pages 215–217)

Activity System Assessment: Evaluating your enterprise strategy
(pages 218–219)

Activation Planning: Assessing how to resource and manage innovation
(pages 220–222)

Value Exchange: Designing the delivery and exchange of value
(pages 223–226)

Reciprocity: Balancing value exchange in the ecosystem
(pages 227–228)

Financial Sensitivity Analysis: Assessing uncertainty and risk
(pages 229–230)

Experiments: Testing the unknowns
(pages 231–232)

Quick Wins: Capitalizing on learning out of the gate
(pages 233–234)

Management Systems: Designing support systems and measuring what matters
(pages 235–237)

PREPARING *for* YOUR QUEST
Setting the Foundation

Many enterprises have found that the best way to prepare for their quest is to do an intense run-through of all 3 Gears as part of their strategic planning process. That helps them set the foundation for Where to Play and How to Win. The following story describes how a team used the 3 Gears of Business Design as their framework for strategic planning, demonstrating the importance of engaging the right individuals to tackle the challenge and utilizing Business Design methods to get the most robust outcomes from your collaboration.[31]

The Nestlé Confectionery Story: *Sweet Success*

The Challenge

In 2008, the Nestlé Confectionery team faced a challenge: How could they reconcile selling chocolate bars in a company that is committed to health and wellness? The need to reconcile a broader corporate ambition with a diverse portfolio is not uncommon in large companies. In the case of Nestlé Confectionery, the Vice-president of Marketing at the time, Elizabeth Frank, saw this strategic tension as an opportunity to innovate. To tackle this challenge, Elizabeth, with the support of Sandra Martinez, then division President, assembled a cross-disciplinary team from marketing, operations, product development, finance, and sales for a two-day strategic planning session, in which the Nestlé leadership team engaged in a full run-through of the Business Design process. The session was designed to examine the current strategy for Confectionery and Nestlé at large, reframe their long-term Confectionery strategy, and align the team behind a new vision and a plan to reignite growth.

From the outset, this team embraced their collective devotion to the happiness good chocolate brings to everyday life. At the same time, they were able to step back and really challenge their current paradigm. Their shared ambition was: to determine how they were going to make Confectionery as "good for you" as every other product produced by Nestlé.

The Breakthrough

The breakthrough came in a number of ways, all of which culminated in a strategic reframing of Where to Play and How to Win, based on a new vision for the business, and a series of initiatives from products to marketing campaigns. The session began with a mapping of their current strategy, to gain important alignment on the current state. The first breakthrough came in Gear 1, when they brought in consumers to tell their stories about looking after their family's health and wellness. The Nestlé team were touched by the insights and meaning they discovered in these stories. There were smiles and even tears during these encounters. The surprise? Consumers believed wholeheartedly that "chocolate is good food." They re-educated the Nestlé team on the virtues of chocolate as part of their everyday well-being. That also inspired the Nestlé team to think longer term, take a more visionary stance, and implement a pragmatic and staged approach to building their business in a relevant and meaningful manner over time.

Gear 2 gave them license to transform this renewed inspiration into new possibilities in the form of three distinct brand experience prototypes, drawing from their collective insight, intuition, imagination, and expertise. They prototyped and role-played their preliminary ideas for consumers, to get early feedback. As an example, for one concept, they presented how their idea fitted into the life of a teenager. They turned one room into a three-scene set, where drawings of high school lockers covered one of the walls for the first scene, a rough mock-up of a convenience store occupied another area to play out the next scene, and a kid's bedroom with a computer constructed out of old cardboard boxes completed the envisioned experience, all at a materials cost of only $17. The teenagers appreciated their creativity and openness, and gave valuable feedback on how to make the Nestlé team's idea even better.

For Gear 3, they rearticulated their strategy and designed a five-year plan to activate their new vision for the business. By reconnecting with consumers, exploring bigger propositions to address wellness in broader and more holistic terms, and visualizing the current strategic model, the team were able to refresh their vision and reframe their strategy. This enabled them to refocus their efforts on a stream of business initiatives that emerged from their shared vision. Passion, laughter, creativity, and determination filled the team's planning session, and they came away ready to make their vision a reality.

The Outcome

The team redefined the meaning of wellness within the context of Confectionery and created a clear and cohesive strategy for enhancing consumers' sense of well-being and supporting responsible and meaningful indulgence. A number of product-related initiatives included using all-natural ingredients, providing smaller-sized portions, offering products with health benefits (such as dark chocolate), and recommitting to Shared Value (a program for fair trade and sustainable environmental practices). Other important initiatives included investment in socially relevant programs that enhanced consumers' sense of well-being on an emotional or social level, like the Smarties *Show Your Colours* initiative aimed at inspiring kids to support important social causes.

A compelling presentation captured the team's vision and inspired the global headquarters in Vevey, Switzerland, with Nestlé Canada Confectionery leading the change in the articulation of the new global Confectionery strategy. In Canada, this new strategy activated numerous initiatives that set the business on a new path toward success and double-digit growth for three successive years. As the Canadian CEO said after the first year, "They've been on fire ever since! The results are outstanding."

"THIS APPROACH TO BUSINESS DESIGN HELPED BUILD TEAM ALIGNMENT EARLY ON AROUND A COMMON UNDERSTANDING OF THE CONSUMER AND A SHARED PATH FORWARD. THE OUTPUTS OF THIS WORKSHOP APPROACH WERE CRITICAL AND SALIENT AND ABSOLUTELY DROVE BUSINESS RESULTS."
— **Elizabeth Frank** *Vice-president, Marketing (2008), Nestlé Confectionery (Canada)*

This example points to the importance of having the right team, high ambitions, and the right design tools to unlock the innate creativity and passion for driving business in a purposeful way. It also underscores the importance of having a strong team leader and a supportive and motivating executive leader.

An Action Plan for Preparing for Your Quest

The first step is to get the right people mobilized on the right development path. Motivated by high ambitions and collectively inspired to create a future vision, this team will help propel the enterprise forward. It's important to have a strong team leader and a supportive and motivating executive leader, as was the case for Nestlé Confectionery.

Collaboration and an open mind are critical from the get-go in the Business Design process, as is empathy by and for all team members. The Tools & Tips section lists a number of activities that can help you in designing and tuning up your team.

FIG. 17 ACTIVITIES AND OUTPUTS IN PREPARING FOR YOUR QUEST

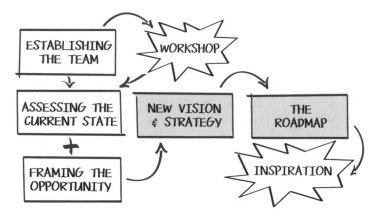

After Establishing the Team, you might conduct a strategic planning workshop, as Nestlé did. You can also pursue your quest through a full-scale project, for which some Tools & Tips are provided in part two. The first step is to capture and assess the Current State of your enterprise from a multifunctional perspective. This will ensure that you have a common understanding of where you stand today. Your next step is Framing the Opportunity. In the case of Nestlé, the team accomplished a Strategy Reframe in a three-day workshop. Finally, you will design a Roadmap to activate your strategy by plotting the steps you will take to deliver on your new vision. In the case of Nestlé Confectionery, the team's vision and roadmap were captured in an inspirational video to present their strategy to global executives. Figure 17 below provides a schematic of the activities and outputs for using the 3 Gears for strategic planning. A more in-depth process for tackling a project (which was done outside the workshop for Nestlé Confectionery) is presented in part two and outlined in the balance of this chapter.

Establishing the Team

This section provides some guidelines on how to establish a powerful and productive team. While many of these principles are common sense, it is surprising how businesses often overlook them in the face of time and resource constraints. Taking the time to get all of the important players on board from the start always pays off in the longer term. Following are some of the key factors in others' success.

Healthy diversity in a team will bring richness to the process and open your enterprise to possibilities and solutions that may be far from obvious. This will also position you to get things done in a well-orchestrated manner and create momentum as you move forward. Establishing a cross-disciplinary team early on will enable you to get to bigger breakthroughs sooner and more effectively. That means having experts from R&D, Marketing, Sales, Manufacturing, Product Supply and Logistics, Finance, HR, and others around the table to tackle the project from the outset. Without this expertise and alignment on commitment to well-integrated outcomes, you will not be able to quickly and collaboratively solve complex challenges along the way. In the case of Nestlé Confectionery, every function that touched the business was brought to the table, which is why there was instant team buy-in and activation.

"WHO YOU SELECT TO BE ON THE TEAM BUILDS ALIGNMENT VERY EARLY ON AROUND A COMMON UNDERSTANDING AND A SHARED PLAN FORWARD. WE HAD THE PEOPLE THAT I KNEW WOULD SEE THE ROADBLOCKS IN THE ROOM TO ARTICULATE WHETHER THEY THOUGHT WE WERE COMPETITIVELY DIFFERENTIATED OR NOT. WE CREATED THIS SAFE PLACE TO BUILD THAT ALIGNMENT." [32]
— **Elizabeth Frank** *Vice-president, Marketing (2008), Nestlé Confectionery (Canada)*

By enlisting team members with a diversity of skills, you will be able to get the job done by the people who do it best. This includes having people who are particularly good at project management, conceptualization, visualization, synthesis, analysis, communication, and other key skills that are valuable to supporting progress along the way. You must absolutely have a designated captain at all times to keep you moving ahead, whether it is one person all through the project or a rotating role. In the case of Nestlé Confectionery, Elizabeth was the driver, but the diverse team brought skills in finance, product supply and manufacturing, and sales and marketing to the table. That's how they cracked the nut in short order.

No one on a design project is along for the ride. Everyone will bring their own unique strengths to the project, and they need to be actively engaged and contributing throughout. Aligning roles with individuals' strengths will give everyone an important role in the process. In the case of Nestlé, all team members had an important role to play in conceiving and activating their renewed vision: for example, the product and nutrition team brought technical expertise; the product supply people brought procurement and operational expertise; and the marketing people brought brand expertise.

While everyone will have important and unique roles, there are some things for which everyone must be on the same page. This will help you get past the friction and enable you to capitalize on the fusion. It will also ensure that you deliver quality in an efficient manner. First, everyone should have a common purpose and mandate. This means having complete alignment on the importance and goals of the project to unify the shared ambitions of the team. Next, team members must share values and commitment. This will serve as the unifying code of conduct throughout the project. When the project gets rocky, as it inevitably will from time to time, the common values and commitment that come from a team built on openness, respect, and collaboration for the greater good will prevail. Another factor involves performance goals and accountability. As part of designing the process, it is essential to articulate the outcomes and deliverables in concrete terms at key points in the process, for both the team and for individuals. You are mutually dependent in your pursuits. And finally, because you're going to work hard and likely be stretched beyond your comfort zone, support for each other and a sense of team spirit will go a long way to facilitate the process. Mutual support can also mean the difference between an energizing and rewarding project and one that is just stressful hard work. Camaraderie and positive energy make the process fun and the breakthroughs and outcomes on the road to success bigger. Fun is important; it shouldn't be underestimated. Such positive energy often contributes to a positive business impact.

Clear, continuous, and transparent communication from the outset will fuel engagement, steady progress, and momentum. Having a clear plan to navigate through the project will give the team a good sense of where they are at all times. Communications must always be timely and without censorship. A cohesive team can raise red flags and help each other, or course correct if things are not going along as anticipated. It is also helpful to establish a means of remote or virtual communication so that every team member will always be able to log in and know where things stand. Many companies have their own intranet or virtual space for check-in. If you don't have one, there are several online resources that can provide an online workspace for the team.

Depending on your current structure and business practices, you might consider either or both of the following two options when designing your team. First, try leveraging intact teams. This will build continuity to the past. Enlist your existing allies who you know have the expertise and passion for carving out new paths. In the first Nestlé workshop, Elizabeth tapped into the intact business team. Second, invite those individuals who would bring valuable expertise and who welcome the opportunity to contribute to new ventures. This will enhance and accelerate outcomes. In subsequent annual strategic planning sessions, the Confectionery team added fresh perspective by bringing in yoga instructors and chefs to the session. Many clients bring in their agency partners as well, as they bring additional creativity and the ability to instantly activate new initiatives that come out of a development session. If you have designers in house, by all means bring them to the table; they will surely bring a valued perspective.

If you are not on the executive team, you'll want to have someone in a leadership position to act as your executive advocate. Getting one-level-up endorsement of your quest will provide "air cover" if you need it. While projects often begin under the radar, if you are committed to seeing a break-through, it is advisable to have a senior coach and sponsor if your efforts are going to be continuous and significant. This will also give you an invaluable sounding board as your developments unfold. All of our programs and proj-ects at DesignWorks have had an executive sponsor. Executive endorsement of the quest gives license to expand thinking beyond "today's business."

It's also a smart move to keep team members' management informed about your plans. Acknowledging participation and securing permission to tap into expanded resources is important in an environment where people need to account for their time and priorities.

Assessing the Current State

Once your team is in place, your first activity should be to take stock of the current state of your enterprise. You need to understand the strategy that is driving your existing outcomes. What are the activities and capabilities in which your enterprise is investing time and money right now? If you are an established enterprise, it is important to appreciate the value your current strategy creates. And it is equally important to recognize the competitiveness of that strategy. This can either give you confidence in your current path or elevate the urgency to explore new paths and models.

The act of visualizing and assessing your current strategy as an Activity

System is a collaborative exercise that requires an open mind, an objective and analytical view of the enterprise, and an aptitude for making connections. In undertaking this exercise with enterprises all over the world, I have found that there is often a lack of alignment within the team on how an organization's activities relate to strategy and how distinct (or not) this set of activities may be. For all the documents and operating systems that exist in many enterprises, there is surprisingly little alignment on what's really driving success in an integrated way. Many operate in functional or business silos, or deal with parallel streams of initiatives and competencies; but when one sees the overarching strategy as an interrelated set of activities, it can provide an entirely new perspective.

Second, the current Activity System often has more power and latitude than most team members realize. What might at first seem a constraint can be the foundation for expansion into either adjacent or totally new businesses. Often, when teams see the power of the system in terms of interrelated activities and capabilities, they are surprised to realize that those interconnected activities are extendable beyond "line extensions" and the business of today. For example, the Four Seasons enterprise excels at providing service to its guests and has been able to leverage this into Residences, as was explained in the second interview excerpt with Isadore Sharp.

As you undertake this phase, there are some key things to keep in mind. First, don't just reiterate what is documented in the strategic plan or annual report; instead, think deeply about where you have allocated resources in activating your strategy, building operational systems, and managing your business on an enterprise-wide basis. Think about the activity systems, capabilities, and assets you have uniquely established. Also recognize the skills it took to build those systems — skills that can also be leveraged.

Take time to knit together all critical activities that impact the distinctiveness and success of your strategy. Get the perspective of all functions. The marketing people will naturally think success is all about building brands. The operations people will think it is all about investing capital in operational excellence. The HR folks will think it is all about recruitment, training, and incentive systems. The R&D people will say it is all about leveraging and extending technical superiority and patents. And so on. Maybe everyone is right. And maybe you have a "silver bullet" that could be the clue to broader success, like the "Golden Rule" of Four Seasons. Most important is how the pursuits of each of your domains connect and contribute synergistically to the central strategy in delivering your value proposition.

And finally, solicit the perspectives of senior executives, those who have a bird's-eye view, to capture a comprehensive, high-level picture. This will help strengthen your foundation as you move forward.

Framing the Opportunity — *The Brief*

By now you will have gathered a variety of insights and information that will need to be synthesized and transformed into a platform for development. This is the time to analyze, synthesize, and crystallize your ambitions — framing the opportunity in a clear and compelling project brief. This activity will lead you to visualize a design process that is tailored to help you achieve your ambitions. It is your opportunity to open the lens and see the world in a broader way.

As the Persian prophet Zoroaster once said, "There are elements of chance, choice, and certainty in every aspect of our lives."[33] Here's how this timeless truth plays out in our current context. Business Design is about anticipating the forces of *chance* (emerging trends and competitive forces), ascertaining the *certainties* (the facts that can anchor you in your quest, such as your current capabilities and contextual forces), and designing the *choices* (your strategy) you make to create a new future. Your best bet lies in combining all three into an intelligent game plan that increases your odds of charting out a valuable new path for growth. The better you are at finding that "sweet spot" of the game, the greater your chances of success.

In staking out new territory, there are a few things to keep in mind. Initially, it will serve you well to look beyond current realities. Whatever business you are in today, you can assume that the context will evolve or even radically change in the future. Now is the time to be an opportunistic entrepreneur. It often helps to think like a start-up, even if you are not one.

The earlier you entertain future possibilities, the better prepared you will be. If you are to be successful in the future, you must be mindful of what is bubbling up around you. That could be emerging trends, rising competitive forces surfacing anywhere in the world, or blind spots your enterprise may have. These blind spots may simply be because certain ideas or plans have been set aside, often for lack of resources, and so are not on the current agenda. The truth is, these forces are often the elephant in the room that you have not faced, either because they do not fit with the current focus of your enterprise or because they are too daunting to face head on.

To position your enterprise for the future, it is valuable to think at least five years out, taking into consideration trends that are long-term and reliable forecasts of what is to come. If you are focused entirely on keeping the cash register ringing today, chances are you are not as prepared for competition in the future as you need to be. It is tough to balance current and future needs, but essential, if you want to position yourself as an enterprise that is on trend. As you will also discover, there is always a place for early wins in the short term that will set you up for bigger successes down the road.

Ignoring challenges now will lead to a greater struggle to compete later on. A foothold is a stronghold in many ways.

In anticipating future competition, it is important to recognize that you are likely not alone in your quest. What may seem like a breakthrough to you may also have been discovered in someone else's development lab. When you identify where you should play in the future, you will discover that there are many others eyeing that playing field. The key is to decide whom you may be up against, or who may be your valued partners in years to come.

In order to ensure that your team's efforts are supported by the organization at large, it is wise to be cognizant and respectful of high-level enterprise visions and agendas. That's where an executive sponsor of future-forward projects can help position efforts in the context of other enterprise initiatives, avoiding duplication or conflicting efforts.

Emphasizing future business/enterprise interests and gains will help gain support for your quest. In your analysis of your opportunity, put some numbers around the gaps and then set your sights high on the potential gains for your business. At the same time, look for and anticipate possible enterprise tensions when framing your enterprise opportunity. All new ventures will inevitably lead to model conflicts that you will have to consider and resolve. For example, if you have established retail relations and foresee opening up new channels, bring the right people to the table so you can find a way to resolve potential tensions early on in the development process. Also, if you are looking at new areas of business that would in some way compete with current lines of business, look for possible ways to integrate new paths into existing streams.

Designing the Roadmap

With an expanded view of the world ahead and the context for your value creation, it is time to design a game plan to guide your next steps. The plan will be a clearly articulated and visualized design process to help you pursue your ambitions.

Process design and management is a core discipline in Business Design. It requires mastery of methods, as well as the commitment of the team. Most teams have a good sense of how to manage projects, but there are some key things to keep in mind throughout the development process. *First,* every project will require a customized approach. That means plotting out not only the broader steps and activities but also the details of each step of research and development, including who will do what, and when. *Second,* the plan will evolve. New information will require adaptation. While the general plan will likely remain intact, it must be kept up to date to reflect the latest discoveries and developments. *Third,* team buy-in of the plan is critical. All team members have to commit to the process, and to their respective roles, and be open to the outcomes at every stage.

At the conclusion of this phase, you will have a clearly defined roadmap to guide your development efforts. The team will be confident that, no matter how complex the project or how uncertain the outcomes, there is a process that will guide multiple players to a unified and productive outcome. Everyone will have trust that the process will allow you to realize your goal.

Remember always to anchor your pursuits in the 3 Gears and trust the process that you have designed to guide your development efforts. While you never know at the outset exactly where the development process will take you, if you stick it out, you will likely be pleasantly surprised and delighted by the outcomes.

The following excerpt from an interview with Elizabeth Frank highlights the value of collaboration in setting the foundation and envisioning a more ambitious future.

It is important to start by capturing and assessing your current state, asking, "What is the current enterprise strategy? How well does the enterprise compete today?" When you have a cross-functional team in a workshop, it is important to realize that everyone's take on that can be completely different. Unless you get that on the table, you'll get nowhere. You won't even understand what your roadblocks are. We created a *safe place* to build that alignment. Being disciplined about it gives everyone a voice.

One thing that's important in establishing a productive team is continuous involvement and shared celebration, with *no one left behind*. When establishing this big team of people, you have no idea how important it is to feel included in a team like this. So if you're going to create a cross-functional work team and sense of shared ownership that becomes part of the culture, I believe you've got to have a commitment to maintaining that all the way through.

A process like this can also truly shape leaders. It's not a side benefit — it's a real intrinsic benefit to this sort of collaborative workshop approach. It inspires greater ambition. Incremental growth does not shape powerful leaders of the future.

ELIZABETH FRANK
VICE-PRESIDENT, MARKETING, NESTLÉ CONFECTIONERY (CANADA)

TOOLS & TIPS
for Preparing for Your Quest

There are many ways to establish your foundation. The Tools & Tips section of this book can help get you started, or add to your current repertoire.

Establishing the Team: Getting the right expertise on board
(pages 118–119)

Team-building Exercises: Fun ways to warm up to work
(pages 120–122)

Competency Mapping: Identifying talent, roles, and passions
(pages 123–124)

Facilitation: Harnessing the best of the team
(pages 125–126)

Team Charters: Creating a shared vision for roles and conduct
(pages 127–128)

Activity Systems (Current State): Visualizing your current strategy
(pages 129–133)

Activity Systems (Competitors): Visualizing competitive strategies
(pages 134–137)

STEEP Analysis: Forecasting future opportunities
(pages 138–139)

Landscape of Players: Identifying future friends and foes
(pages 140–141)

Sense Making and Synthesis: Connecting trends, issues, and players
(pages 142–143)

Project Brief: Framing your ambition
(pages 144–145)

Project Plan: Visualizing the development process
(pages 146–147)

TRANSFORMATION
Embedding Business Design into Your Enterprise

When Claudia Kotchka was appointed P&G's Vice-president of Design Innovation and Strategy, she was given the task of turning one of the business world's most finely tuned, analytical organizations into a design-minded enterprise. Here is her story of how P&G used design thinking to transform their way of working, with the aim of accelerating innovation through the 3 Gears of Business Design.[34]

Procter & Gamble:
An Example of Global Transformation

Procter & Gamble's quest began in 2001 when A.G. Lafley, then CEO of P&G, believed the company needed to look beyond technical innovation and broaden the consumer experience, and looked to design for the solution. In the beginning, some inside P&G viewed the idea as a fad, and something that only involved designers. According to Claudia, "Once they realized that it included everyone, that it is really about multidisciplinary teams and how to get them to work effectively, there were fewer naysayers."

Four things in particular stand out in Claudia's mind as benefits P&G reaps from Business Design. The first is learning to ask different questions. Many times business groups would come in to a design session with one question and an idea of where they should go with it, only to realize that in fact they were asking the wrong question. The second benefit was the value of get-ting different disciplines together, tackling a problem at the same time at the same table. This was a positive break from the usual tradition of working within silos. Third, P&G found great value in a more in-depth consumer look, rather than a strictly quantitative approach, and in the idea of activity-based research rather than product-based research. The fourth benefit was the idea that a prototype is not just something you give to the product supply team and say, in Claudia's words, "Here — we need this to come out the other end." It is really just a tool to further the dialogue, particularly with the end user, not an object that necessarily is going to go into the marketplace.

Above all, they discovered that Business Design is a powerful strategic tool because, in Claudia's words, "It gives you new insights into your customer — what they need and what they're looking for. It gives you new insights into Where to Play and How to Win because it forces you to look at the world differently and not the way you always have."

Today, P&G has trained nearly 300 design-thinking facilitators from multiple disciplines to use this capability to unlock opportunities every day around the world, according to Cindy Tripp, P&G's Director for Design Thinking, Global Design. Cindy played a key role in bringing design thinking around the world and embedding this capability into every region and every business unit.

"AT P&G, DESIGN IS NOW IN THE DNA OF THE COMPANY."
— **Claudia Kotchka** *Vice-president, Design Innovation and Strategy, Procter & Gamble (2001–2008)*

P&G exemplifies on a grand scale how Business Design can help to effectively and productively harness the talents of teams in identifying new opportunities for Where to Play and How to Win. Like P&G, you may begin by leveraging Business Design as a tool for solving problems or unleashing creativity on a single initiative. If it works for you as it did for P&G, you can begin to embed Business Design as a core competency throughout the enterprise as an innovation platform for and a systemic source of competitive advantage. But as Claudia points out, "Know what you're getting into if you decide you truly want to make Business Design a competitive advantage. It is a big job, but it has enormous payout."

Enterprise evolution and transformation do not happen at the wave of a wand. They require a long-term view of the capabilities and culture one aspires to shape. The process takes leadership, commitment, courage, and conviction, along with a thoughtful and well-implemented plan. If you realize the benefits of this approach through early experience and are keen to pursue it as a broader quest, there are some things that are helpful to consider up front. You may be asking: What can we do to embed these practices into our enterprise to enhance collective performance? That's the purpose of this chapter — to present some of the key learning from others' experience in rolling this practice out more broadly across an enterprise. There are no specific tools for doing this; rather, this chapter offers a collection of tips, gleaned from others' experience, to consider in your quest.

Adopting Business Design practices can lead to delivering greater market value; it can also bring value inside the organization, as shown in the table (figure 18) below. For example, iterative prototyping can allow you to explore more breakthrough ideas to create customer value; it can also stimulate dialogue, accelerate progress, and save money in the development process. There is also great value to the enterprise from iteratively prototyping more competitive strategic models. Co-creation can lead to more relevant and robust solutions; it can also help you work out the bugs faster and more cost effectively.

FIG. 18 VALUE TO MARKET AND ENTERPRISE

DESIGN METHODOLOGIES	MARKET VALUE	ENTERPRISE VALUE
Need Finding	Identify new opportunities to better meet customer needs	Create stronger customer focus and sensitivity
Collaboration	Create more robust solutions	Create early alignment and momentum and enhance viability
Visualization and Storytelling	Design a richer, more complete customer experience	Practice more effective and compelling communications to foster internal alignment
Iterative Prototyping	Consider more breakthrough ideas and powerful strategies to deliver customer value	Stimulate dialogue, accelerate progress, and save money in early solution and strategy development
Co-creation	Design more relevant and desirable solutions	Work out the bugs faster and at a lower cost
Mapping Experiences and Systems	Ensure integrated and seamless delivery of new solutions	Ensure greater synergies and efficiencies in your strategic activity model

The process of embedding Business Design into your organization is much like the Business Design process itself. It involves defining a long-term vision for the way you work, putting Quick wins and Experiments into place, and finding the right integration strategy for your enterprise. Business Design can inject a new way of thinking and working together that enhances market sensitivity, constantly evolving value offerings as well as building team alignment and momentum. It can serve as a booster for enterprise collaboration and performance that exercises agility and innovative thinking on a day-to-day basis. That's why many organizations are delivering ongoing programs to train and inspire employees throughout their organization on the 3 Gears, as noted by Thomas Gosline of Frito-Lay. Thomas is spearheading Experience Design at Frito-Lay, and utilizing Business Design training and tenets with cross-functional partners as a way to maximize the impact of his design team. Here's what he had to say on their quest:

> Despite strong growth on our core businesses, we've been challenged in creating the same degree of success in our innovation. In analyzing the underlying issues, we identified an opportunity to be more holistic in our approach to innovation — maximizing not just the consumer desirability, but also the entirety of the proposition. Rotman's Business Design approach has just the ingredients we're looking for: responsiveness to consumer desirability, business system feasibility, and value chain viability. Though we're just in the early stages, it's quite clear that the look of our innovation pipeline can be radically different when we utilize the suite of Business Design tools Rotman DesignWorks developed and trained our teams to use.[35]

Tan Hang Cheong, Principal of Singapore's first polytechnic institution, Singapore Polytechnic, believes in that at an institutional level. That's why he and his team are enrolling faculty in the transformation of a school of 15,000 students. He summed it up well in a recent session in Singapore when he said, "Business Design is the language of change." Business Design *is* a new language — a new way to create and operate. He is not alone in his conviction; Singapore's most ambitious companies are embracing Business Design. That's why there is now an offshoot of DesignWorks known as DesignWorks Singapore.

This chapter is intended to provide you with some things to consider based on general learning and perspectives that we have gained through working with other organizations to move beyond Business Design projects toward the integration of Business Design into the ongoing practices of their enterprises. Topics include:

Tips to Help You Succeed: principles to keep in mind in your journey toward becoming a design-minded enterprise;

Inspiring Innovation: the questions you ask, the language you use, the practices you institutionalize, and the spaces you create;

Business Design as Enterprise Platform: various ways to drive design capabilities and responsibilities throughout your enterprise;

Propagating Design: ways to inspire others and transfer the knowledge and skills throughout your organization;

Measuring Performance and Transformation: considerations on how this fits within other human resources and operating systems and practices, and how you can design your own "dashboard."

Tips to Help You Succeed

Here are my top ten tips to keep in mind as you go about embedding Business Design more broadly throughout your organization:

1. **Make a long-term commitment.** Business Design is not a one-shot vaccine or an event that you engage in periodically; it's a way of thinking, doing, and communicating every day that can become part of your DNA over time.

2. **Build it into your organizational strategy.** Business Design is not just a tactical solution. Making it part of your organizational strategy, from top to bottom and across all areas of expertise, will help you fully leverage the power of Business Design.

3. **Align cross-disciplinary efforts.** Business Design cannot be limited to a single function; it is and must be inclusive. For Business Design to be an effective innovation platform, not only must all participants see their role in the process, they must also see its relevance and value to their own discipline on a day-to-day basis.

4 Prepare to invest. If you want to be really good at this, and in a way that boosts enterprise returns, you should be ready to invest energy, time, and money in all areas of your organization. I always ask, if you regularly put a million dollars into a sales meeting, isn't investing in the capabilities of your entire organization an equally good investment?

5 Integrate Business Design into your existing practices. Business Design, as presented in this book, is meant to be not a disruption but an enhancement. It shouldn't be just an add-on to your existing processes; rather, it should be integrated into your innovation practices as an enhancement.

6 Internalize the practice of Business Design. In the early days, you will need help from experts to get you going, or — from time to time — to get you unstuck. The aim, however, should be to enhance your skills internally. To really get the value out of Business Design and to have it adopted throughout your enterprise, it is important that you acquire and develop the skills internally.

7 Successful transformation requires leadership. For best results, a well-respected and empowered leader with vision and fortitude to lead the transformation should be designated. That's what Procter & Gamble's A.G. Lafley did when he appointed Claudia Kotchka to lead the charge for the company.

8 Inspire, don't legislate. Business Design is not about establishing a strict process or a new set of rules. It's about a culture shift toward deeper values and stronger principles. It is about giving license to people to explore, create, experiment, and learn — both on big projects and day-to-day problem solving. Showcasing and celebrating the outcomes of design quests will create energy in the organization.

9 Feed it and reward it. Chances are, there are a number of HR and cultural implications for adopting Business Design as an enterprise platform. These may include the way people are evaluated and rewarded, allowing more latitude for experimentation and learning, along with more rewards for collaboration and originality.

10 Start now with a tough challenge. Business Design often starts off as an effective problem-solving tool, evolves into a strategic planning tool, and eventually becomes a part of your culture. Start with a pilot group. Conduct a few training and inspiration sessions. Just get started and grow from there.

Inspiring Enterprise Innovation

Business Design is a discipline that aims to elevate the level of innovation and increase your odds of success in a deliberate manner. At the same time, I would argue that its underlying value lies in mindfully nurturing a spirit of innovation and collaboration that unleashes the innate creativity and capacity to rise to any challenge *across* the enterprise. This spirit of innovation has been key in shaping the culture of many successful enterprises.

In the case of Sir Richard Branson, he goes to great lengths to set the tone as a leader at Virgin!

A successful business isn't just the product or service it sells or its supply chain. It is a group of people bound together by a common purpose and vision. In Virgin's case, we fly the same planes as our competitors, and our gyms offer much of the same equipment as other gyms. What separates our businesses from the competition? Our employees. The best designed business plan will come to nothing if it is not carried out by an enthusiastic and passionate staff. This is especially true when things go slightly wrong; a friendly and proactive team can often win people round, averting a potential disaster or even turning it to your benefit.

We at Virgin pride ourselves on trying to find the fun in our businesses, by which I mean that we try to ensure that both our staff and our customers feel a real sense of warmth and affection. I have led from the front on this — dressing up in costumes, trying all manner of stunts (not all going 100 percent right!), and generally showing that I do not take myself too seriously. My approach will not work for all businesses, but keeping a sense of perspective and not allowing management to be seen as aloof will help keep your staff onside. To foster employees' sense of warm, personal interest in customers' needs, it's crucial to ensure that they enjoy what they do and are proud of the company. This is vital to building lasting success and ensuring your service has an edge over the competition.

SIR RICHARD BRANSON
FOUNDER & CEO,
VIRGIN GROUP

Embedding the mindsets and methods of Business Design broadly within an enterprise requires a high-level commitment both to big-picture programs and initiatives and to activating everyday ways to inspire and ignite passion for design-driven innovation. These everyday signals come in the form of questions, language, space, and behaviors. What follows are some ideas that have worked for others and that can re-energize people and foster a culture of design-driven innovation without chewing up the budget.

Begin by asking new questions. As a decision maker, doing this can help you influence the motivations and behaviors of your entire organization. Instead of asking, "Can you prove this will work?" thereby likely killing any new-to-the-world idea, consider asking questions such as the following:

What unmet need does this address? A good starting point when framing the opportunity is to identify how a meaningful and broad-based need might be better met. A rigorous approach to Gear 1 will answer that question. In my experience, if the opportunity is based on the needs of your target users, it's hard to argue against.

What's the big idea that will create breakthrough value? What's the vision for the user experience? This calls for a clear articulation of the proposition and how that may eventually unfold as a multidimensional experience for the user, not just a description of a new product or service alone. I have seen many cases in which teams were given the license to pursue their ideas because they had a unique and compelling vision — a good "future story" that aligned with the long-term purpose and strategy of the enterprise. The Nestlé Confectionery story was one such case. Seasoned executives usually have a good instinct for the merits of a big idea.

Who was involved in the development of this idea? Asking this question will reinforce your commitment to the principle of cross-disciplinary collaboration, reveal how comprehensive the development process was, and signal how much early buy-in and future traction are associated with the idea.

What other ideas did you explore that led you to this one? Multiple prototyping inevitably leads to bigger, more robust solutions. Teams that explore and learn through a number of ideas before converging on one have demonstrated more open-mindedness and rigor than those who started with one idea and focused on making it perfect.

What did you learn from customers, and what do they think of this idea? The co-creation process always reveals valuable insights. Customer feedback, both good and bad, is important to capture. It is helpful to discuss what resonated, what surprised the team, and what bombed. It is a signal that they have stayed close to the customer and are truly creating for and with them.

How could this create sustainable competitive advantage for us? A true break-through will set you apart and allow you to carve out a new space that you can own. The answer to this question lies in a truly distinctive enterprise strategy on Where to Play and How to Win.

Why do you believe in this big idea? While there is no proof for new-to-the-world ideas, a strong sense of conviction will emerge from teams that have been rigorous through all 3 Gears and have identified what is known and what is yet to be tested through experiments and experience. To quote Isadore Sharp of Four Seasons, "It takes courage to do the right thing."

What are you not so sure of, and what do you want to learn as you move forward? It's okay for believers not to have all the answers or 100 percent guarantees. That comes with new territory. Acknowledging what is known and what is not known is healthy. Doing so encourages teams to pursue their path with a learner's mindset and to iterate and advance ideas along the way. It may also encourage them to experiment with different models — such as who pays for what, and what business models to consider.

How can I help? That's a big one. Sad to say, many employees see their senior decision makers as roadblocks to big ideas. The really great leaders offer their wisdom and guidance to support their employees in their pursuit of strong visions and give them the space to experiment and learn.

How does this discovery and development process inform what we are doing now? Through the Business Design Process, teams will most likely discover new insights that can help your business today, with immediate implications for existing priorities. For example, a particular discovery may reveal the need to recast or enhance a current, short-term initiative like a promotion or a product launch. There is always something to be learned in the Business Design process that will affect the here and now.

What should we stop doing based on what you have learned? One of the great benefits of this process is that it leads to a clearer picture of what really matters to the customer and, conversely, what doesn't. Such insight can lead to axing projects on your to-do list that either do not create value or that cost you money in operations, or both. You may find there are projects on the list that do not matter and others that need to be added or activated. By reprioritizing your investment, you will discover not only how good Business Design can *make* money but how it can *save* money.

Use design language. Aside from the way we communicate in our decision-making process, the everyday language we use is a simple clue to whether our activities are design driven. Discussing "needs" and "experiences" and referring to "prototypes" are small clues that signal a design culture.

Create spaces that are conducive to creative collaboration. One of the first things converts to Business Design do is create a visible and accessible space where community collaboration and innovation can take place. While you don't have to redesign your entire office, it is valuable to get out of the cubicle and into a space that's more conducive to collaboration. You may begin by reorganizing and redecorating one meeting room to set your team up for a more creative and productive collaboration. Consider creating a space that is more open, has features like whiteboards and large work surfaces, and is stocked with materials like large rolls of paper, sticky notes, and some prototyping materials. Eventually, you can convert more spaces for creative collaboration, leaving the offices and cubicles to analysis and administration. For those who have taken this all the way, a design orientation is evident throughout their enterprise space. For example, Singapore Polytechnic has built out several innovation spaces, including their "Inspiration Corridor."

Modify your practices. There are many easy and productive ways you can work collaboratively to advance your business through Business Design. Here are some simple ways to get started that have worked for others:

Spend face time with your key stakeholders and listen to their stories. While market research will always play a role in identifying trends and opportunities, spending time with people and *listening* to their stories will give you a more holistic understanding of them and greater insight into their needs. This is important for your understanding not only of customers but of other key stakeholders in your ecosystem.

Have a charrette instead of a meeting sometimes. A charrette is a design session in which challenges get solved on the spot. It is about calling together the right people and organizing an agenda in which you deconstruct a problem, brainstorm solutions, and build out a prototype or two. Instead of reviewing what you said you were going to do in the last meeting, reviewing what you've done since that meeting, and discussing what you will do before the next meeting, why not tackle the job on the spot? There will always be a place for status meetings, but you can often get things done faster and more efficiently with the right people around the table.

Spend as little money as possible on early prototypes. Big ideas don't rely on big spending. Low-resolution mock-ups can often be quite effective in helping to convey your ideas. You can shortcut a lot of recommendations by mocking up products, packages, and retail scenarios at virtually no cost. In our corporate workshops at DesignWorks, we like to limit the early prototyping budget to $20. Consumers love getting involved in the development process and are more likely to give you valuable criticism of an idea when you haven't spent a lot of money on developing it.

Consider multiple options. Before you commit to one solution or idea, always consider other options. I go by the Rule of Three: generate three ways of solving a problem or addressing a need, compare and contrast them with an open mind, and then create the best single solution. Most often, the solution will be none of the original three but some combination of them all.

Visualize more. The fastest way to communicate is often through visualization. Whether it is drawing a diagram, mapping a system of interrelated parts and forces, or creating an experience timeline, visualizing a discussion, challenge, or solution brings clarity and focus to communications and collaboration efforts.

Foster collaboration across functions and business units. With the depth of talent and resources that many large enterprises have, it is ironic that sometimes the biggest barrier to innovation and, more importantly, activation is the structure of the organization itself — the invisible walls between dreams and realization. Often a big idea calls for drawing resources from and leveraging strengths across divisions. Yet, when it comes time to activate an initiative, these divisions may wonder who "owns" the initiative and how it will play out within the organization's current structure. This is a common challenge in large enterprises, and one that must be recognized from the outset of a development project and worked through as big cross-divisional ideas emerge. These big ideas require new structures, new streams of activity, and redefined roles and rewards.

Business Design as Enterprise Platform

While you will need to consider business structures within your enterprise that allow for and reward cross-functional and cross-divisional innovation, you will also need to consider how to embed your Business Design expertise within the organization's structure. There is no single method to build Business Design capabilities and define responsibilities within an enterprise. You will need to do so in a way that naturally enhances how you do business, and in a way that fits with how you introduce new concepts into your enterprise.

A good way to start is to use the design process to design a strategy for expanding the practice of Business Design. This means mapping your stakeholders, assessing your current practices and systems, and understanding the needs of the business and all the players within the enterprise. What you will end up doing is mapping the "enterprise project" as you would map any other design project. Even though it is good to assume a full rollout from the outset, don't be overwhelmed by the magnitude of the task. Rather, use it as a means to foresee what may be required and identify any roadblocks or decisions that may be necessary along the way, whether related to time, resources, or money.

Your first step in the Business Design process should be to engage a pilot team. That is the way most organizations that have worked with Rotman DesignWorks have done it. This process often begins with enlisting team members who are predisposed to the design model — open to trying a new approach and to collaborating. Sometimes it is helpful to focus on a project that is already on a team's list of things to tackle but that the team has either not known how to solve or has not had time to concentrate on. Often those who are riding the wave of success have no interest in new ways, while those who are stuck and have nothing to lose will embrace the opportunity to tackle the challenge in a new way. With one case study under your belt, you can refine your approach and expand to other projects, with an eye to codifying what works best within your organization. Eventually, you will integrate that learning into an expansion effort that will embed this way of working into your organization. Before you know it, people will naturally ask questions like "What need does this meet?" and "Shall we prototype that experience?"

You will also need to identify your sources of expertise. There may already be someone in the organization who understands design, or you may want to hire someone to lead your team in the design process. Some organizations recruit experts on secondment from design strategy firms, or enlist outside trainers or educators to transmit their knowledge and skills in the field to those charged with the task of Business Design. Procter & Gamble and Frito-Lay have done both. It is essential to identify a source of expertise that has depth of knowledge and is committed to an effective and complete transfer of skills. I always advise organizations that if they have centralized expertise, the most valuable role of that group is to teach and facilitate rather than to do the job themselves. The latter approach can limit the scale and impact of Business Design. The best way to accelerate learning and progress will likely be a combination of these.

You will want to design an organizational structure that fits your design strategy. Every enterprise will have a slightly different way of structuring the organization to facilitate design. In some cases, it is a central design group that acts as either a design consultancy or a pool of on-call facilitators to help teams through a development and planning process. Sometimes, design leaders may be embedded into business units. In other cases, over time, the ways and language of design may become so embedded in the organization that teams naturally adopt design principles and practices, which become part of the DNA of doing business. You might also consider establishing a Design Board, bringing in outside advisors to offer expertise, support your mission, and guide your success (see figure 19).

FIG. 19 SOURCES AND STRUCTURE OF EXPERTISE

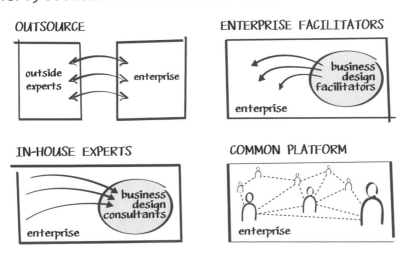

To prevent Business Design from becoming an orphan activity that loses momentum because it is peripheral or contradictory to existing ways of operating, it is important to integrate key practices into your organization in a way that meaningfully enhances the enterprise. That includes thinking about the implications for HR. I often hear comments like, "We are not encouraged to work cross-functionally, try new things, or go outside our current frame of business." This roadblock needs to be addressed head-on. It is an indication that Business Design methods need to be integrated into current strategic planning and innovation initiatives so that they are seen as central to the process rather than dismissed as a sideline activity.

Propagating Design

The adoption of Business Design practices can be accelerated through training and development programs. The goal must be twofold: to demonstrate the power of Business Design to others and to spread the knowledge and skills required to practice Business Design throughout your organization. There are a number of tactics to consider in propagating a design orientation within an organization:

Inspirations: These events can include presentations by inspirational speakers from the business world, or design "lunch and learns" with easy-to-use frameworks and tools, or summits in which a large number of people are exposed to new thinking and tools.

Broad-based Learning Programs: These can include a module on Business Design in training programs for all levels. It is important to induct the junior ranks as well as senior management (in whatever order you choose), to get everyone on the same song sheet. I have found that ambitious people don't like to waste time on theoretical exercises, so it is preferable to train people using real business challenges. This method will reveal how Business Design can change people's perspectives and outcomes in a very short period of time.

Resident Experts: If you don't have enough people in the enterprise to teach others the ropes, it is worth considering a "Train the Trainers" program to develop a talent pool of "masters" in Business Design who can teach others. This may involve putting a select internal group through comprehensive training and certification, with the goal of grooming them to be in-house teachers and facilitators.

How often and how broadly you run these programs will depend on how naturally you can embed them into your current training programs. The key is to map out your training and development program with an eye to making it meaningful and sustained, so you will realize the full potential of an enhanced culture of innovation.

Measuring Performance and Transformation

The big question all analytically minded companies have is, "How do we know it's working?" In some ways, you may just intuitively believe that this all makes sense. At the same time, you might also like to have concrete and measurable evidence of the effectiveness of your programs and the impact they are making. For this, I suggest you create your own "dashboard" (see figure 20), with the goal of establishing a measurable "Gold Standard."

FIG. 20 ENTERPRISE DASHBOARD

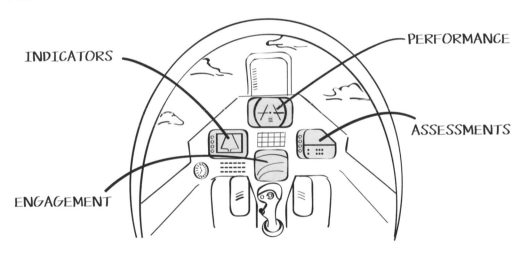

Here are some suggestions to consider when creating your enterprise dashboard:

Performance. Ultimately, this is about better business results, which will take time to realize. Performance, as measured by the market, can also include important measures such as customer loyalty and satisfaction, increased consumption of products and services, and referrals to others. Whatever performance measures you believe to be critical to your success can be built into your dashboard.

360° Assessments. These measure performance on a personnel level — how well an individual performs in his or her job. For example, Business Design is very much about team productivity and effectiveness. As such, it is important to solicit team feedback on the contributions and leadership within teams. Just as in the co-creation process, feedback is the source of learning and advancement.

Indicators. These measure the mindsets and practices of the organization. There are all sorts of profiling instruments that can help diagnose what may be holding teams back and monitor progress in practicing Business Design. You may also have your own indicators of what constitutes innovation. If not, it is important to define and assess these along the way so that innovation is not missed or misidentified.

Engagement and Job Satisfaction. Engagement can be critical to enterprise productivity. A sense of purpose that comes from an inspiring vision and an authentic connection to the customer has the potential to enhance intrinsic motivation. Collaboration brings teams together and gives everyone a voice. Unleashing creativity can energize teams. Progress and shared success have the potential to enhance job satisfaction. All of these possibilities are inherent in the practice of Business Design.

Every enterprise will design its own journey in Business Design. I am hoping the experience of others, as presented in this chapter, provides you with some helpful ideas. As I noted in the introduction, building a culture of innovation by infusing the practice of Business Design is a journey in transforming the ways in which we work — and, ultimately, compete in the marketplace. Big ambitions often start with small initiatives that are pursued with an open mind, strong leadership, and an ability to navigate and stay the course. It only takes one person or team and one innovation challenge to get started.

May you enjoy the journey and realize great success.

Claudia's Top Three Tips for Leveraging the Power of Design

I asked Claudia Kotchka what advice she has for business leaders who want to fully leverage the power of design and run with it in a big way in their organization. Here's what she said:

My first piece of advice is, *know what you're asking for.* My experience is that some people say they want it, but when they realize it's a pretty big culture change that involves all the disciplines in the organization, they're not really so sure. So step one is about knowing what you're asking for.

My second piece of advice is *show, don't tell.* Don't spend a lot a time trying to sell it or trying to explain it. Run some pilots, get it started, and go. That was exactly how you and Roger designed all the workshop training. There weren't a lot of PowerPoint presentations. It was just go, dive in, experience it, which scared the heck out of everyone at first. But I remember one comment: *"This is the best training I've ever attended. Because I'm being trained and don't know it. But at the same time, I'm solving a real problem; a problem that's important to my business."* It is an absolute role model for training — they're working on a real problem. It's not fake, so they're interested. They have a stake in solving the problem, so they show up. And they have no idea what they're getting into, but wow, what amazing results. I can't say enough great things about it. It's incredible! Once you experience it, you come out transformed. And that's true for every single person who experiences it.

The third bit of advice I would give is, *get help.* I always tell people "Don't try to do it yourself. You don't know how to do this. And you don't have to. You just have to make sure it happens in the end." I got help from lots of people, including you [Rotman School of Management]. When I realized I needed to teach management and staff at P&G what we were doing with design, I recognized I don't know how to teach. I'm not an educator. No one at P&G is an educator. So I decided to get help from the best — the experts at educational institutions that know how to teach.

CLAUDIA KOTCHKA
VICE-PRESIDENT OF DESIGN INNOVATION AND STRATEGY, PROCTER & GAMBLE

TOOLS & TIPS
for the Practice of
BUSINESS DESIGN

This section provides a detailed guide to the practice of Business Design. It outlines a selection of the Tools & Tips that have been useful for our students and enterprise teams in tackling full-scale projects. A variety of examples are included to demonstrate the flexibility of these Tools & Tips. The tools can serve as a straightforward guide to using the methodologies, while the tips identify factors to consider in planning activities and synthesizing inputs along your design journey.

This collection of Tools & Tips is only a small sampling of the ways you can unlock thinking and advance development through Business Design, anchored in the 3 Gears.

As noted in part one, Business Design is by no means a formula. It draws upon a flexible repertoire of frameworks and methodologies throughout the design process, including your own tried-and-true methods and new ones you discover or invent. All of these will make up your own "tool kit". Every project quest will demand a thoughtful design of the process that is tailored to the ambitions, scope, and unique considerations of the project at hand.

> **An important reminder:** *You own the process; the process does not own you. The tools are flexible and can be customized and modified as you hone your mastery of the discipline to help you achieve a clear and inspiring outcome.*

What follows (see figure 21) is a visualization of the Tools & Tips as they relate to each phase of the Business Design process, including how the various activities lead to an outcome that serves as the basis for the next phase of development. Tools & Tips are listed on the following pages.

FIG. 21 VISUALIZATION OF TOOLS & TIPS

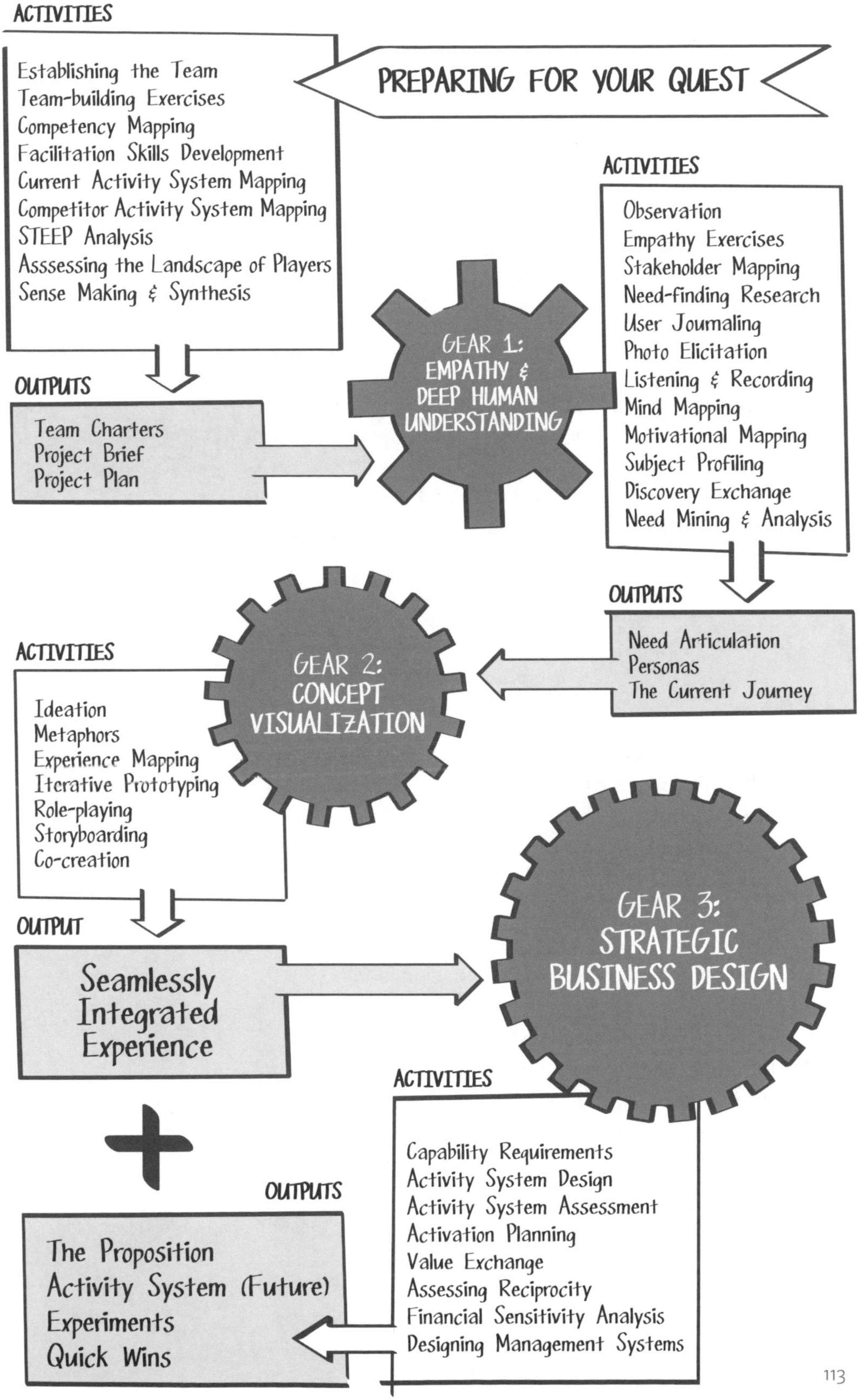

ACTIVITIES

Establishing the Team
Team-building Exercises
Competency Mapping
Facilitation Skills Development
Current Activity System Mapping
Competitor Activity System Mapping
STEEP Analysis
Asssessing the Landscape of Players
Sense Making & Synthesis

PREPARING FOR YOUR QUEST

ACTIVITIES

Observation
Empathy Exercises
Stakeholder Mapping
Need-finding Research
User Journaling
Photo Elicitation
Listening & Recording
Mind Mapping
Motivational Mapping
Subject Profiling
Discovery Exchange
Need Mining & Analysis

OUTPUTS

Team Charters
Project Brief
Project Plan

GEAR 1:
EMPATHY &
DEEP HUMAN
UNDERSTANDING

OUTPUTS

Need Articulation
Personas
The Current Journey

ACTIVITIES

Ideation
Metaphors
Experience Mapping
Iterative Prototyping
Role-playing
Storyboarding
Co-creation

GEAR 2:
CONCEPT
VISUALIZATION

OUTPUT

Seamlessly
Integrated
Experience

GEAR 3:
STRATEGIC
BUSINESS DESIGN

+

OUTPUTS

The Proposition
Activity System (Future)
Experiments
Quick Wins

ACTIVITIES

Capability Requirements
Activity System Design
Activity System Assessment
Activation Planning
Value Exchange
Assessing Reciprocity
Financial Sensitivity Analysis
Designing Management Systems

113

LIST OF TOOLS & TIPS

PREPARING FOR YOUR QUEST

GEAR 1:
EMPATHY & DEEP HUMAN UNDERSTANDING

GEAR 2:
CONCEPT VISUALIZATION

GEAR 3:
STRATEGIC BUSINESS DESIGN & ACTIVATION

PREPARING *for* YOUR QUEST
Setting the Foundation

ESTABLISHING THE TEAM
Getting the right expertise on board

WHY DO WE DO THIS?

To establish a multidisciplinary team that will bring a diversity of functional expertise, perspectives, and management skills to the quest. Setting the foundation for fruitful collaboration is the first step in tackling a Business Design challenge. Establishing the team at the outset of the project will ensure diversity and continuity and enable you to build momentum over the course of the project. Forming a team starts with asking: What functional expertise and management skills will be required to create a comprehensive solution and help activate it? Who are the people who will be critical to *creating* and ultimately *delivering* the solution? Who else may inspire or support us in our quest?

HOW CAN YOU DO THIS?

1 **State your challenge and how it relates to your current business.** This will assist you in determining who can be helpful in pursuing your quest. While the opportunity will become more clearly defined as you develop the Brief (See Project Brief, later in this section), the initial challenge will generally point to the expertise you will want to enroll from the beginning.

2 **Define the core team.** Identify the core interdisciplinary group of individuals, including *intact team members*, who have a vested interest in the project and are able to commit a meaningful amount of their time to it. These individuals should have complementary skills and be committed to being part of the development team.

3 **Identify and recruit additional experts.** Consider who else from professional networks *internally* and networks *externally* can add value to the project. Look for other experts who can add fresh and valuable perspectives. You will want to consider what kinds of expertise would be helpful in creating both the solution and the business system to support it (e.g., technical, marketing, research, sales, logistics, financial). You should also try to identify key partners who will be critical to creating and delivering possible outcomes (e.g., a design agency or other strategic partners who can contribute to both development and implementation).

④ **Establish an advisory team, including an executive sponsor.** Consider whose *wisdom and endorsement* will be needed to ensure that the project is rated as an important priority for the enterprise. An advisory board can be consulted at key points in the development process to help guide your efforts by lending their wisdom to the project. Your sponsor's wisdom and support can help keep your project positioned advantageously within the context of other enterprise initiatives.

⑤ **Define and calibrate requirements for all team members.** This means defining who is dedicated as the *core team* (i.e., those doing the heavy lifting), who is *part time* (i.e., those who will bring expertise or inspiration at appropriate points in the process), and who will be *advisors* (i.e., those brought in on a regular and focused basis).

⑥ **Define the team structure and roles.** It is helpful to identify how different roles relate to the general process and time requirements.

WHAT MIGHT THIS LOOK LIKE?

In a project on food, the core team was made up of representatives from all disciplines, including manufacturing, finance, marketing, product development, sales, and market research. Some were committing more time to the project than others, but all were part of important developmental sessions. Executive sponsors included the business unit president and the corporate CEO; both were scheduled for regular check-ins and counsel. Influencers who were brought in for inspiration from time to time included a nutritionist, a chef, a motivational mountain-climbing speaker, a food columnist, and a yoga and meditation practitioner. While a project leader and a facilitator were assigned, it was clear that everyone on the team had a unique expertise that was valuable to innovation; everyone had clearly defined roles and shared responsibility for outcomes. Members began the project together with clear understanding of the quest, and saw it through together with a shared commitment to contribute, execute, and build momentum as a team.

TEAM-BUILDING EXERCISES
Fun ways to warm up to work

WHY DO WE DO THIS?

To reinforce some design principles and practices early on and get to know each other in a fun way, work through anxieties, and foster collaboration. Here are three simple team-building exercises we've used at Rotman Design-Works to add to your own creative ice-breakers:

Personal Artifact and Story
To understand what makes people tick

Marshmallow Exercise
To practice prototyping and collaboration

Fear in a Hat
To reveal apprehensions and anxieties

Personal Artifact and Story

This simple exercise helps team members explore what motivates them by telling a story that reveals the significance to them of a personal, favorite object.

HOW CAN YOU DO THIS?

Ask everyone to bring an object or artifact that helps tell a story about how this object is meaningful to him or her. Group members then explain why they brought that object and why it is important to them.

WHAT MIGHT THIS LOOK LIKE?

In the first team session of a team project, one of the designers brought a toy car. He told a story about how he collects toys and is intrigued by things that make people more curious and playful. With that insight, we knew we could count on him to bring a fresh and imaginative perspective to any project.

Marshmallow Exercise

The Marshmallow Challenge[36] is a fun and interactive prototyping exercise that encourages teams to experience simple but thoughtful lessons in collaboration and creativity.

HOW CAN YOU DO THIS?

1 Divide the group into teams of five or six people. If you are a bigger group, it is fun to split the group up into competing teams. This also ensures that everyone is fully engaged in the exercise.

2 Gather these materials for each team:
- 20 sticks of spaghetti (the sticks can be broken)
- 1 yard of tape
- 1 yard of string
- 1 marshmallow (the marshmallow must remain intact)

3 Give each team twenty minutes (at the same time) to see which team can build the tallest freestanding structure, using only the materials provided.

4 The marshmallow needs to be on top of the structure.
- At the end of the exercise, reflect on the following:
- What did the team struggle with?
- What did the team do very well?
- What was your process?
- What improves performance? What kills it?

WHAT MIGHT THIS LOOK LIKE?

Visit marshmallowchallenge.com *for more details and examples.*

Fear in a Hat

This is a way for you to understand and appreciate the apprehensions and anxieties your fellow team members may have as you embark upon a project.

HOW CAN YOU DO THIS?

1 On a piece of paper, everyone completes the sentence, "In this project, I am most afraid that _____". People should be as specific and honest as possible, but not in a way that could easily identify them; they should not put their name on the paper. The papers should be placed in a hat (or bowl or bag) and shuffled.

2 One by one, each member of the group reads out the fear of another team member and explains, in his/her own words, what that person fears in this situation. (If you draw your own fear, put it back.) No one is to comment on the fear — just listen and move on to the next person.

3 Members are instructed to avoid implying or showing their opinion about the fear being expressed, to prevent misinterpreting or showing disrespect for someone's fear.

4 When all the fears have been read out, the group discusses what the common fears were and how the team can allay and manage these concerns.

5 At the end of the exercise, the team reflects on the following:
- What are the common fears on the team?
- How can we use insights from this exercise to develop our plan?

WHAT MIGHT THIS LOOK LIKE?

In one team, a common fear that emerged was that all of their exploration and development work would never get executed because of lack of support or conflict with the current enterprise system. That emphasized the important role of the executive sponsor, and raised the team's commitment to Gear 3 and clear activation planning.

COMPETENCY MAPPING
Identifying talents, roles, and passions

WHY DO WE DO THIS?

To ensure diversity and clarity around skills, expertise, and roles. This is a collaborative way to build appreciation for what each team member uniquely brings to the project and reveal personal passions related to the project. Competency Mapping is a deliberate design of your talent ecosystem and answers questions like: What skills do individual team members bring? What knowledge, expertise, and perspectives do they bring? What role can they play in the project? What are their personal interests and passions related to the project?

HOW CAN YOU DO THIS?

1 **Describe competencies and interests.** Ask team members to write on sticky notes up to three pieces of information about themselves in each of the following areas: their area of expertise *(e.g., manufacturing)*, their core skills *(e.g., research and analysis)*, and their personal passions and interests *(e.g., building strong local communities)*. Each piece of information is written on a separate note with the author identified by name or initials (see figure 22).

2 **Cluster and connect.** Keeping the three areas of information separate, begin to cluster the information on the walls. Look for and identify connections and overlaps.

3 **Identify strengths and weaknesses.** Examine the clusters and identify areas of strength (many overlapping areas of expertise and core skills) and areas where there are gaps or weakness (not many skills or overlaps).

4 **Tune the team.** Where areas of weakness exist on the team, ask if those skills are necessary for the project. If they are, find ways of shoring up those weak areas by engaging others who have those skills in the process. Discuss how personal interests and insights may play into the project.

TIPS

These items are useful to have on hand: a big whiteboard or sheet of paper, sticky notes, and markers.

While posting everyone's strengths and areas of interest, take the time to have each person talk about him or herself in more detail. This will help provide a better context to understand everyone's capabilities and interests.

WHAT MIGHT THIS LOOK LIKE?

Through Competency Mapping, a team on a hospital project came to appreciate the diversity of skills and experiences they could collectively draw upon during the project, and the individual passions that could be harnessed. They had competencies including business expertise, architecture know-how, health sciences experience, and information technology expertise, all of which would be important to the hospital project they were about to embark upon. They also realized that they lacked an engineering perspective that would be critical to their project. This led them to recruit a software engineer. Many of them had volunteered in hospitals and could bring personal insights to the project.

FIG. 22 TEAM MAPPING: TALENTS, ROLES, & PASSIONS

FACILITATION
Harnessing the best of the team

WHY DO WE DO THIS?

To ensure the team has designated facilitators who can harness the efforts of every team member and keep the team focused on outcomes. Given the collaborative, outcome-focused nature of the Business Design process, effective facilitation is critical to capturing the most value from the team and the time you spend together. Every meeting, in a sense, is a workshop (or a "charrette," as it is called in the design world). Good facilitation skills help keep the team on track and make sure meetings are productive and outcome-focused.

SKILLS FOR EFFECTIVE FACILITATION

An effective facilitator:
- helps build trusting and collaborative relationships within the group;
- clarifies goals for the group and assigned roles within the group;
- is able to engage everyone in the group;
- does not impose his or her own ideas simply because he or she is holding the pen;
- facilitates productive and effective communication at all times;
- guides the group to stay on track in terms of both outcomes and timing;
- nurtures a productive and collaborative environment ;
- supports effective team decision making when there are choices to make.

These are some of the core skills of good facilitation. If you are really keen to master the skills of facilitation, you can enlist an organization that specializes in facilitation and visualization training.

HOW CAN YOU DO THIS?

1 **Review the list of facilitation skills.** Team members should review the skill requirements and determine their comfort with and readiness to conduct group facilitation. Be honest and open about your interest, commitment, and capabilities with regard to the role of facilitator. It is an important role, but not one that everyone feels comfortable playing. A facilitator's first job is to help the team get the most out of their time together.

2 **Discuss the results of the preceding review and assign two to three lead facilitators to begin the project.** It is advisable to assign this role to your most willing and capable candidates at the outset of the project. You can always rotate in new facilitators as the project unfolds.

3 **Be diligent about helpful two-way feedback.** Effective facilitation is a two-way street. To be an effective facilitator requires discipline and skill. Timely feedback helps the facilitator develop this skill and improve the ability to draw the best out of the team. At the same time, because it takes a respectful and collaborative team to realize productive and fruitful outcomes, the facilitator should also give the team feedback on their behaviors and team dynamics.

TEAM CHARTERS
Creating a shared vision for roles and conduct

WHY DO WE DO THIS?
To articulate the shared vision and codes of conduct for the team. This is best done before project work begins, as it can serve as a simple reference to ground the team throughout the design journey.

HOW CAN YOU DO THIS?
This is a great way to get values and pet peeves on the table early on. As a team, create a Charter with the following headings:
- Project Ambitions
- Team Values
- Roles and Responsibilities
- Meeting and Communication Strategies
- Team Rules and Codes of Conduct

TIPS

Refer to the outcome of your competency mapping to define individual roles.

Remind members that an effective Team Charter calls for clarity, authenticity, unanimity, and candor, especially when it comes to pet peeves.

Try to add a little humor to make it less like a list of overly serious rules. One team had a rule, "No smelly food in meetings." This candid statement was once cited as an effective rule that helped avoid distractions during meetings.

A Team Charter is an important reference when you get off track or the team becomes dysfunctional (as all teams do from time to time).

Identifying key codes of conduct will ensure the discipline and respect required for team productivity.

WHAT MIGHT THIS LOOK LIKE?

Team Charter

Team Ambition
To create a breakthrough technology-based solution that will redefine people's under-standing of the meaning and management of money to help people take control of their financial well-being.

Team Values
Openness, transparency, and respect. Give everyone a voice.

Team Roles and Responsibilities
Mark (Team Lead): Design and oversee master project plan (roles, deliverables, timing)
Eugene (Creative Director): Design clear and inspiring reports and presentations
Grace (Project Manager): Manage all external activities such as research and logistics
Stefanie (Research): Lead secondary research and fortify the business case
Carolyn (Business Advisor): Coach team and counsel on strategy and business viability
Alpesh (Methodologist): Source and design development methods
Job (Facilitating and Sense Making): Facilitate and counsel on prototyping and synthesis

Meeting and Communication Strategies
Meeting Times: Mondays 1–4 p.m., Meeting Room A
Scheduling: Use intranet calendar, hosted by Mark
Meeting Preparation: Agenda and pre-work will be issued 48 hours in advance of meeting.
Communication: Use designated intranet as a portal for all document sharing, online dis-cussions, and planning updates. No external portals.

Team Rules and Codes of Conduct
Arrive on time for meetings, or you bring snacks to next meeting.
No phone calls, texting, or browsing during meetings.
Respond to group email threads in timely fashion to accommodate scheduling and work.
Individuals are accountable for their deliverables.
Decisions will be made on a consensus basis — vote is a last resort.
Constructive feedback only — "attack the problem, not the person"

ACTIVITY SYSTEMS (Current State)
Visualizing your current strategy

WHY DO WE DO THIS?

To gain clarity, alignment, and appreciation for today's enterprise strategy as a system of activities. Activity System modeling is a method of systems thinking and visualization that represents strategy as a unique combination of interrelated activities. Doing this up front on a project will give you a clear picture of your current state that you can reprise in Gear 3 to determine if and how your new vision and strategy fit with your current strategy. This particular approach is used to capture and analyze the current strategy at the outset of a project. It helps address important questions like: What is the enterprise's current strategy to create value? What is uniquely leverageable (in comparison to systems in other enterprises)? How strong is our current competitive advantage?

An Activity System is a visualization of strategy and is made up of:

>   *Hubs:* Core activities that together define how the enterprise uniquely creates value

>   *Supporting Activities:* Specific activities that fortify hubs

>   *Linkages:* How hubs and activities relate to and reinforce each other to create value

A powerful Activity System is one in which a unique system of activities synergistically creates value for the market and the enterprise.

HOW CAN YOU DO THIS?

This approach to building an Activity System is used when you are "on the inside" and have access to individuals who understand the company's inner workings, versus the "outsider" approach used for assessing another company based on publicly available information (presented as a separate tool).

The following outlines a process for building team understanding of and clarity about your current strategy.

Before you convene as a team:

① **Gather input.** Ask team members to think about and list what you do *well* as an enterprise to create and deliver market value and be competitive. It is important to think about activities that create value across the entire business and every function. Input should be based on the questions below:
- What is the overall goal or vision for your business? What is your overarching value proposition? *(e.g., to deliver a seamlessly integrated digital entertainment system).*
- What are the vital activities that your enterprise does well and consistently invests time and money in to deliver value across the spectrum of its activities? *(e.g., building direct one-to-one customer relationships; minimizing costs).*
- What are the specific activities that bring those themes to life? *(e.g., building a strong customer data base; building long-term relationships with vendors).*

② **Consolidate and distill inputs.** You will likely have dozens if not hundreds of possible articulations — and that is normal. Consolidate all of the verbatim inputs that you receive. Aggregate and cluster to consolidate similar inputs down to six to ten activity themes; these are the potential "hubs" of your strategy. Articulate these themes by phrasing them as something you actively *do* — for example, *Build Strong Brands*. In documenting consolidated inputs, there are two lists that will be helpful: a list of hubs (ideally no more than ten) and the complete list of specific activities (potentially a very long list).

When you get together as a team:

③ **Review and discuss your list of themes, and select the most critical as hubs.** Facilitate a discussion about the overarching value proposition and possible hubs. For each hub, ask two key questions:
- How critical is that to our overall proposition and goal of creating value?
- How well do we do that and how extensively does that drive our activities? What is the evidence of that?

It is often helpful for one person who is passionate about a theme to make a two-minute "case" outlining its potential for creating value and why it should therefore be a hub. At this point, you should simply capture the essence of that theme — you can go back and refine the wording later.

Once you have discussed the potential hubs and identified which are most critical to creating value, have team members reflect on the following questions before "voting" for their preferred hubs:

- Is this critical to our value creation?
- Do we invest time and money broadly and consistently to support this?
- Does this contribute to our competitive advantage, relative to systems of other enterprises?

When the team is ready to vote on the hubs, provide five sticky red dots to each team member. Advise them to think about the activity themes that meet the three criteria and allocate one dot per hub. Identify the top four or five hubs and probe for any points of disagreement or deep concerns.

4 **Fortify the selected hubs with specific supporting activities.** For each hub, ask: What are the critical activities that support each hub? Have the participants refer to a handout of specific activities that will be grouped and labeled according to themes for reference.

5 **Visualize and assess the Activity System.** Display the names of the top four or five hubs on large sticky notes or paper plates and place them on a large surface. Discuss as a team how each hub relates to the others and draw lines to show the relationships. Then position specific activities around the hubs and identify linkages within the system.

Have each participant independently rate the uniqueness and competitiveness of your model compared to competitors' systems on a scale of 1 to 10 (1 being identical and 10 being completely different) on a card and give it to the facilitator. Make a quick tally for the group and discuss your intuitive assessment based on the range of numbers and the average of the ratings.

TIPS

Refer to other documents that contain information about your business (e.g., Strategic Plans, Operating Plans, Annual Reports) for insights.

Prototype! At Rotman DesignWorks, we use paper plates and sticky notes to prototype the system early on. This is an iterative process as you gather and distill your inputs and make intuitive connections within your system. Your first version will look like spaghetti and meatballs. That's okay. The key is distillation and making connections.

Aim to get focused. Some of the initial inputs will fall by the wayside. You should have a limited number of hubs; an enterprise cannot have ten hubs and do them all well.

Linkages are important. Understand how one hub connects to another, and/or how one activity can reinforce more than one hub. That's how you achieve synergy.

In assessing your competitiveness, it is particularly helpful to have done a similar exercise on other organizations (see the next tool, on competitors' Activity Systems).

It is often valuable to capture the strategy depicted by your Activity System in a story to explain how the system works. You might construct a one-page narrative that describes your foundational Activity System. This story should describe how you create value through the following:
Overarching Proposition: What does our enterprise uniquely offer the market?
Hubs: What are the core drivers of our business today that define our strategy?
Activities: What specific and concrete activities reinforce those hubs?
Relationships: How do hubs and activities relate to and reinforce one another?

As an alternative method, you can ask members to bring their list of hubs and activities to your work session and transfer them to sticky notes to be clustered into themes and supporting activities, in a similar "organic" method to that presented in constructing an Activity System for competitors (see the next tool). While the process outlined in this tool requires more preparatory work in collecting and organizing inputs, it tends to provide a more rigorous, inclusive, and well-documented foundation.

WHAT MIGHT THIS PROCESS LOOK LIKE?

Figure 23 depicts the process graphically.

FIG 23 VISUALIZING YOUR CURRENT STRATEGY

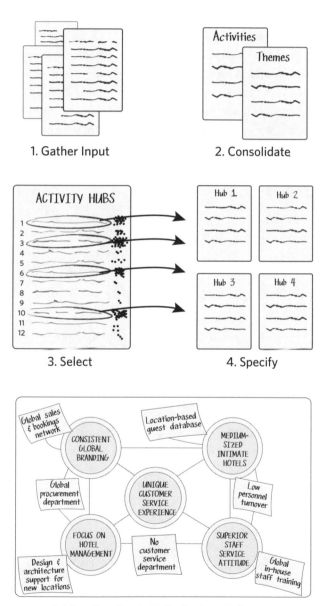

1. Gather Input

2. Consolidate

3. Select

4. Specify

5. Visualize the Activity System & Assess

ACTIVITY SYSTEMS (Competitors)
Visualizing competitive strategies

WHY DO WE DO THIS?

To help bring to light how competing enterprises create value in a distinctive way and, most importantly, relative to the way your own enterprise creates value. This exercise is an excellent way to do a comprehensive deep dive into another company. It will help you get a handle on questions like: What is the enterprise's strategy to create value? What is unique about their system (in comparison to those of others, particularly yours)? How strong is their current competitive advantage?

An Activity System is a visualization of strategy and made up of:

> *Hubs:* Core activities that together define how the enterprise uniquely creates value

> *Supporting Activities:* Specific activities that fortify hubs

> *Linkages:* How hubs and activities relate to and reinforce each other to create value

A powerful Activity System is one in which a unique system of activities synergistically creates value for the market and the enterprise.

HOW CAN YOU DO THIS?

An *outside* approach to building Activity Systems can be used for creating a picture of your competitors or any other organization you would like to understand better. This is how DesignWorks constructs Activity Systems about companies for which we do not have access to proprietary internal strategies.

[1] **Before constructing a competitive Activity System, gather inputs.** Find out as much about the company as possible by reviewing annual reports (which publicly state their vision, strategy, and financial investments) and market-facing sources of information (e.g., a website that presents a comprehensive picture of their offerings). It is also helpful to get a sense of the customer experience by using and interacting with their products and services. Specifically, look for three things:

- What do they offer? Begin by searching through their website.
- Where do they invest? Begin by reading their annual reports.
- What's the experience? Begin by immersing yourself in the customer experience by visiting a store, investigating a service, or purchasing one of their products.

When you have gathered this information, you can take the following steps to aggregate, synthesize, and map your inputs into an Activity System:

2 **Lay out what you know.** As a team, share all of the information you've gathered. List all of the inputs on sticky notes (one per note) and discuss what they signify.

3 **Find patterns and cluster them.** Begin to group together related inputs as potential hubs and ask: *How is this critical to their success in creating value?*

4 **Articulate, position, and connect the hubs.** Once you have three to five large clusters, begin to label each one as a hub. As noted earlier, articulate these hubs by phrasing them as something the company actually *does: For example, Minimize Costs.* Through this process you will begin to see connections between hubs. Find these connections by asking, *How does one hub relate to others? How does this combination of interrelated hubs uniquely create value?*

5 **Build out the Activity System.** Position specific supporting activities around the hubs, and then identify linkages among all of the hubs and the activities. *For example, long-term vendor contracts might be a specific activity that contributes to minimizing costs.* Identify relationships by asking: *How does activity reinforce each of the hubs?* The more connections, the stronger the system. Your final Activity System should be a one-page visual representation of the organization's strategy as defined by hubs and supporting activities.

6 **Discuss Uniqueness and Competitiveness.** Have each participant in-- dependently rate the uniqueness and competitiveness of the enterprise's strategy by comparison with those of other companies on a scale of 1 to10 (1 being identical and 10 being completely different) on a card and give it to the facilitator. Make a quick tally for the group and discuss your intuitive assessment based on the range of numbers and the average.

TIPS

Use any accessible information or intelligence that helps you create a robust picture of the company's strategy.

Prototype! At Rotman DesignWorks, we use paper plates and sticky notes to prototype the system. This is an iterative process as you gather and distill your inputs and make intuitive connections within the system.

Aim to get focused. You should have a limited number of hubs; an enterprise cannot have ten hubs and do them all well.

Linkages are important. Understand how one hub connects to another, and how one activity can reinforce more than one hub. That indicates synergy.

As in building your own Activity System, it is often valuable to capture the strategy in a story to explain how the system works. You might construct a one-page narrative that describes the enterprise's strategy. This story should describe how the enterprise creates value through the following: ***Overarching Proposition:*** *What does our enterprise uniquely offer the market?* ***Hubs:*** *What are the core drivers of our business today that define our strategy?* ***Activities:*** *What specific and concrete activities reinforce those hubs?* ***Relationships:*** *How do hubs and activities relate to and reinforce one another?*

WHAT MIGHT THIS PROCESS LOOK LIKE?

Figure 24 depicts the process graphically.

FIG. 24 VISUALIZING COMPETITIVE STRATEGIES

1. Lay out what you know

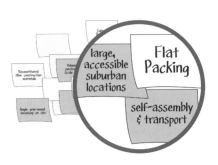

2. Find patterns and cluster

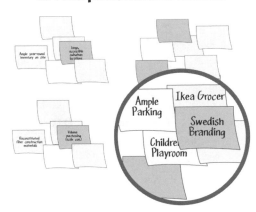

3. Articulate the hubs & identify linkages

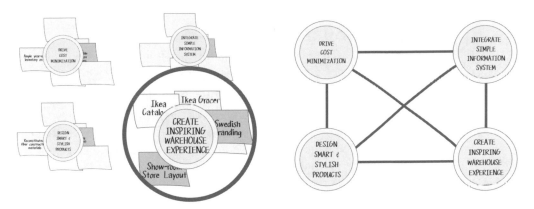

4. Position activities around hubs, connect, & visualize

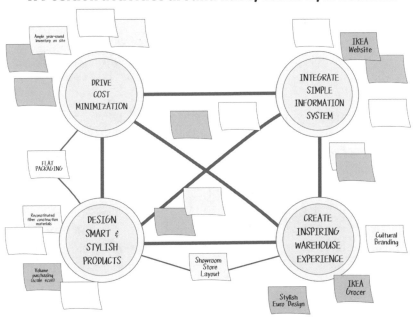

STEEP ANALYSIS
Forecasting future opportunities

WHY DO WE DO THIS?

To discover and define relevant trends that will impact the project. A STEEP Analysis is used to identify broad trends in the areas of Society, Technology, Economy, Environment, and Politics (STEEP). The objective of this exercise is to contextualize your challenge in order to seize "on-trend" opportunities. Your goal is to define the three to five influential trends that will have the greatest impact on your project's development and outcome.[37]

HOW CAN YOU DO THIS?

1 **Cast the research net wide.** Using information from articles, books, blogs, or your own observations, select a total of three to five interesting trends based on your project topic in each of the areas of Society, Technology, Economy, Environment, and Politics.

- *Society:* What are the most relevant social, demographic, or lifestyle trends?
- *Technology:* Which technology trends could influence future scenarios?
- *Economy:* What are the emerging issues, forces, and industries shaping the economy and business climate?
- *Environment:* Which environmental issues and developments could have a real and dramatic impact?
- *Politics:* What are the policies and regulatory issues that might make a difference?

Gather both qualitative and (more importantly) statistical data to substantiate emerging trends. Make sure to state your references and sources.

2 **Analyze your findings.** Create a two-by-two framework and judge each trend on the likelihood that it will occur and how greatly it would impact the context of your project. Label one axis with "likely to occur — unlikely to occur" and the other axis with "high impact — low impact." Plot your research findings onto the framework.

3 **Select three to five trends.** Based on your research and intuition, select three to five trends that would have the greatest impact on your project outcomes. The most notable trends will be in the "high impact/likely to occur" quadrant of your two-by-two framework.

TIPS

Broaden your perspective on the world by learning about topics outside your area of expertise as a route to achieving new contextual insights.

Consult a variety of research resources (e.g., newspaper and magazine articles, the Internet, books, government reports, third-party research). While you might do some sleuthing in "social media" and opinion pieces for intuitive insights, you should place priority on credible sources of intelligence.

Remember that identifying trends is not a way to predict the future but a way to anticipate and plan for the future.

WHAT MIGHT THIS LOOK LIKE?

Figure 25 illustrates the outcome of a project on healthy eating that shows that the rise in obesity and diabetes, government regulation of foods and of food labeling, increased consumer interest in organic and all-natural foods, and increased consumption of prepared meals all point to opportunity gaps in the market.

FIG. 25 STEEP ANALYSIS MAPPING

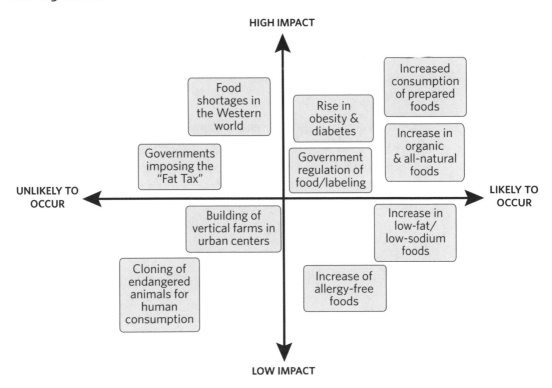

LANDSCAPE OF PLAYERS
Identifying future friends and foes

WHY DO WE DO THIS?
To identify which other players are conducting business in the market space.
This helps you determine which players pose competitive threats and which
ones could bring a complementary strength to your enterprise and be leveraged into strategic partnerships.

HOW CAN YOU DO THIS?
1 **Define the space and identify a broad base of players.** Define the
business space in the broadest terms — both within the direct space you
are considering (e.g., healthy packaged foods) and in adjacent spaces (e.g.,
businesses that address other dimensions of healthy living like weight-
management services, makers of supplements, food services). There is no
such thing as too many players to consider at the outset of this exercise.
Research as many as possible of the companies, organizations, and categories that are considered to be part of the industry you have selected.

2 **Prioritize.** Once you have the long list, prioritize who is best positioned
to make an important move in this space, including both direct and indirect
competitors, as well as those that may become allies.

3 **Cluster your findings and create a framework to organize them.** Begin to
cluster your findings depending on what each offers. For example, in healthy
eating, clusters may include food manufacturers, service companies, communication companies, and others. They may also cluster by commercial
versus public or not-for-profit.

4 **Review and analyze.** Conduct a review of the activities, trends, and
financial results of key players within each cluster. This should provide you
with an informed perspective on what is happening with each sub-sector
and organization. Use this information to better understand the industry
you are working in, as well as during Gear 3 when you may want to identify
partners to help deliver your solution.

TIPS

Your STEEP Analysis will reveal some of the players in your targeted space.

Consider companies from as many different industries as possible. Many companies are now crossing over into different industries — for example, from products to services or from retailing to information services.

WHAT MIGHT THIS LOOK LIKE?

Figure 26 gives a summary of a few of the players in the "healthy lifestyle" business, to demonstrate the diversity of players. Depending on the enterprise strategy, some of these may serve as potential partners in the delivery of a new solution.

FIG.26 SUMMARY OF PLAYERS

FOOD MANUFACTURERS	**PEOPLE AND SERVICES**
Nestlé	Food experts (e.g., nutritionists)
Kraft	Wellness coaches
PepsiCo	Aramark
Campbell Soup Company	Fitness clubs (e.g., Curves)
Del Monte	Weight-management services
General Mills	(e.g., Weight Watchers)
OTHER PRODUCT PROVIDERS	**MEDIA AND INFORMATION**
Grocers (e.g., Whole Foods)	Online services (e.g., Diet.com)
Lifestyle products (e.g., Nike, Lululemon)	Health organizations (e.g., Mayo Clinic)
Supplements (e.g., GNC, Amway)	Publications (e.g., Prevention)
Pharmaceuticals (e.g., Pfizer)	Not-for-profits (e.g., Heart & Stroke)
Retailers (e.g., drugstores)	Self-help books

SENSE MAKING AND SYNTHESIS
Connecting trends, issues, and players

WHY DO WE DO THIS?

To identify intersections between the various factors and forces influencing the quest. As preparation for defining your Brief, you will want to consider all of the foundational work you have done, extract the most pertinent discoveries, and synthesize the "sweet spot" of opportunity by making connections between your capabilities, future trends, competitive forces, and important stakeholders. At Rotman DesignWorks, we often refer to this as "Mapping the Mess." While it may be a complex web of considerations at first, mapping all of your insights onto one surface can help bring clarity to the opportunity.

HOW CAN YOU DO THIS?

1 **Identify forces, factors, and players in aggregate.** Refer to your Activity System Models, STEEP Analysis, and Stakeholder Map (Gear 1 tool) to help you define business capabilities, future trends, and significant stakeholders. Put all of your discoveries and work to date on one surface (like a wall) so you can take in the full picture.

2 **Determine relationships.** Analyze the forces, factors, and stakeholders to determine how they influence or can be influenced by one another. Visualize these aspects and their connections by mapping them out.

3 **Identify the opportunity.** This is the intersection or "sweet spot" for your Brief. Tensions between forces are often an opportunity for innovation. For example, the rise in obesity concurrent with diminishing access to healthy food presents an opportunity to reconcile tensions in trends.

TIPS

Consolidating and mapping inputs can lead to a clearer picture of the most pertinent issues and dynamics relating to the challenge by harnessing the insights of a team around a visual summary of discoveries.

This is really a thinking process. Your intuition and logical thinking will lead you to the conclusion that you have found an opening to a meaningful and well-defined opportunity.

It is helpful to have a huge surface that can hold a lot of data and insights in view. Sticky notes and a whiteboard can be helpful, as this will be an iterative mapping process.

WHAT MIGHT THIS PROCESS LOOK LIKE?

Figure 27 shows a simplified visual representation of how three project inputs feed into a Project Brief for enhancing the well-being of seniors through the arts. You can imagine how many other inputs are considered on a large-scale project. In this case, the three important inputs that contributed to defining the Brief were: Stakeholder Mapping on caring for seniors, the foundational Activity System of the enterprise, and a STEEP Analysis that pointed to important economic, population, and social trends that would give purpose to the quest.

FIG. 27 SENSE MAKING & SYNTHESIS

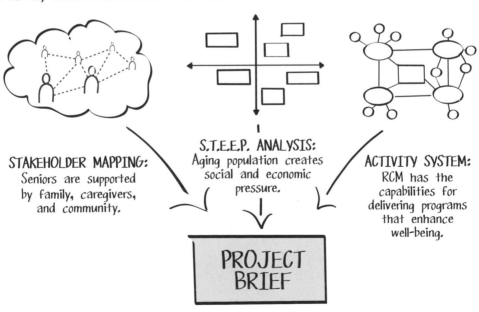

STAKEHOLDER MAPPING:
Seniors are supported
by family, caregivers,
and community.

S.T.E.E.P. ANALYSIS:
Aging population creates
social and economic
pressure.

ACTIVITY SYSTEM:
RCM has the
capabilities for
delivering programs
that enhance
well-being.

PROJECT
BRIEF

PROJECT BRIEF
Framing your ambition

WHY DO WE DO THIS?

To crystallize the ambitions of the project, key issues, and stakeholders to be considered, and the business motivation for the project. A Project Brief must be specific enough to make the objectives and challenges clear while being open enough to allow for opportunities and new possibilities to emerge. A good Project Brief is succinct and brings together all of your foundational discoveries into a focused framework for development.

HOW CAN YOU DO THIS?

Here are some questions that can be helpful in distilling your Project Brief:

What are our goals and ambitions for this project?
What are the issues or conditions that inspire this opportunity?
How could this create value for the market and the enterprise?
Who is our primary target? Who are other important stakeholders?
What is the activity around which we want to create value?
What can we bring to contribute to the solution?
Are there any analogies or references we can learn from?
Who do we need to better understand and recruit to help provide insight into the activity?

TIPS

Useful inputs include: your Activity System, your STEEP Analysis, the Landscape of Players, Stakeholder Maps (initial cut), and any other pertinent data or insights.

At the beginning of a project, briefs are often too narrow or too broadly defined. The key is to "right-size" the project according to what you feel is aspirational yet within scope.

To keep your Brief focused (a one-page Brief is ideal), you may capture more detailed information as supporting documents.

New information will surface during the discovery process. While your Project Brief will provide an important touchstone in your development, don't ignore unexpected discoveries that can either enhance or call for a reframing of the quest.

WHAT MIGHT THIS LOOK LIKE?

Project Brief: Living Well (The Royal Conservatory)

What are our goals and ambitions for the project?
To develop a breakthrough, revenue-generating solution for The Royal Conservatory that will improve the physical and mental well-being of seniors.

What are the issues or conditions that inspire this opportunity?
Too often, seniors internalize ageism, disengage from activities, and deteriorate mentally and physically. They may become reclusive or dependent on family member support, limiting their psychological independence and engagement. In an aging society, there is pressure to find solutions to support seniors in a socially and economically responsible manner.

Who is our primary target? Other important stakeholders?
The primary target is seniors seventy years of age and older who find joy through engagement in the arts and self-expression. Other important stakeholders are the people who provide lifestyle support and care to elderly family members and friends.

What is the "activity" around which we want to create value?
Enhancing the physical and mental well-being of seniors.

What can The Royal Conservatory bring to contribute to the solution?
The Royal Conservatory's current sponsored "Living Through the Arts" program leverages the beneficial aspects of music therapy through a variety of Outreach Programs and Creativity Workshops. The program has been proved to enhance individual and community potential through artistic self-expression and creativity, with measurable evidence that these programs enhance well-being on both cognitive and emotional levels. The Conservatory is the largest and oldest independent arts educator in Canada and has offered extraordinary opportunities for learning and personal development through music and the arts for more than 125 years.

Any analogies or references we can learn from?
SM(ART)S: Seniors Meet the Arts, Young @ Heart

Whom do we need to recruit? (As preliminary input to designing the research)
Twenty seniors — mixed by gender, type of residence, and cultural background
Ten caregivers of seniors — a combination of family members and paid caregivers

PROJECT PLAN
Visualizing the development process

WHY DO WE DO THIS?

To visualize how the Business Design methodology will be used on a project, including the activities, the timing, and the desired outcomes. This can help to guide the team and to communicate to others how the project will progress. It serves as the backbone for development by organizing Business Design tools and activities to tackle the challenge at hand. It will answer the question: What are the flow of activities, methods to be used, deliverables, and milestones?

HOW CAN YOU DO THIS?

1 **Create a timeline.** Draw a line on a large piece of paper representing the project timeline, and designate each major phase of development and the desired outcome — Foundation, Gear 1, Gear 2, and Gear 3.

2 **Map the methods and activities through all three Gears.** This will show how you will sequence activities and how you move through divergence and convergence toward outcomes for each phase of activity.

3 **Plot the milestones.** Mark down the important deadlines and deliverables. Consider the start date and end date for each activity and phase.

4 **Supplement with project details.** For each key activity, consider the events necessary to reach due dates and deliverables, and indicate the actions and activities necessary to reach those goals, including research, development work sessions, and presentations. Assign roles and responsibilities to individuals on the team.

5 **Visualize.** Illustrate your timeline visualization to identify key elements, including development activities, methods, and deliverables. Visualizing your roadmap helps keep all of these activities in context, providing a vision of how they all come together.

TIP

Keep the plan open and high-level at the beginning. This will allow you to plot out the major milestones and deliverables before focusing on the detailed plan.

WHAT MIGHT THIS LOOK LIKE?

Figure 28 shows a three-month project plan visualization that began with Gear 1 at Rotman DesignWorks, showing how the methodologies, activities, and outputs were sequenced.

FIG. 28 DEVELOPMENT MAP

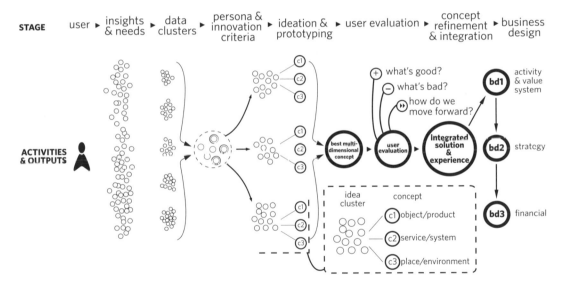

The Business Design Process

GEAR 1: EMPATHY & DEEP HUMAN UNDERSTANDING

Reframing the Opportunity

OBSERVATION
Absorbing context and human behaviors

WHY DO WE DO THIS?

To discover fresh insights by studying people in their natural environments. This exercise helps us address what is actually happening rather than simply relying on preconceived notions. By following a structured approach to perceiving human behavior relative to objects, the environment, and other people in a specific context, we can frame a situation in concrete rather than hypothetical terms. Key questions to consider in this activity include: What are the "observable facts" — the people, objects, and activities that are present? How are people interacting with each other, objects, and their surroundings? What is *really* going on here? What could that mean or suggest?

HOW CAN YOU DO THIS?

☐ **Define an activity and select an observation site.** Think about the situations you would like to know more about and select a location that best suits the conditions of your project. Select a well-defined site that is relevant to your quest *(for example, kids eating lunch at school).*

☐ **First-level observation — see things objectively.** Conduct your first phase of observation for 30 to 60 minutes. Record only the factual aspects of what you see and do not disregard anything. Watch for the physical elements that can be objectively verified by scientific methods whenever necessary. It is important *not* to assign meaning or pass judgment on what you see at the time of observation. Collect the following facts:

- What kinds of people are present?
- What objects are present?
- Where is the activity taking place? What is the environment?
- Are there any "workarounds" taking place (where the user is trying to solve a problem without any existing solutions at hand)? (For example: The kids are swapping food. Some are throwing their lunch in the garbage.)

[3] **Develop a hypothesis.** Do this only after you have exhausted your ability to take in objective data. Based on what you have observed, develop a hypothesis for what you think is happening in the location you have selected. *(For example: The kids are swapping food and throwing their lunch in the garbage because they don't like what's in their lunch box.)*

[4] **Second level observation – look for meaning.** Conduct a second level of observation for 30 to 60 minutes. Based on what you are seeing, begin to make note of what you *think* is happening – the *meaning* behind the actions, interactions, events, and objects. These aspects are highly subjective and will tap into your intuition. Ask yourself:
- Why is this happening and why are people doing these things?
- What objects are important? What role do they play?
- How are people engaging with each other, with objects, and with their surroundings?
- What is the context (social or practical) that is motivating them to do these things? (For example: The look on their faces suggests they think some of the food in their lunch box is disgusting. The kids don't like what was packed for them at home. If they can't swap it, they throw it out.)

[5] **Articulate insights.** Analyze your notes to see if your hypothesis was correct and if it revealed anything new about the world that you did not know before. These new insights should be captured and used as part of your user understanding research.
(For example: If kids had a say about what went into their lunch box, they might be more likely to eat a healthy lunch and develop better eating habits.)

TIPS

You'll want to have a camera and a notepad in which to write and sketch.

Effective field observation is a structured and disciplined exercise. Unstructured observation runs the risk of focusing only on the things that interest you rather than all the things that are going on.

Be mindful of ethical considerations. Be respectful of local norms of conduct; mask or secure the identity of people or places you are observing, and avoid intrusive or disruptive behavior.

WHAT MIGHT THIS LOOK LIKE?

Figure 29 depicts the subject of an observation exercise. The notes that follow show what might emerge from the exercise.

FIG. 29 OBSERVATION — FIRST LEVEL AND SECOND LEVEL

OBSERVATION NOTES

First level: Just the facts.

It is 10:30 a.m. This man is in an open office space, at his desk, in front of his computer — it's a Mac. There is a mug on his desk. There are toys on his desk (that he keeps picking up), including a "Russian doll," a miniature Eiffel Tower, and a pink rubber brain. There are drawings and sticky notes on the wall behind him. There is a bike and helmet beside him.

Second level: What could that mean?

This man is working. All of the objects and his surroundings suggest he is in a creative role. The toys suggest he has a playful outlook. He approaches his work in a creative way and visualizes his ideas as he develops them. He appears to have created his own little inspiring workspace in this open office.

EMPATHY EXERCISE
Living the experience

WHY DO WE DO THIS?
To build empathy by experiencing the world from someone else's perspective, and to help enhance the depiction of the Current User Journey. Through this exercise, you will come to genuinely understand a person's challenges, have greater empathy, and generate fresh insights based on your experience. As you put yourself in someone else's shoes, ask: What does this person experience and feel? What are his or her points of pain?

HOW CAN YOU DO THIS?
1 **Define the target subject.** Based on the challenge, identify whose perspective you would like to better understand and appreciate. *For example: Let us assume your end user is an elderly person.*

2 **Outline the challenge.** Think of a situation in which this person struggles. It could be a situation where there is a physical or mental challenge or a difficulty or barrier in everyday life. *For example: Let us say the elderly person has trouble with dexterity in everyday life.*

3 **Describe the activity.** Create an activity that will enable you to experience the world from your target's perspective. Do this by defining the person, her situation, and an activity that presents a challenge for her. *For example: Let us say that the person has trouble doing daily tasks on her own at home.*

4 **Recreate the experience**. Use props, aids, or artifacts that help to simulate the experience. *For example: To simulate what it is like to be an elderly person living alone, you may don thick rubber gloves to simulate challenges in lost manual dexterity.*

5 **Execute the exercise.** View the world through this person's point of view by living her life for at least an hour. Fully immerse yourself into the activity to truly experience the world from the user's perspective. *For example: To experience what the elderly person does, try preparing a meal and making a phone call while wearing thick rubber gloves.*

6 **Reflect on the experience.** Reflect on what you experienced and how it made you feel. Define the most powerful emotions you experienced and your most compelling insight into how it must be to live that person's life.

TIPS

When defining the activity, a direct simulation may not be possible because of physical or circumstantial limitations. In this case, define an analogous situation that parallels the core challenges the person experiences. *For example: To appreciate living with chronic pain, put some stones in your shoes for a day — not to create pain, but to appreciate what it is like to be plagued by distraction and discomfort for hours on end.*

When you execute your exercise it is important to try to experience the world from your users' perspective as much as possible. This means eliminating distractions and focusing on the task at hand.

WHAT MIGHT THIS LOOK LIKE?

To understand the challenges that seniors face as they age, one team member wore rubber gloves to recreate the experience of the decreased sense of touch and dexterity that many seniors face (see figure 30). She wore the rubber gloves all day while she attempted to carry out common tasks such as paperwork, making meals, and brushing her hair. She found these tasks to be much more difficult and had to adjust her speed and concentration just to accomplish these easy, everyday tasks. As a result, she became quite frustrated and tense. Through this process, she discovered that decreased physical functions of the elderly negatively affect not only their physical abilities but also their emotional state.

FIG. 30 EMPATHY EXERCISE

STAKEHOLDER MAPPING
Identifying and connecting people who matter

WHY DO WE DO THIS?

To identify all the players who matter to the project and how they relate to and influence each other. Stakeholder Mapping defines stakeholder roles and visualizes their relationship to others in the "human system." While you may likely do a preliminary version of this before framing your Project Brief in broad strokes, a more in-depth analysis will create a more definitive picture of the dynamics at play, as it did in the healthcare case in the chapter on Gear 1. This tool helps to frame the challenge and increases the chances of success in a solution that will address all stakeholder needs during implementation by appreciating how all of the key stakeholders (users, enablers, and influencers) interact and influence one another.

HOW CAN YOU DO THIS?

1 **Identify all stakeholders relevant to your project quest.** List each stakeholder on an individual sticky note. A stakeholder is any person or organization who can be positively or negatively affected by, or cause an impact on, the actions of an end user. In a business-to-business context, this may include various decision makers inside the company, as well as customers, suppliers, distributers, and vendors. Arrange the sticky notes on a large piece of paper or a wall.

2 **Define roles and relationships.** Analyze the group of stakeholders to define their respective roles and relationships in the human ecosystem.

3 **Visualize the human system as a pathway or network.** Represent relationships in a visual manner in order to bring clarity to the picture. Position and connect the stakeholders who influence each other the most. This can be organized around the user journey, as it was in the chapter on Gear 1, or depicted by a general "network map" of stakeholders pertaining to a common issue, as shown below (in figure 32).

TIPS

Stakeholder mapping begins at the start of a project and is refined on a regular basis, as new information is uncovered that leads to a better understanding of the challenge.

It is important to consider a broad range of stakeholders. Think about all possible stakeholders who influence the decision-making process, and consider the web of interrelationships among them.

This exercise can also be helpful in mapping key stakeholders within a business customer's company (e.g., executive officer, procurement manager, project manager) and in relation to external partners, vendors, and the ultimate end consumer.

WHAT MIGHT THIS LOOK LIKE?

The healthcare company Stakeholder Map in the chapter on Gear 1 was laid out according to the patient journey (see figure 31).

FIG. 31 STAKEHOLDER MAPPING ALONG A PATIENT PATHWAY

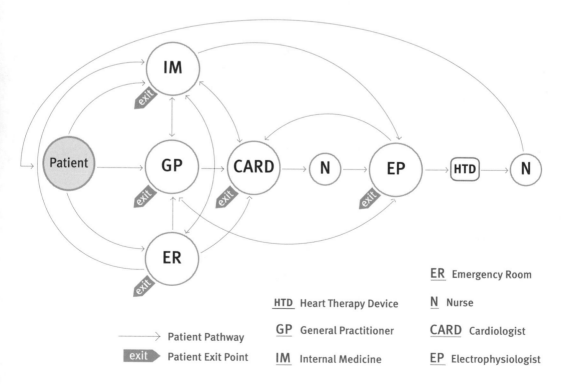

ER Emergency Room	
HTD Heart Therapy Device	N Nurse
GP General Practitioner	CARD Cardiologist
IM Internal Medicine	EP Electrophysiologist

·······> Patient Pathway
exit▶ Patient Exit Point

*In another analysis of institutional healthcare decision making, the stakehold-
ers were depicted as a network of commercial players, healthcare procurement
decision makers, medical professional administrators, and important influencers,
as shown in an early, low-resolution diagram (figure 32).*

FIG. 32 STAKEHOLDER MAPPING IN HEALTHCARE DECISION MAKING

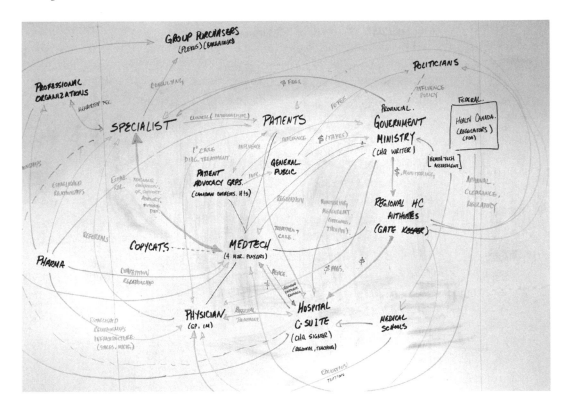

NEED-FINDING RESEARCH
Designing a deep dive

WHY DO WE DO THIS?

To define the people to be recruited as research subjects in order to better understand their needs. This activity involves identifying key stakeholders (and the defining variables within each group), specifying what activity you want to explore, selecting the research exercises you will do, and determining logistical criteria for recruiting. Designing Need-finding Research will address: Who do we need to better understand? What is the right "sample profile" that will ensure we have a varied representation of each stakeholder group? What is the right research design? How many people do we need to recruit, against what specifications, and for what activity?

HOW CAN YOU DO THIS?

1 **Define your target subject, with an emphasis on the end user.** Refer to your Stakeholder Map and Project Brief to define who matters most. Be sure to explore all the needs of all important stakeholders. Limiting your stakeholders to a single group may prevent you from discovering new insights along the way and reframing the challenge more precisely. *For example (to keep it simple), the end user might be a patient, and the key advisor might be the doctor.*

2 **Define the activity.** Define the broad interrelated activities that are most relevant to your Project Brief. *For example, a patient's activity might be "managing my heart condition," and a doctor's activity might be "managing patients with a heart condition."*

3 **Diversify the sample.** Diversify your research by looking at a variety of types of people in your sub-samples. These contrasts will help you see similarities and differences in the way the same activity is done by different people. *For instance, if the activity is "managing a heart condition," you might select patients who are young, middle-aged, and elderly.* You might want to further diversify by gender and socioeconomic status, rather than focusing on a homogenous group.

4 **Define criteria.** Create a table to help you determine recruiting profiles and logistical criteria. The number of people you intend to interview, their

geographic distribution, and the interview site will all have to be factored into the research planning.

⑤ **List research exercises.** Specify the various exercises or activities you would like your research participants to take part in (e.g., User Journals, Photo Elicitation). Be aware that the more activities you have users take part in, the more they may have to be compensated for their time.

⑥ **Define an action plan.** Consolidate all of this information into a recruitment and field research plan. This document should be reviewed with your team and a professional recruiter. A professional recruiter will recruit people who meet your criteria and are willing to participate.

TIPS

Refer to your Stakeholder Map and Project Brief for whom to include and what activity to explore.

In considering how to diversify your sample, use your intuition to con-sider subsets in your sample. For example, you might want to include patients who are both compliant and non-compliant with medical recommendations, and people of different ages, genders, and ethnic backgrounds, and from different geographic locations, if you believe this will reveal differences in perspective and behavior. Ultimately, you will be looking for needs that are common to a diverse cross-section of people.

How many people should you recruit in total? An MIT Sloan study suggests that in-depth one-on-one interviews with ten to twenty customers per segment should be adequate to identify customer needs. I suggest beginning with a minimum of ten per stakeholder group, and increasing your sample size if significant differences emerge. The key with this relatively small sample is to aim for quality and depth so as to identify both common underlying unmet needs and important differences that are worthy of expanding your research sample.

If you discover that meaningful differences emerge within important stakeholder groups, you should consider increasing the number of people in your research sample to ascertain how representative these differences are.

Prepare to over-recruit research participants to make up for participants who drop out of the study. It is normal to over-recruit two to three people for every ten.

WHAT MIGHT THIS LOOK LIKE?

Figure 33 shows what an initial recruiting plan for a healthcare project might look like. The key is to ensure a good mix and an appropriate sample size for each important stakeholder group.

FIG. 33 HEALTHCARE RECRUITING MATRIX

PATIENTS AND FAMILY (25 total)	NURSES (10 total)	DOCTORS (20 total)	OTHER HEALTHCARE SPECIALISTS (5 total for insight only)
Patients (age 65+) Patients (age 41–64) Patient Partners (for insights only)	Nurses: EP Hospital and General Nurses	Specialists: Electrophysiologists Hospital Cardiologists and Community Cardiologists Generalists: General Practitioners and ER Physicians	Psychologists Pharmacists

USER JOURNALS
Understanding the current user journey

WHY DO WE DO THIS?
To stimulate dialogue with participants and reveal new insights based on user-generated content. This method is used to draw out personal stories from people in order to understand them holistically, revealing new insights. These stories serve as the basis for discovering unmet needs among important users of your ultimate solution, particularly the end user. User Journals are an effective way to engage users, either as a supplement to or instead of Photo Elicitation (for example, in situations where photo-taking is prohibited). This will reveal answers to questions like: What is this experience like from the users' perspective? What kind of insights and unmet needs do their journeys reveal?

HOW CAN YOU DO THIS?
1 **Select a target group**. Identify the key stakeholder group whose current journey you would like to better understand, according to your field research plan.

2 **Define the experience.** A User Journal exercise asks individuals to document their experience within the context of a specific activity. They record their activities, thoughts, and feelings in a journal over the course of a few days. Rely on the Project Brief to help you define the experience you would like to know more about. For example, in a project on chronic pain management, we asked patients: *"For each of your visits to a doctor regarding your pain condition, please document your experience, using this journal."*

3 **Design the package.** A User Journal Package is a kit that is sent out to individual users. Each kit contains three documents: Participant Instructions, Journal, and Informed Consent.
- *Participant Instructions.* These include an overview of the package plus details of contact information, exercise instructions, exercise duration, important dates and times, and a request for a follow-up interview.

- *Journal.* This provides detailed instructions for completing the User Journal exercise. It states the purpose, procedure, and research activity, and provides thought starters. It also includes a number of blank pages that the user will write in.
- *Informed Consent.* This outlines the ethical conditions governing how the research exercise will be conducted. It states the purpose of the research, the procedure that will be followed, confidentiality provisions, contact information, and what the participant is giving consent to.

④ **Recruit and schedule participants, and deliver the research package.** After participants have been recruited, a follow-up interview of approximately 60 minutes should be scheduled to take place at a location that is most convenient and comfortable for the participant. When the participant has been recruited and the interview has been scheduled, the research package can be placed with the participant.

⑤ **Conduct the interview.** Conduct a follow-up interview with subjects to discuss the journal they have created (which you should keep for reference). The purpose of this interview is to listen to their stories to gain deeper insight into their needs.

TIPS

Tips on conducting an interview may be found below in the Listening and Recording tool.

User Journals are a handy tool to use in conjunction with a Photo Elicitation exercise. Journals allow users to record their thoughts and experiences when they are not comfortable taking photographs (because of sensitivity issues).

Journals are also a good tool to use in environments (such as an office or a hospital) where picture taking is not appropriate or is not allowed because of confidentiality or privacy restrictions.

You can design the journal to elicit input on a number of levels, including feelings, timing, location, thoughts passing through the user's head, and so on. The key is to make it user-friendly and not overly complicated.

Finding individuals to participate in your research is something best left to professional recruiting firms who recruit for market research. Work with them to identify the profile of the people you would like to recruit, the number of subjects, what they will do, and how they will be compensated, as per your Field Research Plan. Alternatively, a lower-cost way to recruit individuals is through your own professional and personal network, though this may result in a less representative sample.

Be sure to compensate research participants for their time.

WHAT MIGHT THIS LOOK LIKE?

In a study on chronic pain, we asked patients to keep a journal (see figure 34) on their way to and during visits to the doctor (where taking pictures was not allowed). These journals prompted them to tell stories about their experiences that revealed deeper insights and unmet needs.

FIG. 34 PATIENT JOURNAL ENTRIES

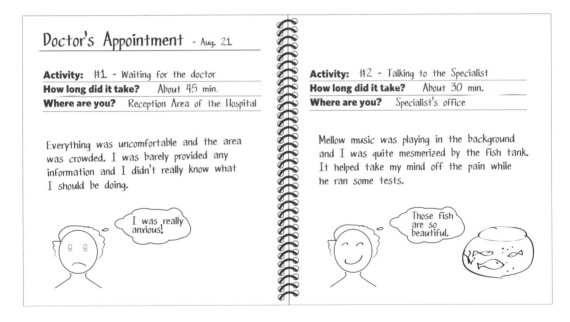

PHOTO ELICITATION
Discovering unmet needs through storytelling

WHY DO WE DO THIS?

To trigger insightful stakeholder stories through subject-generated photographs. These stories will help you discover unmet needs by drawing out personal stories around a broadly defined activity. Photo Elicitation is an effective way to solicit important stakeholder stories and discover insights not normally uncovered by traditional market research. This methodology is much like the Journal exercise, but provides more specific and tangible "triggers" that generally reveal even more powerful stories and insights. It will help answer questions like: What helps and hinders people in carrying out the activity of interest? What are the POEMS (people, objects, environments, media/messages, and services) they encounter? What are their unmet needs?

HOW CAN YOU DO THS?

This methodology is inspired by the early work Rotman DesignWorks did with the Illinois Institute of Technology's Institute of Design.[38] The following is a synopsis of the method that has proved to be very fruitful in our need-finding explorations.

1 **Define target participants, with an emphasis on the end user.** Refer to your Stakeholder Map and Project Brief to define who matters most.

2 **Define the activity.** A Photo Elicitation exercise asks individuals to use a camera to take pictures relating to an activity in their life, exploring both positive and negative aspects of their experience. (This could be done with a digital camera or, if subjects do not have access to one, a disposable camera provided by the researcher.) Rely on the Project Brief to help you define the activity you would like to know more about. This assignment leaves room for broad exploration. The following are a few examples:

"Take photographs that tell your stories about managing your health and wellness — what helps and hinders you."

"Take photographs that tell stories about how you manage your personal finances — what helps and hinders you."

"Take photographs that tell stories about commuting to and from work — both good and bad experiences."

3 Design the package. A Photo Elicitation Package is a kit that is sent out to individual users. Each kit contains three documents:
- *Participant Instructions.* These include an overview of the package plus details of contact information, exercise instructions, exercise duration, important dates and times, and a request for a follow-up interview.
- *Photo Instructions (and camera if provided).* This provides detailed instructions for completing the exercise. It states the purpose, procedure, and research activity, and provides thought starters.
- *Informed Consent.* This outlines the ethical conditions governing how the research exercise will be conducted. It states the purpose of the research, the procedure that will be followed, confidentiality provisions, contact information, and what the participant is giving consent to.

4 Recruit and schedule participants, and deliver the research package. After participants have been recruited, a follow-up interview of approximately 60 minutes should be scheduled to take place at a location that is most convenient and comfortable for the participant. When the participant has been recruited and an interview has been scheduled, the research package can be placed with the participant.

5 Follow up and collect photos. Once each individual has completed the exercise, arrange to have the photos emailed to you if they are digital. If a disposable camera was used, collect the camera and have the photos developed.

6 Conduct the interview. After you have received the photos from the participant, organize (but do not change the sequence or edit) the photographs. Conduct a follow-up interview with the subjects to discuss the photos they have taken. Your number one job is to listen with empathy and an open mind to their stories, not to ask direct questions.

TIPS

Photo Elicitation is a valuable exercise that requires time and focus. It is often best to use this technique with key stakeholder groups.

There is no such thing as a "bad" picture. Do not filter out pictures before you begin the interview. Even bad pictures usually have a story behind them.

See the Listening and Recording tool below for interviewing tips.

WHAT MIGHT THIS LOOK LIKE?

FIG. 35 PHOTO ELICITATION —
INSPIRATION THROUGH STORYTELLING

This photo (figure 35) was taken by a police officer who was undergoing chemotherapy treatment. He described the empty feeling he felt every morning when he woke up and saw his police uniform hanging in his closet. It reminded him that he was not actively serving his community and being a productive member of society. His sense of self-worth suffered during his period of chemo treatment. (That alone inspired an idea for a "chemo buddy" program.)

FIG. 36 PHOTO ELICITATION —
THERE ARE NO BAD PHOTOS

This picture (figure 36) shows that there are no bad photos. This dark photo was taken by a woman with an extended family overseas. While the interview team was ready to delete this photo, it turned out to provide a valuable insight. The woman described the glowing computer screen in a dark room. Since her family is on the other side of the world and there is a twelve-hour time difference between her and her family, she often calls them in the middle of the night. This led to a story about the importance of keeping in touch with her "roots" and the value she placed on her cultural identity. That was a rich story for a bad picture!

LISTENING AND RECORDING
Getting the most out of interviews

WHY DO WE DO THIS?
To glean the deepest understanding and most powerful insights out of time spent with others. A mindful and disciplined interviewer can draw out stories about an individual's life that reveal fresh insights and unmet needs and that eventually serve as criteria for creating innovative solutions. Interviews may use prompts (like photos or journals) or be conducted by simply asking people to tell you a story or recount an experience.

HOW CAN YOU DO THIS?
[1] **Prepare and define roles.** Interviews are best conducted in teams of two. One team member takes the lead and guides the interview. The other individual takes notes on *everything* they hear and see, making sure not to leave out any details of stories, defining quotes, or observations. It is also important for this person to manage any voice or imaging devices you may use to record the interview. Prepare your roles, materials, and prompts (e.g., user photos or journals) before the interview begins.

[2] **Explain the interview process.** The start of the interview should be used to welcome the interviewee and make him feel comfortable. Below is an example of how you might begin your interview:

"Today we want to hear your stories about (subject matter). This is meant to help us understand your experiences on this topic."

In a situation where photos are used as prompts, you might like to add:

"To help you tell us your stories we want you to keep five things in mind. These five things are: [39]
People: Who are the people you encounter and interact with during this activity?
Objects: What are the things you use and interact with?
Environment: What are the places where this activity takes place?
Messages and Media: What information are you looking for and how do you get it?
Services: What are the services and support systems you use?

"We've asked you to take pictures of (activity). Keeping these things in mind, can you begin by telling us what this first picture is about?"

③ **Probe with open-ended questions.** Continue to ask about their stories in an open-ended manner, by asking, *"Tell me your story about (this picture or this subject),"* *"Tell me more,"* or *"Why is that important to you?"* It is important to ask open-ended questions in order to hear subject stories. Asking direct, product/service-specific questions will not reveal the same depth and breadth of insight in the search for important unmet needs.

TIPS

Conducting a proper interview with the user is key to getting the richest and most unfiltered insights. Here are some practical tips:

Make it natural. It is crucial for the interviewee to feel at ease and able to talk freely without pressure or judgment. That will result from a balance of genuine empathy with an appropriate dose of neutrality (i.e., control your reactions to their stories).

Let them do (all) the talking. Empathy and insight will come only if you are not attempting to steer the conversation and are openly and intently listening. For at least the opening part of the interview, try asking only two questions: "Could you tell me more?" and "Why is that important?" Product/service-specific questions will lead to largely uninspiring responses and will rarely uncover an unarticulated need.

Be comfortable with silence. We are often uncomfortable with "dead air." It is important to overcome this discomfort, as these moments of silence will allow people to be free with their stories. Often the biggest burst of insight comes after four or five seconds (an eternity!) of silence.

Be mindful and pay attention. Capture any nonverbal clues there may be in emotions *(he got teary-eyed when . . .)*, behaviors *(he was fidgeting during his recount of . . .)*, and body language *(he looked like all his energy was zapped out of him when . . .)*.

Record everything. As a note taker, capture the stories and quotations to bring to life the pictures, journals, or other prompts. Be on the lookout for moments of excitement or frustration. Record information in the user's terms, including the obvious or seemingly unimportant.

WHAT MIGHT THIS PROCESS LOOK LIKE?

Figure 37 depicts the interviewing and note-taking process graphically.

FIG. 37 INTERVIEW ROLES & NOTE TAKING

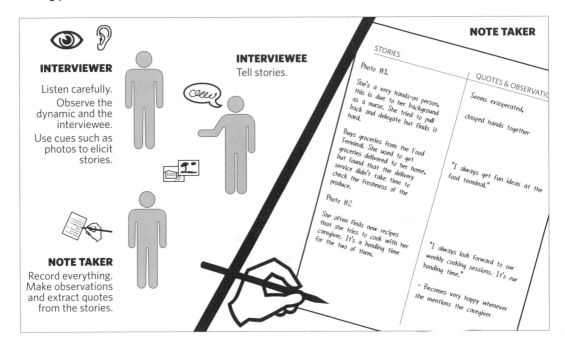

MIND MAPPING
Making connections to understand the whole person

WHY DO WE DO THIS?
To map thoughts and ideas "organically" to help make connections between seemingly unrelated data points and observations. This method of visualization is a thinking tool that helps make the thoughts and ideas (the "stuff" in your head) explicit for you and other people. It is used for a variety of purposes, including interview debriefing, organizing your thoughts, or making sense out of the research findings. It helps you think through questions like: What's really motivating this person? What are the main themes emerging from this interview, and how do they connect?

HOW CAN YOU DO THIS?
1 **Center your map on the individual.** Start in the center of a piece of paper with the interviewee's name. Draw a line to the first theme or topic it makes you think of in the context of the interview. Refer to your interview notes to help you recount what you heard. Ask yourself:
- What was the most surprising insight from that interview?
- What does that mean?
- What was the overall theme behind what the subject said?
- How does that connect with other things the subject said?

2 **Expand the map.** Work outward in all directions, putting similar ideas close to each other. This process encourages you to recount the stories you heard in a fluid and natural way.

3 **Look for patterns and connections.** When you believe you have most of your insights out on paper, consider how they all link together. Use circles or lines to highlight these connections. Ask yourself: What's really motivating this person? What are the main themes emerging from this interview, and how do they connect?

TIPS

Things to have on hand: User Journals, interview photographs, and notes.

Make sure your paper is large enough so you have room to expand upon your thoughts or ideas.

This is an excellent way to debrief an interview with your interview partner(s).

Try not to filter what you put down; write down every thought or idea that comes to you. Along the way, ask yourself: Why is that important to this person? You can cross-reference the next tool, Motivational Mapping, for tips on how to do this.

WHAT MIGHT THIS LOOK LIKE?

Figure 38 depicts a Mind Map based on an interview with a patient.

FIG. 38 MIND MAPPING A PATIENT INTERVIEW

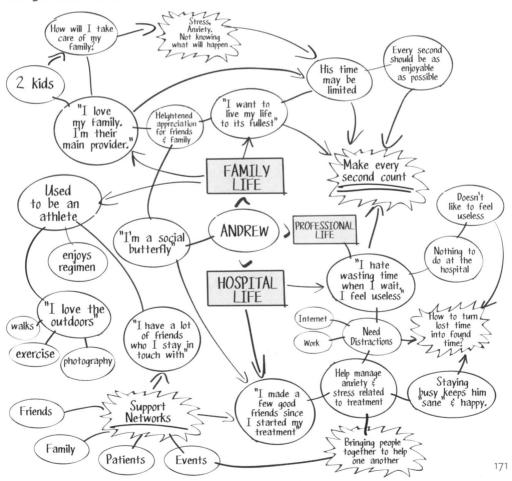

MOTIVATIONAL MAPPING
Searching for deeper meaning

WHY DO WE DO THIS?
To think more deeply about what interviewees have done and said, and to articulate their underlying motivations and unmet needs. This will help give deeper meaning to observations and elements of the interviewees' stories and quotations, and reveal more than the obvious statements and insights. *This can be used in conjunction with the following tools: Mind Mapping, Discovery Exchange, and Need-mining and Analysis.*

HOW CAN YOU DO THIS?
☐ **Select an interesting comment from a story.** In the center of a piece of paper, write down a comment or activity for which you believe there is deeper meaning. *For example: "I sat for hours staring at the wall with nothing to do while I just waited endlessly."*

☐ **Define insights.** Branching off from your initial observation or quotation, consider what that might mean to the participant on a more subjective level. *For example: "I have no time to waste. My time is valuable."* Consider other insights the central statement might suggest, and draw another branch on your map.

☐ **Articulate the need.** Go one level deeper to consider what unmet need an insight may point to. *For example: "I need to find time, and make the best use of it" or "I need to be productive."*

TIPS

Like the observation exercise, Motivational Mapping will enhance your empathy and understanding on a deeper level.

Look for needs that are deep enough to do something about but not so abstract that they seem vague and uninspiring.

Intuition plays an important role here. Through all of your research, you will have an intuitive sense of what really matters to and motivates your subject.

WHAT MIGHT THIS LOOK LIKE?

Figure 39 shows a visualization for the Princess Margaret Hospital project referred to previously.

FIG. 39 MOTIVATIONAL MAPPING

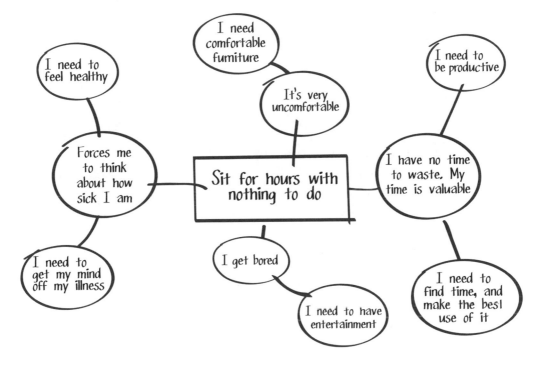

SUBJECT PROFILES
Synthesizing the interviews

WHY DO WE DO THIS?

To synthesize and record the important aspects of each interview within the context of a project and provide a quick way to identify participants and their details. Subject Profiles can serve as a helpful reference guide to individual interviews, including key motivators, defining quotations, and insights gained from each person's story. You will have many interviews, and proper recording of each one will ensure thoughtfulness and robustness in your research.

HOW CAN YOU DO THIS?

Here are some tips on how to summarize an interview, with an example of a format and content provided (see figure 40).

- Refer to your interview notes, Mind Map, and Motivational Map.
- Include defining quotations — these are valuable for keeping your discoveries in understandable language and are helpful in articulating need statements.
- Keep each Subject Profile brief and succinct — one page is best, as this will force you to synthesize, and you may have dozens of interviews to consider.
- Use the Subject Profiles throughout the research process as a quick and easy way to recall different interview subjects at a glance.

WHAT MIGHT THIS LOOK LIKE?

FIG. 40 INTERVIEW SUMMARY

SUBJECT NAME	Ben Shipley
AGE	62
DATE & TIME	05/07/10 @ 12:30am
INTERVIEW LOCATION	Coffee Shop
INTERVIEW TEAM	Alex, Alana
INTERVIEW DURATION	1 hour

Provide a brief overview of the user

Ben is the owner and operator of the Over The Top Sox Co. for over 20 years. He has a background in management and has helped sustain and grow the 80-year-old company his grandfather started. He is an extremely hard-working owner who works 12 hours a day and never seems to tire of the constant challenges his manufacturing business has to offer. Ben is proud of his staff, his business, and especially of all the socks they make and sell ... "Everyone always thinks of socks last, but we always think of socks first!"

Describe your user's habits and practices relevant to the project

Ben is a huge believer in the power that technology brings to his business. He feels that without technology, he wouldn't be efficient enough to compete with goods produced in China. Though the company does manufacture socks, a big part of their competitive advantage is R&D for large clients. Ben a makes a habit of constantly using the latest knowledge to further their understanding of product development and how technology can help him. In the plant, much of the production is automated, which cuts down much of their labor costs.

Ben makes sure to visit all of their large clients face-to-face to establish a good rapport. He also realizes the potential for great staff: he now has many potential hires coming his way due to the recent downturn in manufacturing jobs. He tries to choose those who have great skill and something to offer even if there is currently not a position for them at the plant.

What is this person all about — what drives him/her?

Ben is an entrepreneur and business enthusiast. He loves the fact that every day there is a new challenge to tackle and he can use his management skills to solve it. He values his employees. He sees the silver lining in everything, so he always sees problems as opportunities.

What is this person's biggest point of pain?

His biggest point of pain is competing against large brand names who can easily undercut his prices. This can lead to a loss of profit and can easily affect the established relationships he has with his clients. Control of his inventory is another point of pain. Ben needs to be aware of what is going on in his warehouse at all times to make sure things are running smoothly. He has to keep the cash register ringing to keep the people he values on the payroll.

DISCOVERY EXCHANGE
Making intuitive connections and building a framework for analysis

WHY DO WE DO THIS?

To visually synthesize collective research insights, as a means of creating shared empathy, consolidating discoveries across the team, and providing a framework for subsequent analysis. As team members share their interview stories and insights, you will intuitively formulate a hypothesis on common issues and needs, thus making sense out of the volume of research findings. This is useful for making links between numerous insights across many interviews and volumes of research data. During this exchange, patterns, themes, and common needs will begin to emerge.

HOW CAN YOU DO THIS?

1 **Assign a facilitator and a visualizer.** They will record the exchange and lead the group discussion. All team members should be prepared to share their interviewee stories and should have their research notes handy.

2 **Begin with one compelling story.** One team member should begin by recounting an interview story that comes vividly to mind. It is most powerful (and empathic) to *recount the story in the first person* (i.e., as if you are the interviewee) and not "interpret" or filter the story through your own lens. While the story is being recounted, the visualizer should mark down defining quotations, key themes, and words that emerge from the story. The visualizer will start to create a consolidated map of the research findings.

3 **Build on insights.** Other team members who have similar stories or related insights should share them. This will help to build on the number of insights and help to flesh out the visual map.

4 **Share stories.** Once the first story and insights have been exhausted, other team members should take turns sharing other (quite different) research stories that they feel are important. The team should do this until a good cross-section of stories has been shared and clear patterns emerge.

5 **Pause for reflection and look for connections.** Use circles or lines to highlight patterns and connections, looking for important themes and common needs.

6 **Articulate a short list of hypothesized needs.** Based on your exchange and the patterns that emerge, articulate a short list of needs that you believe are common to a particular stakeholder group, keeping the SPICE framework (social, physical, identity, communication, emotional) in mind to define needs holistically. Ideally, you will get this down to no more than five needs. This will serve as an initial framework for need analysis.

TIPS

Some useful things to have on hand: User Journals, interview notes and photographs, Mind Maps, and Subject Profiles.

Capture defining quotes. *(e.g., "I was terrified on my first day of school. Everything was new.")*

Use a large whiteboard or poster paper to ensure that you have enough space to develop connections and links.

This is an intuitive process. Look for deeper meaning and common needs across all of the interviews. Motivational Mapping can help take the conversation to a deeper and more meaningful level.

WHAT MIGHT THIS LOOK LIKE?

In u project that explored what people value (right after the 2008 market drop), a bank of insight-rich stories revealed common patterns around community, cultural identity, and balanced living. Figure 41 shows an early-stage visualization of the Discovery Exchange.

FIG. 41 CAPTURING STORIES & MAKING CONNECTIONS

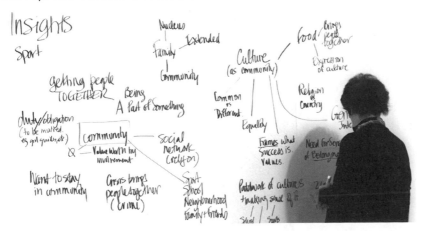

NEED MINING AND ANALYSIS
Turning soft data into hard data

WHY DO WE DO THIS?

To bring rigor and depth to need finding, and ensure that discoveries are broad-based and meaningful, as opposed to just momentary inspirations. The goal is to extract insights from your research and to translate those into a set of well-defined, universal needs, keeping the SPICE framework (social, physical, identity, communication, emotional) in mind to ensure that you consider the many dimensions of your end users and other stakeholders.

There are many approaches to analyzing needs, ranging from an organic method that clusters insights on sticky notes (which can give you a sense of the patterns in insights and needs to inspire fresh thinking) to a more rigorous analysis, like that presented here. I recommend this more rigorous approach if you are undertaking a significant project for which you would like a strong foundation you can refer to on an ongoing basis. It is the method we use at DesignWorks on all large-scale projects to ensure we are working from a platform of thoughtful and rigorous need-finding research.

HOW CAN YOU DO THIS?

This process is guided by the framework you will have intuitively built in your initial group debriefing and exchange. It is best done if you have transcribed all of your interviews into a typewritten format from your interview notes or from a recording on an audio device. (A transcription service can quickly and cost-effectively do this for you.) You should refer to the full text from each interview. You will continue to discover "hidden" insights and needs within these stories and quotations as you deconstruct them into a comprehensive collection of data points. The spreadsheet below will show you how you can turn your wealth of data into a powerful foundation for innovation.

1 **Deconstruct your interviews into insightful quotations and snippets of stories.** These will become your insight "data points." Insights can come from the stories you've heard, a great quotation, or something relevant that you've observed in the environment or the interviewee's behavior. Record each of these insights into individual cells of an Excel spreadsheet. Using excerpts from the stories and quotations from your interview transcription, begin to identify insights that are:

- *Revealing:* a glimpse into deeper motivations and needs
- *Authentic:* supported by the story/observations
- *Practical:* trigger ideas on ways to help the subject

[2] **Analyze the insight and connect it to your initial need framework.** Referring to your list of hypothesized needs identified in your initial framework (see the Discovery Exchange tool), consider which of these needs may be underlying each insight. One insightful story or quotation may point to more than one need. During this process, be cognizant of emerging new needs and be prepared to adjust your need analysis framework and revisit insights in light of newly identified needs.

[3] **Tabulate the universality and intensity of these needs.** To gain an idea of the intensity and universality of needs, cross-reference the interview insights with the intuitively hypothesized needs. You can do this by creating a spreadsheet with columns as follows:
- Spreadsheet Column A: Identify the subject (the interviewee).
- Spreadsheet Column B: Profile the interviewee briefly.
- Spreadsheet Column C: Capture each interview "snippet" with either a single revealing quotation or a segment of the subject's story that you feel revealed a profound insight.
- Spreadsheet Column(s) D+: Each column will represent one of your hypothesized needs (maximum of 7 needs).

For each entry in Column C, connect it to the appropriate needs in columns D+ by putting "1" in each column with which you believe the data point is associated. Tabulate the intensity and universality of needs by calculating each column on the Excel sheet. This will help you to verify the needs in your initial need framework and provide you with a flexible database of all your interviews that you can use to analyze and substantiate your need-finding conclusions.

   This process should leave you with four to six deep, unsatisfied needs that will serve as the criteria for innovation and value creation.

TIPS

Use the outcome of your collective Discovery Exchange as an initial framework going into analysis, but be prepared to alter it — it is only an initial hypothesis. Don't force-fit needs to your initial hypothesis. If a new need emerges, add it to the list of core needs and revisit the assignment of data points to needs.

This is a highly iterative and intuitive process, though it culminates in an analytical output.

Needs often cannot be articulated by individuals themselves and only surface once the need-finding process is complete. Motivational Mapping can help define a deeper need.

Any given data point may be associated with multiple needs. Ask yourself the following question: Could this comment relate to other needs? For example, a comment on "waiting for hours" could be related to a need to be more engaged and productive or a need to have more information.

WHAT MIGHT THIS LOOK LIKE?

Figure 42 shows a section of a spreadsheet illustrating how the individual insights and quotations were broken out, analyzed, and linked to needs.

FIG. 42 SPREADSHEET ANALYSIS OF SOFT DATA

COLUMN A Subject	COLUMN B Profile	COLUMN C Stories & Quotes	COLUMNS D+ Support & Connectivity	Engagement	Effortless Simplicity	Empowerment	Healthy Healing
(1) Police Officer	48 y.o, Married. 3 months of chemo therapy	I get anxious just sitting there (waiting room)		1			
		I never talk about cancer	1				
		I have no time to waste		1			
		Going to work is the greatest part of my life				1	
		Waiting is the most painful time		1			1
(2) Retired Nurse	63 y.o., Active in her community. Just starting chemo	I cover my face a lot — my face looks good, but in my heart I cry	1	1			1
		There is nothing to help pass the time		1			
		Spending time with my grandson is 'happy time'		1			
		There are a lot of people with different backgrounds (hard to start a conversation)	1		1		
		The walls are gray and the air is stale		1			

NEED ARTICULATION
Defining a platform for innovation

WHY DO WE DO THIS?

To articulate unmet needs in a way that inspires the development team and creates a vital platform for innovation. Creating new human-centered value stems from a deep understanding of people's needs. This step is the culmination of all of your need-finding research. In combination with your Personas and a depiction of a user's Current Journey (see the following two tools), these needs will serve as the basis for creating and evaluating new solutions going forward.

HOW CAN YOU DO THIS?

Now is the time when you turn the "hard data" back into "soft data" to create an inspiring need-based springboard for innovating. Now that you have used your analysis to validate the broad and important needs to be met, it is time to capture them in a human and compelling manner. The following steps should be taken for each of the top four to six needs.

1 **Headline the need.** Summarize the motivating need in a short phrase, using simple, user-friendly language and avoiding abstract or generic terms. You will need a shorthand phrase to refer to in development. *For example, on the Princess Margaret Hospital (PMH) project, one of the key needs was "engagement."*

2 **Define the need clearly.** Provide a clear definition of what you mean by that need, and ensure that everyone understands and buys into that definition. Nothing is more likely to derail you in Gear 2 than the question: That's clever, but what does it mean? *For example, on the PMH project, "engagement" meant turning lost time into found time by giving patients the means to make more productive use of their time (both while waiting for and during treatment) and engaging them emotionally, physically, intellectually, or spiritually.*

3 **Provide a defining quotation.** Looking back through your notes and Subject Profiles, select a quotation that captures the spirit of the need as voiced by a real person. *For example, a defining quotation for "engagement" was: "Waiting is the most painful time. I'm here for five hours; there is an opportunity to learn and make me productive."*

TIPS

Things to have on hand: User Journals, interview notes and photographs, and Subject Profiles.

Needs should be articulated in a human way that is easily understood (i.e., something a "real person" would say) and reinforced with insightful and compelling quotations.

Needs must be relevant to the project and broad enough to create opportunity, but not so broad that they are vague and do not inspire solutions.

PERSONAS
Creating human archetypes

WHY DO WE DO THIS?
To depict important stakeholders in holistic terms and put their needs into context. Personas are fictional composite characters based on data from real people. They are to be used to keep "real people" at the table throughout the development process and frame the project challenge in human, holistic terms.

HOW CAN YOU DO THIS?
[1] **Define important stakeholder groups.** Select the most critical stakeholders, with priority always on the ultimate end user of your future solution.

[2] **Determine if there are important differences within these groups.** Analyze the data generated from research and look for differences within groups in terms of motivations, attitudes, and behaviors. If one stakeholder group clearly contains more than one type of character, feel free to create more than one Persona for that group to avoid over-generalizing about one group and eventually creating solutions that could alienate others. *For example, On the Princess Margaret Hospital project, there were distinct subgroups of patients who shared a common set of needs but expressed them in different ways. Profiling them separately ensured we delivered a patient experience that served all of them.*

[3] **Personify.** Characterize each of the distinct stakeholders you've identified. Your Personas should depict key differences you have observed among diverse users. Craft your Persona to feel like a real person by bringing him or her to life in the "first person," (i.e., using the pronoun "I"), citing defining quotations, and including visuals that reflect personal interests and lifestyles. Remember to create fictional characters based on real research data — make them "real" and not bland or idealized.

TIPS

Refer to the Needs you have identified, as well as observations from your Subject Profiles and interview notes for inspiration.

Personas serve as criteria for innovation. Done well, they can aid others in empathizing with your users as well as inspiring you throughout the development process and keeping the "human factor" at the center of value creation.

While needs may be universal, sometimes it is helpful to create more than one Persona to avoid over-stereotyping users. Each Persona should have a clear point of view. This will stretch your solution development in a way that maximizes universal appeal.

Respect confidentiality; do not use real names, personal data, or photos from your interviews.

WHAT MIGHT THIS LOOK LIKE?

In the case of Princess Margaret Hospital, we developed a number of Personas to reflect the various patient groups that were identified. Two of these are shown on the next page (figures 43 and 44) to illustrate their distinct motivations in the context of their shared needs. One patient subgroup needed a greater awareness of what was happening to them and support from others, while the other patient subgroup had a more intense need to be productive and have control over their treatment. While they all had needs in common, their needs required different solutions.

FIG. 43 PATIENT PERSONA

ANDREW McKENZIE

Age: 46
Occupation: Auditor
Status: Married, 2 Kids

I live with my wife and two kids in a modest house in Ajax. As a former high school athlete I enjoy sports and the outdoors; jogging with friends, boating, and hiking. My family and I try to stay engaged with the local community. I participate in environmental activities such as volunteering to coach the local kids' hockey team and helping to maintain local parks. Since I've been diagnosed with cancer for a second time, I would have to say that I'm fairly knowledge-able with the treatment process. I still try to work full-time although I worry more about deadlines and whether or not I will be able to take care of my family from time to time. My friends and family (especially wife) help a lot through the tough moments of my healing process. I don't want to feel like a burden so I try to drive myself to the hospital for treatment, although on occasion my friends may tag along. If asked, my friends and family would probably describe me as hardworking, generous, and focused.

FIG. 44 PATIENT PERSONA

PAMELA THOMAS

Age: 63
Occupation: Retired Nurse
Status: Widow

I've had cancer for 2 years now. I come in for treatment once a week, usually Wednesdays. I live by myself in a small house in Barrie. Cynthia, my longtime caregiver, comes by once a week to check up on me. I have 4 children and 10 grandchildren, who occasionally visit me from time to time. I wish I could see them more frequently.

Since the start of my treatment I try to keep myself busy with things I enjoy doing the most. Every day I take a long walk with my dog in a nearby forest. Every Sunday I volunteer at a local church. Tuesdays and Thursdays I cook for my friends, and every Friday I go to the nearby community center to meet my knitting group. The center is a great place to spend time with some of my old friends and make new ones. On treatment days I take the hospital shuttle service. I look forward to coming there. I know it sounds weird, but treatment days are the highlight of my week. I see the hospital as a way to connect with others.

THE CURRENT JOURNEY
Contextualizing the opportunity through empathic storytelling

WHY DO WE DO THIS?

To bring to life a current end user experience by depicting actions, struggles, and feelings. Storytelling is a useful way to evoke empathy for the user and to humanize and contextualize the opportunity for those on the development team as well as others with whom you will share your project. Your storytelling should reveal opportunities for solution development. Note that this can (and should) be done in a more mechanical manner early on in Gear 1, so you can have a framework for investigating your user's experience. Throughout Gear 1, you will gather new insights into the person's journey, and the feelings, people, and places that are part of it.

HOW CAN YOU DO THIS?

1 **Create a timeline.** Begin to sketch out a user's story by drawing a line on a large piece of paper that represents the period of time a current user experience lasts. This timeline may represent a few hours, a few days, or even a few months.

2 **Plot the experience stages.** Using your insights gathered from Gear 1, plot the beginning, middle, and end of the experience along the timeline. Consider the POEMS (people, objects, environments, messages, and services) that the user encounters.

3 **Detail the journey.** Thinking about the logical progression of events uncovered by your research, create a narrative story that encompasses the typical journey for your user as he or she currently experiences it. Consider the user's struggles, emotional state, functional requirements, and interactions with other stakeholders along the way. Avoid being vague about stages in the experience by injecting tangible elements from the POEMS framework to shape your depiction. If you get stuck, refer to your interview notes, needs, and Personas.

④ **Visualize your story.** Bring your story to life by illustrating the current journey through pictures, sketches, graphics, and even a short inspiring "slide show" or "movie" set to music. This story will be most powerful if it captures the user's struggles on both a practical and an emotional level.

TIPS

Highlight the needs and behaviors of users without going into unnecessary detail, capturing the journey in a holistic and human manner.

An effective way to communicate the experience to others is to create a simple animated movie using still images, text, and music. This can easily be done using presentation or basic movie creation software.

WHAT MIGHT THIS LOOK LIKE?

The following is a script from a simple yet compelling three-minute depiction of the opportunity to improve the patient experience by capturing the despair of the current journey and the needs that inspired a new vision for a journey of hopeful healing on the Princess Margaret Hospital project. The use of select copy and the transition from slow and sad music and the black-and-white photography of the current scene to colorful visuals and inspiring music set the tone for the creation of a new vision.

MUSIC	STORYLINE — WORDS	VISUALS
Sad and slow	PMH Systemic Therapy Treatment Centre 2007	Outside of the Princess Margaret Hospital
	This is where patients **enter** …	Long, dreary hall with chairs lined up against one wall
	This is what they **see** …	Gray wall with an old framed print
	This is where they **wait** for hours …	Line-up of institutional chairs with no space between
	This is what they **look** at …	A dull wall with a thermostat and a glaring light
	This is what they can **do** …	Tattered old magazines
	This is where they **sit** for hours …	Crowded treatment room, with a chair facing the hallway
	This is where they **rest** …	An institutional gurney extending into the hallway
	This is what they **see** …	A bright fluorescent panel of light and an air vent
	This is their experience. How can we make it better?	Dull, dreary shot of an endless corridor of waiting
Transition	Through **generous** support and the vision of PMH … **This space is a canvas to create** …	Big empty white space (a racquetball room)
Inspiring and upbeat	**An experience** that gives patients **hope**	Skyline with sunshine breaking through the clouds
(Build)	Where they **know** support is **always** there	Team of friendly and caring healthcare professionals
(Build)	Where **confidence** is acquired through **knowing**	Scheduling board (airline arrivals)
(Build)	There is a constant sense of **calm** … **comfort** … and **peace**	Zen roof garden Comfortable living room Woman meditating in a robe
(Build)	A place where **relationships** are created	Smiling nurse with patient
(Build)	… and **waiting** is just a **frame of mind**	Woman painting a canvas in a sunlit studio
(Build)	Where your **mind** is at **work** … and **play**	Close-up of a work-station Close-up of a chessboard
(Build)	Where new **discoveries** … help you **forget** that you are in a **hospital**	Gallery wall of art Close-up of woman watching a goldfish in a bowl
Optimistic	There **can** be such a place … Princess Margaret Hospital	Princess Margaret Hospital Brand imposed on the big empty white space (a racquetball room)

GEAR 2: CONCEPT VISUALIZATION

Refreshing Your Vision

IDEATION
Generating new possibilities

WHY DO WE DO THIS?

To generate a large number of ideas for satisfying unmet needs. Structured, collaborative idea-generation around a central theme can yield a wide range of ideas by tapping into the experience and imagination of a diverse team. From a plethora of seemingly outrageous and unorthodox solutions, new possibilities for solving unmet needs will emerge. Ideation addresses the important question: How can we best meet this person's needs?

HOW CAN YOU DO THIS?

1 **Ideate.** This first step is designed to generate hundreds of ideas.

- *Begin by picking one Persona and one need.* You can start with any one of the Personas or needs. It is important to focus on one at a time, so you can maximize your sense of empathy in serving a personal and specific need. This will also generate a *lot* of ideas from different angles.
- *Frame the need as a question.* Identify your Persona and one of the top unmet needs. Use these two inputs to create a question based on the unmet need. For each need, begin with a question like: "How can we help (the Persona) to (unmet need)?" *For example: How can Princess Margaret Hospital help Andrew feel more productive?*
- *Generate ideas.* Thinking freely and without judgment, generate ideas that address this need. The goal is to generate as many ideas as possible in a short amount of time. Aim for quantity over quality in your ideas — the more ideas the better.
- *Repeat for every need and Persona.* This will give you a wealth of ideas, all of which touch on a different dimension of human need and collectively feed the creation of a rich and multidimensional solution. Every round of ideation will generate fresh ideas, taking new needs and variations in Personas into account.

② **Cluster and identify larger concepts.** Across your vast pool of ideas, common solutions will emerge. Look for patterns, cluster similar ideas together, and identify the bigger concept in these clusters. *For example, a number of ideas may add up to a communication access service that may be relevant to all Personas and serve more than one need.*

③ **Expand on the most breakthrough concepts.** Choose your top concepts using the following criteria:
- Does this concept address a need and create value for users?
- Is this a breakthrough concept that could *dramatically* enhance their experience?

One concept at a time, ask the following questions: What might that look like? How could that work? What kind of POEMS (people, objects, environments, media/messages, and services) could that entail?

TIPS

Allow yourselves to think outside your current business offering. Often, the *intent* of concepts that are totally outside your business can be reconfigured in other ways. Don't edit at this point.

Defer judging ideas until the end; build on the ideas of others. Every idea is valid; sometimes breakout ideas are right next to the absurd ones.

Keep ideas flowing by capturing the essence of the idea and quickly moving on. Don't stall by going into detail.

Doodle or sketch to make your ideas visual. Visuals are easier to understand and will in turn stimulate new ideas.

Use metaphors or analogies to come up with ideas. Imagine yourself as someone famous or as a successful company; then ask yourself what kind of ideas they would come up with to address the needs. (This process is covered in more detail in the next tool, on Metaphors.)

WHAT MIGHT THIS PROCESS LOOK LIKE?
Figure 45 depicts the process graphically.

FIG. 45 IDEATION & CONCEPT ENRICHMENT

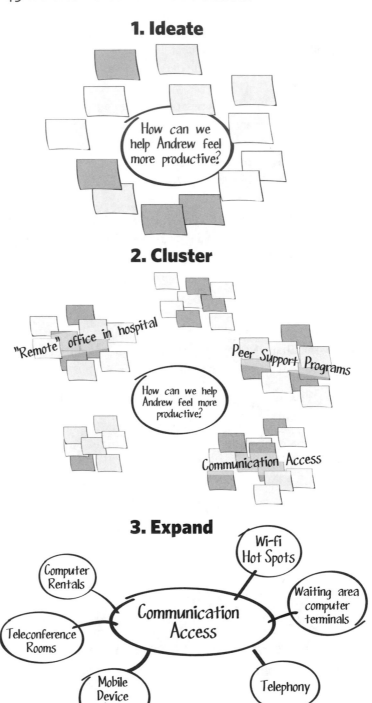

1. Ideate

How can we help Andrew feel more productive?

2. Cluster

"Remote" office in hospital

Peer Support Programs

How can we help Andrew feel more productive?

Communication Access

3. Expand

Computer Rentals

Wi-fi Hot Spots

Waiting area computer terminals

Teleconference Rooms

Communication Access

Mobile Device Apps

Telephony

METAPHORS
Using analogies to stimulate imagination

WHY DO WE DO THIS?
To stimulate our imagination by creating an analogy between two unlike things. Metaphors can be used to fuel brainstorming by relating qualities or traits from one context to another. This tool is helpful for expanding the pool of breakthrough ideas.

HOW CAN YOU DO THIS?
1 **Describe the "feeling" or outcome you would like to create.** Based on your unmet needs, describe the ideal outcome you would like to achieve through a new experience. *For example, in the activity of early childhood education, you found that kids wanted it to be more fun and engaging.*

2 **Think of analogies.** Based on that desired response or outcome, think of other things that elicit that reaction or deliver that result. Look to different industries to help open up a broader range of possibilities. *For example, if you were trying come up with ideas to help kids learn in a fun and engaging way, you would think of other ways that kids have fun — such as sports and games. If you chose games as the metaphor, you would pose the metaphorical question: If learning were a game, what might that* entail? What might that look like?

3 **Transfer those attributes to your own challenge.** This will help you to find alternative solutions and build on the ideas you already have. *In the case of childhood education, games are active, fun, competitive, and interactive. A possible idea might be a math game in schools with teams of students playing to win prizes.*

TIPS

The greater the difference between the two things you are comparing, the more powerful the metaphor you will create *(e.g., education as a game).*

Finding the right metaphors may take some practice; it may take time to think of one that is truly inspiring.

WHAT MIGHT THIS LOOK LIKE?

For the Princess Margaret Hospital project, a first-class airline seat was used as a metaphor to create a new chemotherapy experience. The need: to turn lost time into found time. Since patients sat in a chemo chair for hours on end and could not move, the team thought about other situations where people had to sit down for hours with limited mobility. They felt that a first-class airline chair was an appropriate metaphor. First-class chairs on airlines are designed to be luxurious, comfortable, and provide many amenities to passengers. While this may some-day lead to the design of a new chair, it also inspired new services and access to activities to help patients pass the time during treatment.

EXPERIENCE MAPPING
Designing a new and ideal experience

WHY DO WE DO THIS?

To design a multidimensional, seamlessly integrated user experience. Experience Mapping describes the stages of an experience and begins to tell the story of how a new solution will play out over a period of time. Building your ideas and concepts into a seamless experience will help close the gaps and enhance user value, moving from knitting together the "mechanics" to creating a compelling story. It helps you address questions like: How does this new solution come to life? How does this experience address unmet needs in a seamless manner? Are there gaps in this experience? Are there aspects of this experience that need to be further developed?

HOW CAN YOU DO THIS?

1 **Create a timeline.** Begin by drawing a line on a large piece of paper that represents the span of time during which your user will experience your envisioned solution. Depending on the amount of time it takes to complete the full product or service experience, this timeline can represent a few hours, a few days, or even a few months.

2 **Plot the experience stages.** Along the timeline, create stages that begin with the user dilemma and move through the user's discovery of your solution, his experience with it, and the outcome or memory. Consider specifically how the user first finds out about the solution, how he interacts with various components of the solution, and how he reflects on how well the solution met his needs.

3 **Build out the experience.** Thinking about the logical and seamless progression of events in this experience, create a story that encompasses the ideal experience for your user, keeping in mind the POEMS framework (people, objects, environments, media/messages, services). Consider the user's points of pain, emotional state, functional requirements, and interactions with other stakeholders. Be as detailed as possible. If you get stuck, role-play from the user's point of view (as described below in more detail in the tool on Role-playing).

4 **Visualize the experience and tell the story.** Illustrate the experience by using pictures, sketches, and graphics. Create a compelling narrative to capture the full experience, and the role of key design elements.

TIPS

Things to have on hand: selected ideas from Ideation, as well as the Needs and Personas (always keep them at the center).

Having difficulty deciding where to begin your experience map? Begin with the moment of discovery and usage — where the "big idea" peaks; this may be in the middle of the journey. From there you can work out the "after stage" (where it leads) and the "before" stage (how the user got there).

The ideas that you did not move forward with from ideation can filter back into your experience map, to help fill in gaps and enhance the solution.

Avoid being vague about stages in the experience; be as detailed as possible by using the POEMS framework to guide your exploration. Weave the details into your narrative in a relevant and natural way.

WHAT MIGHT THIS LOOK LIKE?

Figure 46 is a simple schematic that shows a segment of a patient experience and how ideas were built into the experience along a timeline to continually enrich it and close the gaps.

FIG. 46 EXPERIENCE MAPPING

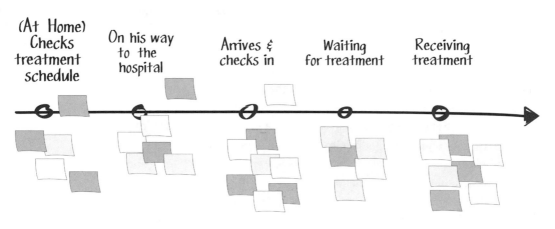

(At Home) Checks treatment schedule

On his way to the hospital

Arrives & checks in

Waiting for treatment

Receiving treatment

ITERATIVE PROTOTYPING
Making the abstract concrete

WHY DO WE DO THIS?

To stimulate thinking and dialogue by making abstract ideas concrete. While any representation of an idea is a "prototype" (including an Experience Map or Storyboards) this method refers to the building of a physical component of your envisioned experience. Prototyping helps you think through key components by building them out in a low-resolution, physical form. This will help advance concept development through experimentation and is useful in getting instant feedback from users, particularly in combination with Role-playing or the presentation of Experience Maps or Storyboards. It brings the solution to life by addressing questions like: What could this component look like? How might it work? What aspects of this idea need to be further developed?

HOW CAN YOU DO THIS?

☐ **Pick a component of your experience that's only abstract at this point.** Based on your ideas from Ideation and Experience Mapping, select one of the important conceptual components that you would like to develop further. It may be one of those ideas that all team members get excited about but may picture differently or have different ideas about how it could play out.

☐ **Prototype the idea.** Make your idea concrete using inexpensive and easy-to-acquire materials (e.g., cardboard, markers, Popsicle sticks). When building your idea, think about what it might look like, how it might play out, what context it is in, or how it could be "built" to satisfy the user's specific need. Your prototype should not resemble a finished, polished product, but should rather communicate the desired intent. A rapid prototype (i.e., one you devise during the course of development) is:
- *Quick and timely.* The less time you spend on it, the better.
- *Inexpensive and disposable.* Use inexpensive means and materials.
- *Plentiful.* Produce as many possible "expressions" as you can.

☐ **Explore how it works.** Place the prototype in the context of a user experience to see how it functions or operates. Use Role-playing or Storyboarding to present and explain the prototype to gain feedback (explained in more detail below in the Role-playing, Storyboarding, and Co-creation tools).

4 **Iterate and enhance.** Use your own intuition and feedback from others to improve the prototype for further testing. Critical feedback and continual testing will help to create a solution that satisfies all stakeholders.

TIPS

Low-resolution prototyping refers to physical representations of ideas that can be made with a low investment of time and money. Creating low-resolution prototypes helps you to visualize ideas, learn quickly, and reduce risk.

Prototypes should not be of a higher resolution than what is needed to communicate the desired intent.

It is helpful to use this method in conjunction with Role-playing and Storyboarding. This helps you in playing out your solution as a team to close the gaps, and in presenting your low-resolution concepts to stakeholders in Co-creation.

WHAT MIGHT THIS LOOK LIKE?

A student team wanted to test an idea of an in-home organic waste disposal system. To explore how that idea might work in the home, they mocked up their concept of an in-home organic waste disposal system in low-resolution, physical form with easily accessible materials (tape, cardboard, markers, pipe cleaners) and role-played their idea (see figure 47). They discovered that placement of the organic waste disposal within the kitchen to fit in with the user's normal kitchen routines was important. This inspired them to find ways to easily dispose of their waste while keeping it out of sight and under the sink.

FIG. 47 PROTOTYPING A SYSTEM FOR ORGANIC WASTE DISPOSAL

ROLE-PLAYING
Playing out the experience to close the gaps

WHY DO WE DO THIS?

To play out solutions in order to identify gaps, solicit feedback, and create a natural and seamless solution for the user. Role-playing uses improvisational acting to describe a multidimensional experience. It uses actors, props, a set, and a good storyline to communicate and demonstrate a new idea in real time. By role-playing your solution, you will figure out which aspects of the solution work and which do not work. You can do this as a team to enhance your ideas, or with users to get feedback on your ideas in Co-creation.

HOW CAN YOU DO THIS?

1 **Develop a plot.** Based on your newly envisioned experience, define and develop a plot line to demonstrate how the experience would work for the user.

2 **Set the stage.** Define and design the set, props, prototypes, and roles that people will play. The set, props, and prototypes should not be highly detailed and polished; rather, they should simply imply the setting and give a sense of the environment and objects.

3 **Role-play.** Walk through the experience as a role-play. The key is to improvise without a detailed script. Do this first in front of your team (to discover gaps or unnatural actions) and then, with a more well defined role-play, in front of others to gain feedback on what's working and what is not.

4 **Refine.** Evaluate what worked and what didn't work. Refer to the Co-creation exercise for tips on eliciting feedback.

TIPS

Use your Experience Map, storyline, and Prototype props in designing and playing out your solution.

It is important not to make the role-play too comical or absurd. Humourous interpretations of sensitive subject matter, such as personal or healthcare situations, must be handled with respect and care. Also, since a role-play is supposed to reflect real life, a comical interpretation may take away from the message being communicated.

This exercise should be coupled with the Co-creation exercise in order to gain user feedback to help improve the experience.

WHAT MIGHT THIS LOOK LIKE?

To gain feedback from their target users, the Nestlé Confectionery team created multiple role-plays that were targeted to different types of consumers, using low-resolution prototypes as props (figure 48). They gained instant and valuable feedback as input to help in enriching their concepts.

FIG. 48 ROLE-PLAYING AN EXPERIENCE USING PROPS

STORYBOARDING
Capturing the story in key frames

WHY DO WE DO THIS?
To capture key elements of the ideal user experience in a sequential, scripted, and visual way. Storyboarding is a cost-effective way to capture an experience to elicit feedback about the concept from the user. It is a less "theatrical" and more distilled and consolidated alternative to playing out the solution for users in Co-creation, and can be used as a synopsis of your idea in internal presentations, by capturing the key elements and benefits of your idea.

HOW CAN YOU DO THIS?
1 **Create a narrative.** Refer to your Experience Mapping exercises to create a frame-by-frame story, including:
- *the beginning,* introducing the point of view, where the story takes place, and the conflict or situation;
- *the middle,* describing the experience offered to the user in key stages — how they become aware of the solution, their experience with the solution, and the completion of that experience;
- *the ending,* concluding the story and summarizing the outcome.

2 **Select critical events.** Select the important parts of the story that reveal the design moments, using the POEMS framework (people, objects, environments, media/messages, services). Design moments are parts of the solution that help influence the outcome of the story. These can be captured in anywhere from five to twenty frames, depending on how multidimensional and extensive your concept is.

3 **Detail these moments.** List the actions and key components that need to be visualized though photography or drawings. Be as descriptive as possible, and identify the imagery that needs to be created in order to visualize the critical events. Create rough sketches to work through the visualization. This step helps to provide a coherent plan and focus communication.

4 **Complete the storyboard.** Refine your visuals and combine them with the written story to create a clear story of how your experience plays out.

TIPS

A storyboard is much like a comic book or a frame-by-frame outline for a commercial or a film. The story is communicated using text and key images to deliver important messages.

Make the design elements as specific and concrete as possible and avoid generalizations.

WHAT MIGHT THIS LOOK LIKE?

Figure 49 shows a few frames from the Princess Margaret Hospital storyboard that was used to convey the ideal experience for a patient, beginning at home and traveling to the hospital.

FIG. 49 STORYBOARDING KEY EXPERIENCE POINTS

Checks Hospital Portal **1**

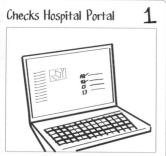

When Andrew wakes up, he checks his treatment time online. The portal allows him to book his treatment pod and select his personalized services.

Uses Hospital Shuttle Bus **2**

The shuttle bus that comes every 10 minutes picks up Andrew at the designated station and takes him straight to the hospital.

Arrives, Begins Treatment **3**

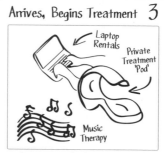

Andrew begins to receive the treatment in his personal pod. He has access to a laptop, which is connected to the Internet, his e-mail, media channels, and a variety of music.

CO-CREATION
Engaging others in the development process

WHY DO WE DO THIS?

To engage others (particularly end users) in the early development process in order to enhance and refine ideas. A representation of your concept is presented in a way that elicits honest, open feedback about ideas and concepts. Co-creation prevents team members from getting too attached to their ideas and provides them with an outside opinion — most importantly, that of the end user. This practice can be helpful in soliciting feedback from a variety of "users" of the solution, who will bring a valuable perspective to what will work and not work. It will also reveal new insights and stimulate fresh ideas on how to make your solution even more user-centered. This is not a method of "evaluation"; it is an exercise for making your solution as relevant and rich as it can be.

HOW CAN YOU DO THIS?

1 **Set up.** Before users are brought in to see your experience concept (as Experience Maps, Storyboards, or Role-plays, and often including physical prototypes), be sure to assign tasks to individual team members. Assign people to present, tell the story, take notes, and observe.

2 **Introduce the exercise.** The presenter should introduce the team and explain the purpose of the exercise and the feedback session. Make it clear that the ideas are not final and that you would like open, honest feedback.

3 **Present the prototype.** Present the experience for no more than 10 to 15 minutes. Be professional when presenting, and avoid anything that might be insensitive to the participants' feelings about the situation. It is important to show empathy in order to engage participants and convince them you are making a genuine effort to serve users better.

4 **Solicit user feedback.** The presenter should lead the feedback session by asking the following questions:

- What don't you understand?
- What's working for you?
- What's not working for you?
- How could it be better?

As the user provides feedback, someone else should take good notes. The other team members should sit to the side and take care not to distract or influence the discussion; they can ask questions once the presenter is done.

5 **Debrief as a team and refine your idea.** Discuss and capture the opportunities to enrich your ideas. If you presented a Storyboard or Experience Map, work through the entire idea and note what worked and what did not and how it could be improved. Discuss what you learned about where and how the idea added value for the user. Enrich the ideas based on the feedback you received.

TIPS

There are a variety of prototyping methods that can be used for Co-creation — including Role-plays, Experience Maps, and Storyboards. In early development, it is often preferable to use low-resolution methods to give the audience the sense that you are "inviting them into the lab." The most important thing is being clear about your idea; just because your idea is presented in rough form doesn't mean you should be ad hoc in your presentation. Have a cohesive and compelling story to tell.

Give users a lot of credit. They are imaginative, intelligent, and generous in their effort to give you valuable feedback. They are your customers.

Avoid defending your ideas. Be open to criticism and graciously accept comments. In fact, you can even show enthusiasm for criticism — learning that something that doesn't work gives you the opportunity to fix it. That critical feedback will allow you to better refine your concept.

Remember that this is a learning experience for the team. Ask open-ended questions and let the users freely express their opinions.

Do not be discouraged with negative feedback. Try to distinguish between feedback on the intent and feedback on the execution.

This exercise also reveals new insights into your users, which may inspire more ideas that can enrich the concept.

WHAT MIGHT THIS LOOK LIKE?

The Nestlé Confectionery team wanted to test out their new idea that targeted teens. Acting out the experience provided the team with insights into how teenagers would experience a new idea. They did this by playing a typical day in the life of a teenager, moving from a scene by the lockers in the hallway of a school to a mock-up of a convenience store to a computer in a teen's room at home (figure 50).

FIG. 50 CO-CREATION AND RECREATING THE HIGH SCHOOL EXPERIENCE

GEAR 3: STRATEGIC BUSINESS DESIGN
Refocusing and Activating Your Strategy

THE PROPOSITION
Synthesizing the opportunity

WHY DO WE DO THIS?

To capture the outputs of Gears 1 and 2 and translate them into a value proposition. This will help summarize and clarify your business idea to be used as the foundation for Gear 3 and defining Where to Play and How to Win.

HOW CAN YOU DO THIS?

Summarize your progress as a team by articulating and synthesizing your findings as follows:

1. The Inspiration (Gear 1): Who is our target and what need will we satisfy?
- Reprise the Persona. What's the opportunity? How does this fit into her life?
- What unmet needs are you satisfying? Use the SPICE framework (social, physical, identity, communication, emotional) to help you think of the opportunity holistically.

2. The Idea (Gear 2): What will you uniquely deliver?
- Step back and discuss the big idea and the intent behind it.
- What is the overarching idea that will get the Persona excited?

3. Value to End User (Connecting Gear 1 to Gear 2): What's the benefit?
- How will the Persona benefit from this idea?
- How does the idea add value to her life in a meaningful way?

4. Value to Enterprise (Gear 3): What do we have to gain from this?
- What will it do for your business (at a high level)? (e.g., improve loyalty, provide notoriety and buzz, increase revenue stream, increase employee engagement)
- How will it set you apart from competitors?

5. What's the Overarching Proposition? (Synthesis of the above)
- What will you uniquely offer? (This is a synthesis of target, offering, and need fulfillment.)

TIPS

A really robust idea has many virtues. A strong central proposition will serve as a lighthouse in your ongoing quest to deliver the ultimate vision.

If necessary, prompt discussion by asking questions such as:
What inspired you in the first place?
How does this idea benefit end users in the most meaningful way?
What appealed to them most?

WHAT MIGHT THIS LOOK LIKE?

Figure 51 shows a synopsis of the Singapore WISH idea:

FIG. 51 SYNTHESIZING THE OPPORTUNITY

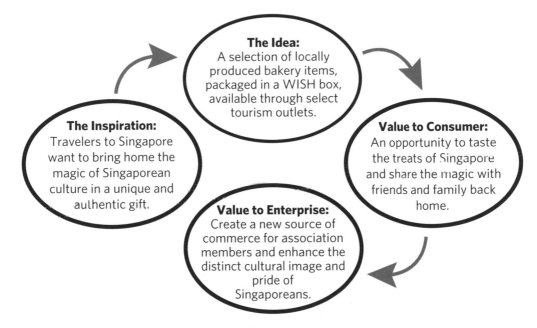

The Idea:
A selection of locally produced bakery items, packaged in a WISH box, available through select tourism outlets.

The Inspiration:
Travelers to Singapore want to bring home the magic of Singaporean culture in a unique and authentic gift.

Value to Consumer:
An opportunity to taste the treats of Singapore and share the magic with friends and family back home.

Value to Enterprise:
Create a new source of commerce for association members and enhance the distinct cultural image and pride of Singaporeans.

SINGAPORE WISH PROPOSITION
Deliver an authentic cultural experience and a unique gift collection of carefully selected, locally produced Singaporean bakery items to delight travelers from abroad.

CAPABILITY REQUIREMENTS
Delivering the breakthrough

WHY DO WE DO THIS?

To deconstruct the ideal experience and mindfully identify the capabilities required to deliver critical components of the experience. This exercise translates design tactics into capabilities, and then aligns those to internal or external resources. It can be a useful way to identify new or enhanced capabilities and options for strategic partnerships. It addresses the following questions:

- What are the tactical components of your envisioned experience?
- What will be required to develop and deliver the experience? What will you need to do well to win?
- What current enterprise capabilities could be leveraged?
- What are the requirements and costs to develop this?
- What external sources of expertise and potential partnerships are there?
- What is the strategy to develop or access new capabilities?

HOW CAN YOU DO THIS?

This exercise is best done in tandem with designing your Activity System, and will shape your strategy for developing capabilities, defining what you do internally and externally and revealing important priorities for investment and effort. By breaking down the critical components of your envisioned experience, you will be faced with important choices for the enterprise. Your first step is to determine the jobs to be done and who is best to do them.

1. **List all of your envisioned design components.** Identify the key components of the experience, including the people, objects, spaces, communications, and services (POEMS).

2. **Identify the capabilities required to develop and deliver each component.** Capabilities are the expertise and capacity required to deliver a product or service embedded in your envisioned experience. *For example, if you are designing a new coffee system (as Nespresso did), you will need machine design and manufacturing expertise.*

3. **Identify current enterprise capabilities.** Determine which current enterprise capabilities can be leveraged to fulfill those requirements. If capabilities do not exist now, you will need to decide whether you will develop them internally or draw on expertise external to your enterprise.

4 **Estimate costs to develop new or expanded capabilities internally.** If you do not know specific numbers, use your intuition and define the relative measures of High/Medium/Low as working measures. The amount of effort likely to be required is also a good measure of the cost. *For example, the cost associated with Nespresso's developing an appliance manufacturing capability is high, while the cost to advance and perfect proprietary capsule technology is lower.*

5 **Identify external sources of expertise.** If capabilities do not exist within your enterprise today, identify external sources of expertise through potential partnerships and suppliers. *For example, Nespresso could partner with world-class machine manufacturers like Krups and Magimix.*

6 **Define your capability-building strategy.** For each capability required to deliver your winning experience, assess your options on whether to leverage or expand existing internal capabilities or to leverage or establish external partnerships. Weigh the pros and cons of each scenario. After exploring and assessing your options (which will take a thorough and complete investigation over time), choose and define your capability-building strategy.

TIPS

It is helpful to refer to your final Experience Map or Storyboard and consider all components and design elements that make up your envisioned offering that will set you on a path to win.

Have your Current State Activity System in hand to identify which current enterprise activities and capabilities could be leveraged.

Keep your stakeholder Personas and needs on hand. You will want to preserve the integrity of your vision as it relates to serving your end user in particular.

Brainstorm possible options for how you could build these capabilities. Include creative options outside of typical practices and imagine all possible partners who might be involved. The Landscape of Players you may have developed earlier will come in handy.

Strategic partnerships are an ideal way to leverage the capabilities of other organizations, if those capabilities do not exist with your own organization. While you may begin by exploring a longer list of possible partners, you will need to assess the fit and viability (both operationally and financially) of these important decisions as you make critical strategic choices.

WHAT MIGHT THIS LOOK LIKE?

Figure 52 is a simple table showing how Nespresso might have assessed the capabilities required to deliver some of the key components of their vision:

FIG. 52 CAPABILITY REQUIREMENTS

Tactical Component	Capabilities Required	Current Enterprise Capabilities	Cost to Develop Internally	External Sources of Expertise	Development Strategy
Coffee Capsule	Quality coffee and delivery technology	Sourcing, patented technology and production expertise	Medium (to advance, perfect, & expand)	Not needed	Develop internally
High-Style, Quality Coffee Maker	World-class industrial design	Limited	Medium (but not currently core expertise)	Alessi	Work with top external designers
	Appliance expertise & manufacturing capacity	None	High	Krups, Magimix	Develop strategic partnerships
Brand Marketing	Branding & communications	Access to world-class marketing expertise & agency partners	Low-medium	Marketing partners	Develop internally, working with brand marketing partners
Direct Marketing	Data-base management, call center, & fulfillment excellence	Some corporate experience, though not core practice	Medium	Direct marketing partners	Work with of marketing partners
Fair Value Program	Grower relations & practice expertise	Nestlé expertise & established practices	Medium, if leverage parent company	Not needed	Develop in tandem with Nestlé

ACTIVITY SYSTEMS (Future)
Designing a strategy to win

WHY DO WE DO THIS?

To translate a rich new vision into an enterprise strategy to win and provide a framework for activation. Visualizing your strategy as a distinct system of interrelated activities will synthesize how you will create value in a distinctive and competitive way. It will focus your efforts on the areas of activity that matter most to your success. Value Exchange (described in a later tool) will also inform how you design your Activity System.

An Activity System is a visualization of strategy and is made up of:

> *Hubs:* Core activities that together define how the enterprise uniquely creates value

> *Supporting Activities:* Specific activities that fortify hubs

> *Linkages:* How hubs and activities relate to and reinforce each other to create value

A powerful Activity System is one in which a unique system of activities synergistically creates value for both the market and the enterprise.

HOW CAN YOU DO THIS?

Like much of the Business Design process, Gear 3 is an iterative process and incorporates the work you do in several areas, including Capability Requirements, Value Exchange, and Reciprocity. Your Activity System for the future takes all of these areas into account and sets the stage for activation. Here is a general guideline on how to go about designing a future-state Activity System:

1 **Reprise your proposition.** This is your synthesis of the opportunity and value proposition that serves as the anchor in your quest.

2 **Decide what combination of core activities will be most critical to your success.** These are the key four or five "hubs" that will enable you to deliver on your proposition, create the most value for your end user, and ultimately provide the greatest return on investment for the enterprise. These hubs will capture what you must do well both internally and through

any important outside alliances you will cultivate. Because they are activity based, these elements should be phrased as something you actively *do*: for example, *Build Strong Brand/Consumer Relationships, Leverage Scale.* I have reprised the Nespresso system as an example of this methodology (see figure 53). In this case, key strategic activities included: deliver a premium coffee experience globally, deliver a uniquely integrated and stylish coffee system, cultivate direct relationships with consumers, and create shared value (social and environmental responsibility). These are the core, inter-related hubs in the system.

3 **Define how these hubs relate to one another.** All good systems are synergistic — that is, their components are mutually reinforcing. In the case of Nespresso, many of the hubs are mutually reinforcing. For example, delivering a premium coffee experience is related to delivering a uniquely integrated and stylish coffee system.

4 **Identify specific activities related to these hubs.** These are specific activities that focus efforts on delivering tangible outcomes. In the case of Nespresso, partnerships with appliance manufacturers specifically reinforce the delivery of an integrated and stylish coffee system. The proprietary capsule reinforces both this coffee system and the delivery of a premium coffee experience.

5 **Assess, iterate, and define your strategy as a distinct and synergistic system.** As with the exercise of capturing your current state, this process of synthesis and visualization is iterative. You will want to work through the design of your system until you believe you have a tightly connected, synergistic, and unique system of activities.

TIPS

Value Exchange assessment (described in a later tool) will also inform how you configure your Activity Systems.

It is valuable to capture the strategy depicted by your Activity System in a story to explain how the system works and uniquely creates value. This story should describe how you create value through the following:

Overarching Proposition: *What does our enterprise uniquely offer the market?*
Hubs: *What are the core drivers of our business today that define our strategy?*
Activities: *What specific and concrete activities reinforce those hubs?*
Relationships: *How do hubs and activities relate to and reinforce one another?*
Distinctiveness: *How is this system distinct from others? How will it create competitive advantage?*

In assessing your new Activity System, refer to the Activity System Assessment tool that follows.

WHAT MIGHT THIS LOOK LIKE?

Figure 53 is a visualization showing how Nespresso might have integrated their distinct activities into a system.

FIG. 53 NESPRESSO ACTIVITY SYSTEM

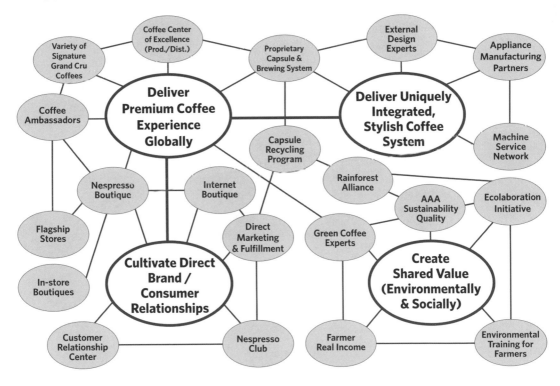

ACTIVITY SYSTEM ASSESSMENT
Evaluating your enterprise strategy

WHY DO WE DO THIS?

To evaluate the chosen strategy for How to Win as a means of creating value and advancing competitive advantage. This is the ultimate test of your strategy, inspired by Roger Martin's work on Activity Systems as a strategy consultant.

HOW CAN YOU DO THIS?

Ask yourself the following questions:

Does your envisioned strategy create value?

- How will the envisioned strategy create value for end users? How will this system of activities meet users' unmet needs in a new and meaningful way?
- How do the activities create value for the enterprise?
- How does the strategy create value for other key stakeholders? How will they win? (See the Value Exchange tool.)

Is your strategy a breakthrough?

- To what extent does your new Activity System enable you to deliver a new and meaningful proposition to the market?
- How does it change the rules of the game vis-à-vis the competition and within the current Landscape of Players?
- Does it represent a meaningful evolution of your current strategy?

Is it distinctive?

- Is your market-inspired idea and set of enterprise activities distinctive in the market relative to known competitors in this game? (See Activity Systems: Visualizing competitive strategies.)
- Could it preempt other (anticipated) players on the landscape?
- Does this strategic Activity System give you a distinct advantage?

Does the system fit?

- How do the activities complement and reinforce each other? Is it a cohesive and synergistic set of activities?
- How does it leverage what you are already good at doing? Does it fit with your current strategy or does it represent a significant departure from your current strategy? (See the tips in the Activation Planning tool on how to manage different scenarios.)

Does this system create a sustainable advantage?

- How long can you sustain an advantage with this strategy?
- How likely is it to be imitated?
- What aspects of your envisioned system are difficult for others to replicate?

TIPS

Now is the time to be objective and analytical rather than enthusiastic because you are in love with your ideas and vision. If your system "fails the test," revisit it and design ways to make it stronger and more distinctive.

This is best done as a group, with candor and objectivity. This will solidify your collective commitment.

Get the objective input of others; it is helpful to call on senior mentors and trusted advisors.

ACTIVATION PLANNING
Assessing how to resource and manage innovation

WHY DO WE DO THIS?

To determine the best way to structure resources to pursue your vision within the context of the current enterprise. Too often we try to squeeze innovation initiatives into our current "To Do" list, or force-fit them into current operations, thereby jeopardizing the integrity of the bigger idea.

HOW CAN YOU DO THIS?

Here are some possible ways in which you might activate and manage your new vision.

Evolution: Embed your new thinking into your existing business. Pursue this option if the new vision offers the potential for a natural lift in your business — that is, if it represents a step up and forward from where you are today, if it has the potential to drive growth in a more accelerated fashion, and if it can be activated in the short term without risking current business. *For example, the Nestlé Confectionery team reframed their opportunity and refocused their long-term strategy for their core business, activating a stream of initiatives that both supported the current business and set them on a path toward their longer term vision.*

Parallel Stream: If your vision requires a dedicated focus on establishing your new strategy to accelerate progress or before anticipated competition emerges, you may decide to set up a separate team internally to work in tandem with the team that is working on keeping the cash register ringing today. If your current and future strategies are leveraging the same system to a strong degree, and the individual teams can benefit from working side by side and informing each other's work, this can be a good way to build both the current, short-term business and the longer-term business. *For example, in my days at Procter & Gamble, we sometimes split the Brand team into Current Business and Future Business. That allowed us to stay focused on keeping today's business strong while positioning us for greater competitive advantage in the future.*

Separate Unit: Sometimes it makes more sense to completely split off the new business and think of it as a start-up. To assess this option, it is helpful to think of your current Activity System and Management Systems. Setting up a new working unit is a good move if there is any risk that the new idea could be "watered down" in the current system or, worse, forced to conform to current practices in a way that would compromise the intent of the new strategy. This does not mean that you can't call on the parent enterprise for counsel and collaboration, but it allows you to operate with more freedom and a more customized decision-making system than you would have if you were working within the current enterprise structure. *For example, Nespresso has operated as a separate unit of Nestlé since its inception, and has been allowed to pursue a compatible but demonstrably different business strategy than the parent enterprise.*

Here are some things to consider in activating your strategy:

1 **Compare your new Activity System to your current one.** Ask yourself the following questions:
- How different is this new strategy (as defined by the system of activities) from your current one? Is it radically different, or a natural extension of your current strategic direction, or somewhere in between?
- Are there tensions between the current strategy and the new one? Tensions are ways of working or going to market that could come into conflict. For example, you might want to pursue a new way of marketing that does not fit with your current route to market; or the management systems that are effective in managing today's business may be different from those required to support the new strategy.
- How much of your current system will be leveraged in pursuing the new strategy?

2 **Reflect on the resources required.** This is a matter of both the people that will be needed to carry out your plans and the dedicated effort required. Consider the following questions:
- Do these resources and people have other (immovable) priorities? Will this plan cause them distraction either way? Can they recruit and designate other people in their group to do the work under their guidance?
- Will this pursuit demand more resources than the enterprise currently has in place? Does this require additional investment in staffing and development?

▣ **Consider the alternative organizational structures that may be required and the cost implications.** Your ultimate objective is to pursue your vision in a steady and focused manner without disruption to the current business or operations. Assigning a cost to that will make the business investment and accountability explicit. Costs may include people, research, development, and capital.

TIPS

Clearly, this is not a small decision, but one that requires you to develop a well-thought-out case for doing what is right for the enterprise today and in the future.

Prototype a number of scenarios and consider the costs, benefits, and risks of each. Finding the most appropriate and productive path is both a creative and an analytical process you can take on as a team.

This is where your executive sponsor can help you in designing and implementing the right organizational strategy. Your considerations will demonstrate commitment to both the current business and the future of the enterprise.

VALUE EXCHANGE
Designing the delivery and exchange of value

WHY DO WE DO THIS?

To translate design elements and the sequence of events in your envisioned experience into a value-creation exchange system among stakeholders. This helps you synthesize and visualize how value is created and, importantly, reveals opportunities for you and other stakeholders to *make* money through revenue streams and *save* money by finding the most effective and efficient ways to deliver your solution. This exercise will help you answer questions like: How does the market idea get created and delivered? Who are the key stakeholders and how is value exchanged among them? Where's the money? How can we be most effective and efficient with resources and expertise?

HOW CAN YOU DO THIS?

This exercise is best done in tandem with defining your Capability Requirements and designing your strategic Activity System, as you will ultimately need to decide what you will do internally and what you will do through partners. You will begin to explore the financial side through this exercise. The Reciprocity exercise (described in the next tool) broadens the assessment of value to ensure that this is a win-win for everyone in a broader sense, because value does not always have a clear price tag on it. An example from the Singapore WISH project is included as a real-life illustration.

1 **Define stakeholders and their roles.** Based on the outcome of your Capability Requirements, identify all of the relevant stakeholders who are a part of your solution and what they uniquely bring to the delivery of your envisioned solution. *For example, in WISH, the role of the producers could be to produce, manufacture, and co-package multiple products from various network producers, as well as to inventory and distribute finished gift boxes.*

2 **Define the key design elements (POEMS) and how they are delivered.** This defines how the design elements get created, produced, and delivered to the customer, including how value is created through enablers and influencers. *For example, in WISH, customer-facing elements include various promotional components (e.g., branding, communications, merchandising), the flagship shop, and the WISH box itself.*

3 Define how all parties may benefit and make money. While it is important to define what each stakeholder contributes to value creation and what each gets in return in the broadest sense, this exercise focuses on if and where stakeholders make money — one of the important incentives in business. While this is a conceptual exercise to intuitively explore the financial exchange, you will also need to work through the specific financials within this exchange. Reciprocity expands the definition of value to ensure that everyone wins in these broader terms. *In the WISH example, the most obvious source of revenue is the sale of the WISH box (from which retailers and producers benefit), but there are other partners who need to be paid in order to create and deliver all of the necessary design components.*

4 Visualize the exchange of value among them. Now is the time to begin to prototype your system into one ecosystem that links stakeholders to the delivery of the solution. Use sticky notes and large surfaces to begin to prototype your delivery and value exchange system.

5 Look for additional sources of financing and revenue. While you may already have identified the obvious ways to make money (for example, through selling a core product or service), this is the time to look for additional revenue streams. *In the case of WISH, would others interested in the promotion of Singapore find it beneficial to join the network and contribute their expertise or sponsorship?*

6 Look for efficiencies. Think of the cost of developing capabilities, as well as the effectiveness of the value chain. *In the example of WISH, utilizing existing capacity would be the most cost-efficient approach in production and co-packaging. While an alternative was to outsource co-packaging to a third party, this would have added extra cost to the value chain. Also, collaboration with others in the tourism business offered opportunities for quick and broad access, as did distribution through existing high-traffic retailers.*

7 Explore, prototype, iterate, and refine. Starting with an initial prototype, ask yourself the following questions: Is this the most effective and efficient way to deliver our envisioned solution? Are there other ways to go about this, ways to do this more cost-effectively, or ways to establish other potential streams of revenue? *In the case of WISH, there are future possibilities for capturing revenue from tourism sponsors and public enterprises interested in promoting Singapore.*

⑧ **Evaluate the unique role of your enterprise.** Determine how you (in this case the Industry Association and the member producers behind Singapore WISH) are uniquely positioned to create this solution and succeed. Reflect on the existing capabilities and interdependent relationships, and determine if these can be distinctly leveraged to contribute to success and competitive advantage. *In the case of Singapore WISH, the tight network of collaborative producers that deliver authentic Singaporean treats is not something anyone else could preempt or replicate, as it is anchored in "authentic" Singaporean products.*

TIPS

Your envisioned Experience Map will be an important reference, as you will want to preserve the intent of your envisioned solution.

Your Stakeholder Map, Personas, and Needs are helpful references to ensure that you deliver value to key stakeholders — the end user in particular.

Identifying Capability Requirements and designing your future Activity System are interrelated exercises that together will shape your strategy.

This is an iterative process; stakeholders and elements can be rearranged to reveal different models of value exchange. Using tools such as sticky notes and an erasable whiteboard lets you quickly plot and reorganize your visualization.

Consider ways to refine the system and improve both viability and efficiency by looking to external partners and technology. The Landscape of Players you may have developed earlier will come in handy here. Imagine all possible partners who could help you deliver your new idea, and how they could deliver and receive value.

After consolidating and refining your system of Value Exchange, refer to the tips on Reciprocity (see the next tool) to consider how best to sustain the system.

WHAT MIGHT THIS LOOK LIKE?

In the following example from Singapore WISH (figure 54), the roles of all the stakeholders involved in developing and delivering key components of the envisioned experience were mapped and refined to create the following visualization. Dollar signs indicate where there is a financial benefit to stakeholders.

FIG. 54 SINGAPORE WISH VALUE EXCHANGE

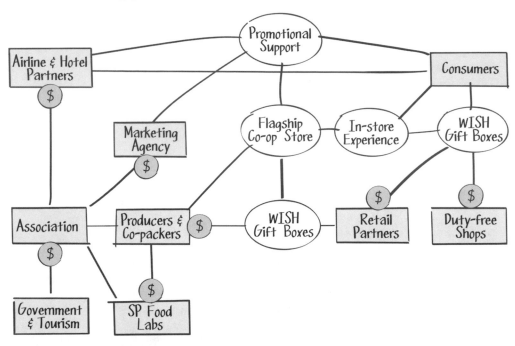

Capabilities & Roles

Association – Brand marketing, orchestration of alliances, orchestration of producers.

Producers – Product and manufacturing experience, supplying quality products, co-packing, inventory, and delivery.

SP Food Labs – Technical expertise on formulations and packaging.

Retail Partners – Consumer access and distribution.

Airline & Hotel Partners – Traveler access and distribution.

Marketing Agency – Branding, packaging, marketing services, and communications (advertising, merchandising, etc.).

Government & Tourism – Potential financial support or sponsorship finding.

RECIPROCITY
Balancing value exchange in the ecosystem

WHY DO WE DO THIS?

To ensure that there is a balanced give and take among stakeholders within the new value-creation ecosystem. "Reciprocity" means that everyone is giving and receiving value, both financial and non-financial. Ensuring reciprocity is a key factor in a sustainable solution. To determine if you have done so, you will ask questions like: Is everyone providing and receiving value in a balanced fashion? Is this a sustainable exchange system?

HOW CAN YOU DO THIS?

1 **Identify all of the stakeholders who are critical to success.** This includes your end customer, key strategic partners, enablers, and your enterprise as a whole. They are all connected to your Activity System. They are your key to activating your strategy, creating value, and fortifying your competitive advantage.

2 **Articulate what value each of them gives and receives.** This could be financial (they receive money), emotional (they feel better in a relevant and meaningful way), reputational (they experience enhanced status or brand image), or practical (they gain access to new markets or to information that benefits them). This value is easily captured in a simple "balance sheet" chart.

3 **For each stakeholder, assess the balance of give and take.** However value is defined for that stakeholder, it is important to design for a fair and balanced exchange. This will keep stakeholders motivated to participate and stay committed to a sustained effort.

4 **Assess how your enterprise adds unique value.** Most important in the end is to ensure that your enterprise is uniquely positioned to drive the system, and that you cannot be swapped out for another enterprise.

TIPS

It is helpful to refer to your work on your envisioned Activity System, Capability Requirements, and Value Exchange.

Value should not be seen only in monetary terms or in terms of strictly equivalent transactions. In this exercise, you address the broader motivation and benefits for each stakeholder to be "in the system," considering the many ways in which all stakeholders can benefit.

This exercise requires an ongoing commitment to understanding the needs of your important stakeholders as a way to sustain the ecosystem and fortify your position within it over time.

WHAT MIGHT THIS LOOK LIKE?

An excellent example of an enterprise that has a well-balanced ecosystem is Nespresso. They have multiple stakeholders — consumers, retailers, farmers, environmental alliances, machine designers, manufacturers, and servicers. Nespresso is fully committed to ensuring that everyone wins through an ongoing effort to bring value to every stakeholder in the system. They also bring unique capabilities to the system — in marketing, proprietary capsule technology, quality assurance, and global access. The following chart (figure 55) is a simple snapshot of what some of the stakeholders give and receive and of how Nespresso adds value for them.

FIG. 55 ASSESSMENT OF BALANCED EXCHANGE

STAKEHOLDER	WHAT THEY GIVE	WHAT THEY RECEIVE	HOW NESPRESSO ADDS VALUE FOR THEM
Machine manufacturers	Manufacturing capability and capacity	Capacity utilization, revenue, quality brand name visibility and association	Access to global distribution, proprietary capsule technology, commitment to quality, marketing expertise, and a strong brand
Retailers (outside the flagship boutiques)	Consumer access through mini-boutiques	Revenue from sales, merchandising support	Marketing expertise and strong brand image/ demand
Coffee bean growers	Quality beans	Revenue, help in business and growing practices	Shared value through a commitment to fair trade and expertise in business and growing practices

FINANCIAL SENSITIVITY ANALYSIS
Assessing uncertainty and risk

WHY DO WE DO THIS?

To assess and mitigate investment risk by identifying unknowns that could have significant impact on financial outcomes. This information will help you to design your development plan and enterprise strategy to maximize success. It will also inform both your Activity System and Value Exchange and help you determine which Experiments you want to conduct (as described in the next tool).

Most companies have strong financial acumen and can run lots of numbers to calculate revenue scenarios and variations in known costs. The method described here is designed to help you isolate and examine the *unknown* variables (often operationally based) that can have unexpectedly negative financial effects if not considered and allowed for properly. Having defined tangible solutions and the play-by-play of the experience, you will be equipped to determine which variables present risk. This is the time to take a critical and analytical look at what could go wrong, what the financial impact might be, and, most importantly, how you can design both your Experiments and your system to reduce risk and maximize the chances of success.

This exercise involves building confidence in your model by studying variables and planning for them in order to make the financial model more robust. By identifying key variable costs for each stage of a proposed solution, you can plan for potential vulnerabilities and identify ways to manage risk.

HOW CAN YOU DO THIS?

1 **Deconstruct your experience and assess the degree of certainty associated with executing specific design elements.** Identify the key components that make up the solution and identify which are more certain and which are unknown. *For example, if you are strong in the area of manufacturing familiar products, you can likely predict the quality and cost of delivered goods. If your solution calls for a new mode of delivery, like mobile service units or distribution through new sites, you may have less experience in how that works and the sales or costs associated with it.*

2 **Identify the variable costs and revenue drivers associated with key elements.** For each stage of your solution, identify:

- *Variable costs:* expenses that change in proportion to business activity (e.g., call-center activity, service calls) and operational uncertainties, particularly things that might go wrong (e.g., vending machines or trucks breaking down in a new delivery channel or product returns associated with a money-back guarantee);
- *Revenue drivers:* activities that determine the amount of money a company receives in a period of time (e.g., number of units sold, or sales by channel of distribution).

③ **Isolate the unknown factors and test financial sensitivities.** Based on your collective experience and intuition, determine which of the unknown variables can have the biggest impact on financial performance. These are the ones you will want to explore first in spreadsheet form, and subsequently test in the real world through Experiments. If you have negative outcomes, you will want to find ways to design around them in order to mitigate risk. *For example, you may explore the relative daily sales through two different points of distribution (e.g., an office site and a convenience store) or the use and durability of a vending machine in a high-traffic site.* These will become elements of your experimentation plan.

④ **Design learning experiments.** Experiments are not necessarily aimed at go/no go decisions (though they can be); rather, their purpose is to help you identify what you need to consider and do to mitigate risk and maximize success. As noted in the Experiments tool (the next tool), you will want to design the experiment to produce measurable outcomes with a clear articulation of how the results will be used.

TIPS

Helpful things to refer to: your Experience Map, Capability Requirements, Activity System (Future), and Value Exchange.

This exercise does not include fixed costs such as capital costs or the costs of building a website, though such costs will definitely factor into your overall payout plan. This exercise focuses on identifying high-risk variables.

Conversely, those elements that represent a low risk may proceed in development or be rolled out as Quick Wins (see the tips in the Quick Wins tool, below).

EXPERIMENTS
Testing the unknowns

WHY DO WE DO THIS?
To gain valuable learning that will shed light on uncertainties and potential risks, giving the enterprise the confidence to move to the next level of development and rollout. Experiments are a form of prototyping that provide observable and measurable learning outcomes about whatever part of your new idea has never before been done (by you, and even others). This is a good way to "test the waters" on market uptake, explore risk variables from your Financial Sensitivity Analysis, and gain valuable learning on how to deliver the best user experience. The goal of Experiments is not to collect "proof" but rather to gain learning on how to design the best means of delivering your vision and fortify your *reason to believe that you are on the right track.*

HOW CAN YOU DO THIS?
1 **Isolate the elements of your idea that present the most uncertainty and potential risk.** These are the elements that, if they go wrong, the user experience or business model is at risk, often revealed through Financial Sensitivity Analysis of variables. These could include uncertainties about the product itself, the way it is used or breaks down, uptake in a new distribution channel, the effectiveness of an important new communication element, or a logistical challenge. These are the elements you are dependent upon for success.

2 **Create a hypothesis.** For each experiment, use your intuition to predict how it will help you learn how to increase the odds of success. *For example: Will doctors appreciate and use patient counseling tools? Will people be drawn to a product that is made available at a new site? Will they use and appreciate a technical hotline? Will an institutional dispensing machine be usable and durable in a designated high traffic site?* Use this prediction to generate a hypothesis.

3 **Design an experiment.** Create a small-scale experiment to test your hypothesis by brainstorming a number of options to gain more insights or information. *For instance, if you are wondering about the viability and relative sales of a product through two different channels, or the impact of having a sales person on site, or aiding purchase decisions through an on online kiosk, set up a paired comparison experiment.* Make sure you are clear on what needs to be measured and how you will measure it.

☐ **Define your expected use of results.** It is important to anticipate the range of results you might get, including worst-case scenarios. Define what kinds of results you are hoping for (in measurable terms) and what you will do if you don't achieve those results. This is not necessarily a go/no-go experiment, but rather a way to gain learning so you can design alternatives to mitigate risk and be more assured in the path you subsequently decide to take. Even if you fail, you will get valuable insights on how to resolve or improve your solution.

☐ **Execute, evaluate, and refine.** Determine what you will do with the learning to move the idea forward. Use this information to refine each element or to revisit your Activity System or to provide evidence that your idea will work and your strategy is sound.

TIPS

Refer to your envisioned Experience Map, Prototypes, Activity System, and Financial Sensitivity Analysis when identifying key experiments.

Time and money spent testing and validating executional variables at an early stage can help both "test the waters" on market interest and avoid costly mistakes, improving your payout in the long term. With a small investment in time and money, you can create Experiments that can help enrich your idea and ultimately grow your business. Try imposing financial constraints to think of new ways to test your assumptions. *For example, re-skin an existing piece of equipment in a new location instead of redesigning something new that will take more money and time.*

Experiments should produce measurable outcomes and actionable learning.

WHAT MIGHT THIS LOOK LIKE?

In the early days of Nespresso, former CEO Jean-Paul Gaillard's team went out to home-appliance outlets in Geneva, Lausanne, and Nyon and started selling machines to individual customers. His goal was to try this out for a week to see if they could sell 100 machines. In the end, they sold fifty-eight (in addition to twenty-five sold to offices), which helped Gaillard and his team learn that there was a market for these products, though previous market research had concluded that there was no market. From there, Gaillard moved ahead and launched Nespresso nationally in Switzerland.[40]

QUICK WINS
Capitalizing on learning out of the gate

WHY DO WE DO THIS?
To activate new learning and ideas in a way that will benefit the enterprise in the short term, and set it on the path toward the new vision. Unlike an Experiment, there is little or no risk associated with a Quick Win. On the contrary, this will enable you to leverage new insights and ideas to make an immediate positive impact on your business. Sometimes Quick Wins are about taking something you were already doing and doing it better. Sometimes they are about replacing a tactic that you now know does not create much user value with one that does. Often, the Quick Win can be knocking something off your "To Do" list that wasn't really going to create value at all. These are all Quick Wins. That is where Business Design can help you both *make* money and *save* you time and money. This is the opportunity to take stock of all of your learning and ideas and ask: How could we create value *now*?

HOW CAN YOU DO THIS?
1 **Reflect on the learning from your development process that is relevant to your current business.** This may be a new insight that inspires a tactical move to help you address a short-term challenge or an idea from your grander vision that fits well with your current strategy and activities. *For example, new insights may lead you to recast a short-term promotional effort to be more relevant and in keeping with your new vision.*

2 **Identify the smaller, tactical elements of your idea that can benefit your business today.** These are the elements for which you are confident that there is virtually no downside and a good potential upside for better meeting your stakeholders' needs. This could include ways to better serve the end user or to enhance the motivation and engagement of an important enabler. These are the ideas that you should not hold back, as they are valuable to stakeholders and/or the enterprise today. Ideas may come in any form — process improvement, revenue-generating opportunities, new distribution channels, better communications, or an improvement to a product or service that can make it better almost right away. *For example, in the healthcare case presented in the chapter on Gear 1, implementing an expanded "fast track" initiative for patients who presented specific symptoms was immediately doable and valuable.*

☐3 **Leverage your learning and make a plan to activate Quick Wins.** The beauty of this process is that there is always instant value to your discoveries and development efforts. You have gained new understanding of your stakeholders, have fresh ideas, and can show value for your efforts right away.

☐4 **Execute, gather learning, and celebrate your early wins.** This is a great way to build confidence in the value of Business Design. This will also signal the start to pursuing your longer-term vision and motivate the team.

TIPS

Ideas do not have to be expensive. Sometimes a small, simple tactic at the right place and time can generate surprisingly positive outcomes.

Don't forget to cut things off your current project list that you now know aren't going to create value.

MANAGEMENT SYSTEMS
Designing support systems and measuring what matters

WHY DO WE DO THIS?

To design systems to support the job to be done and define what needs to be measured to monitor and assess performance against goals. New value-creating solutions and a new enterprise strategy to deliver them often call for an evolution or even revolution in management and measurement systems. Inserting a new solution and strategy into existing systems can sometimes be counter-productive and can impede progress. By identifying what support systems are required and what measurements need to be put in place to gauge the success of a new strategy, the enterprise will be able to make business decisions that support responsible progress. It is critical to be explicit in these areas and ensure alignment at the outset of your quest. The key questions you will need to address are: What systems need to be put in place to implement and manage the new vision effectively? What do you need to measure and how will you measure the things that matter most?

HOW CAN YOU DO THIS?

Management Systems

Consider what management systems are needed to support your quest, using the following as guidelines:

[1] **What systems need to be in place to execute effectively?** These could include new go-to-market systems, inventory-management systems, quality-control systems, communication systems, or recruiting practices. These are essentially the systems and protocols that will enable you to move forward effectively and efficiently, in order to ensure responsiveness, quality, or management of critical factors in delivering your solution to the market. Systems are important because they bring order and alignment, accelerate progress, and enable you to scale effectively.

☑ **What systems are currently in place?** Assessing your current management systems and processes will identify what systems are already in place and embedded in the way you do business. In an existing enterprise, these are often a key factor in your go-to-market and operational success.

☑ **Leverage and reconcile.** You may have some systems that will give you a good start. There may also be systems that could impede progress because they support the current way of doing business but not the new strategy. Identify what you can leverage, what new systems you will need to establish, and, importantly, where there may be conflict in management systems.

☑ **Design how your system will integrate and be explicit about conflicts.** This is important in assessing how you will manage your new initiative or strategy and getting alignment from others on how you will move forward. This should be considered in tandem with your Activity System Assessment.

Measurement

Define what metrics and methods of measurement will be most relevant and actionable. Using an approach similar to one for designing management systems, ask questions like: How will you measure progress? How does this fit (or not) with your current decision-making measures? Often a new idea calls for measuring new dimensions of progress. Here are some things to consider:

① **Business Results.** Define your goals and the key factors that will demonstrate business performance, and include sales (dollars or units), costs, profit, points of distribution, turnover, and so on. These may be the same measures you currently use, or you may adjust them. *For example, moving from a low-cost, mass-market product to a premium, high-end product may require an adjustment to dollar sales (if you are historically a "volume-driven" manufacturer that aims to maximize capacity utilization).*

② **Quantitative tracking research.** These are key "indicators" that you might want to track. Questions are often closed-ended and focus on predetermined indicators of success. These could include awareness, trial, satisfaction, referrals, repurchase, loyalty, or frequency of use. These are the quantitative measures you will want to keep your eye on and course-correct as necessary.

③ Qualitative research. This will provide new insights that may emerge unexpectedly and can give you new ideas on how to enhance customer value or correct a deficiency. If certain expected results aren't being achieved, explore this openly with customers. Who knows better about what is working, or not working, than your customers? Instead of assuming what is broken, conduct interviews with your customers to find out their key complaints. This type of research is open-ended, and is a source of ongoing discovery, inspiration, and valuable feedback.

TIPS

When you begin defining metrics, prioritize measures, putting what matters most at the top of the list. Focus your measurements on those that are of high value to your business in both the short term and the long term. That way you can begin to gather valuable learning and take immediate steps to maximize success.

As with the design of management systems and processes, it is critical to get alignment with key decision makers on measurements up front. Be clear on what will be measured, why, and how you will measure it. Also include decision-making criteria, much as you defined the "expected use of results" in Experiments.

ACKNOWLEDGMENTS

I am always inspired by insightful and generous people who have a genuine devotion to helping others learn and succeed. This book is written in that spirit, and is a reflection of all of those who have made the advancement of Business Design a collaborative and important quest in enhancing personal and collective potential, either within an educational institution or in the enterprise world at large. There have been many people I'd like to recognize and thank for their contributions and support throughout this journey.

At the top of the list is Roger Martin, Dean of the Rotman School of Management at University of Toronto. A visionary leader with perspective, intelligence, and foresight, Roger staked out important new territory in integrating design into business education and practice. He invited me to join him in this quest in 2004 and has been an invaluable inspiration and coach to me since the day I joined Rotman. Co-founding DesignWorks, Rotman's Strategy Innovation Lab, and developing the relevance and practice of Business Design together has been an incredibly fulfilling mission. Roger has been generous in sharing his wisdom and bringing his sharp strategic mind to advancing the discipline of Business Design, and advocating the importance of this practice in both education and industry. He also provided invaluable feedback on the development of this book.

DesignWorks would not be a force today if not for the support of our benefactors who are committed to advancing business education. Marcel Desautels' vision and generous contribution to the Rotman School funded the start-up of DesignWorks. Joseph Rotman spent time with students on many occasions, inspiring them on the need for fresh thinking and an entrepreneurial design-inspired approach to building a business. Both of these men are intuitively 'design thinkers' and appreciate the need to inject a new way of thinking into business education and practices.

Within the educational space, there are some particularly important people who have contributed to the integration of design and business. David Kelley, a life-long innovator who co-founded IDEO and established Stanford's d.school, was one of the original DesignWorks collaborators, as was Patrick Whitney, Dean of the Institute of Design at Illinois Institute of Technology, along with Vijay Kumar in the early days of our Procter & Gamble training. Jules Goss of the Ontario College of Art and Design University brought his design perspective and Industrial Design students to our first Summer Fellowship Program and our first joint course in 2006. Job Rutgers, also from

OCAD University, has been a dedicated ongoing design partner in advancing our educational collaboration over the past five years and contributing to our quest in Singapore. Jeanne Liedtka of the University of Virginia's Darden School of Business, Sara Beckman of the University of California's Haas School of Business, Nathan Shedroff of the California College of the Arts, and I have openly collaborated to bring value to our respective students, culminating in our shared 2010 award from the Academy of Management in teaching design principles and practices to MBA students.

Our pursuit would not have been as relevant or pragmatic if not for enterprise leaders who embraced the principles of Business Design as a means to unleash greater potential in their organizations through both DesignWorks training and project work. At the top of that list is Procter & Gamble, my alma mater and one of the most forward-thinking companies on the planet. Claudia Kotchka, who led the charge of expanding design thinking across the organization globally, also made important contributions to this book through her reviews of drafts of the manuscript and through the interviews featured in this book in which she shares her wisdom. Cindy Tripp was instrumental in codifying and expanding design thinking training to every corner of the P&G world.

There were other industry pioneers that gave us a canvas to hone training methodologies and demonstrate the potential of Business Design through projects: the world-class Princess Margaret Hospital (led by Sarah Downey at the time), the team at Medtronic, Sandra Martinez and Elizabeth Frank of Nestlé Confectionery, Veronica Piacek of Pfizer, and Ann Mukherjee and Thomas Gosline of Frito-Lay. There were a host of other companies who engaged in learning programs and supported research projects. There have been others whose participation has been mutually beneficial, but whose identity will remain confidential; to those, I say: "You know who you are. Thank you. You have made a valuable contribution to the development of an important discipline."

I have to call out Singapore as a country of pioneers who have fully embraced the potential of Business Design. Philip Yeo saw huge value in bringing Business Design to Singapore in his role as Chairman of SPRING and Special Advisor for Economic Development in the Prime Minister's Office in 2008. Debbie Ng helped make that happen. The Singapore Polytechnic team, led by Principal Tan Hang Cheong and Deputy Principal Hee Joh Liang, took on the mission of bringing this new discipline to their country as a means of both educating a new generation and bringing out the best in established entrepreneurs. There is now a long roster of Business Design pioneers in Singapore who are breaking new ground in their quest to innovate and grow.

Our bank of knowledge and evidence that Business Design *works* would not be where it is today without the commitment of the DesignWorkers — the graduates and collaborators who have joined the pursuit with passion, intelligence, and a dedication to advancing the discipline. Haris Blentic was the first to enlist in the P&G challenge. Mark Leung and Eugene Grichko signed up in 2006 and have shown unwavering commitment to our mission, contributing to many important research projects, including the Princess Margaret Hospital project presented in this book. Eugene is also the caretaker of the Rotman DesignWorks brand and the illustrator of this book. Mark keeps the DesignWorks operations running smoothly as we grow and expand internationally. Grace Park brings energy and fresh insight to our executive workshop programs and enterprise coaching. Stefanie Schram, dedicated to the cause from her first day at Rotman, has contributed to research and projects while developing and delivering our executive training programs. David Brown, also a dedicated Business Design graduate, brought an entrepreneurial spirit to our quest in Singapore, along with Stewart Shum. Carolyn Meacher, lifelong colleague and collaborator, has brought wisdom to the team with her many years of experience and expertise in innovation coaching. Danielle Waxer helped immensely in orchestrating the many interviews and clearances required for the publication of this book. This core team has made an important contribution to MBA student learning, executive training, and research.

A special thanks to Alpesh Mistry, a long-standing member of the Design-Works team, my longtime teaching partner, and my primary collaborator on the book. He helped gather input for the development of methods and cases, and kept the project running smoothly with his organizational skills and diligence.

There have also been a number of other Rotman collaborators who have brought expertise and insights to our work over the years. There is an incredible wealth of talent and insight at Rotman. Those who have made a distinct contribution include Mengze Shi, my partner in the first MBA Business Design Practicum; Brian Golden, who invited us in to redesign the Princess Margaret Hospital experience; Melanie Carr, a psychoanalyst with insights into human nature and behavior; Maria Rotundo, an expert in organizational behavior and culture; and Ken McGuffin, Manager, Media Relations, who continually opens doors to propagate our message. Steve Arenburg, Executive Director of Advancement Events and Strategy, and Karen Christensen, Editor-in-Chief of *Rotman Magazine*, both brought insights and expertise in plotting out the original vision for this book and bringing it to market.

That brings me to the book itself. Contributing to an international publication is a true sign of generosity. While some of the research and project work we have done at DesignWorks is confidential for good reasons, we have benefited from those who have been able to share their cases and wisdom to help others learn from their experiences. I'd like to thank each of them in order of appearance in the book. Tim Brown of Nestlé Canada introduced me to the folks at Nespresso, Guillaume Le Cunff and Hans-Joachim Richter, who were very open-source about their path to success. Isadore Sharp of Four Seasons Hotels and Resorts, an incredibly gracious and highly successful entrepreneur, shared his insights on both the human and the strategic side of building a successful enterprise. With the support of Andrew Bridge and Christine Choi, I was introduced to Sir Richard Branson, the visionary behind the Virgin Group, who shared his insights on how to build a customer-centric business and an enterprise culture of breaking the mold in a strategic way. Sarah Downey of Princess Margaret Hospital shared her DesignWorks story to inspire other organizations in creating a new vision for patient care. Earl Bakken, co-founder of Medtronic (the world's leading medical device company), shared his wisdom on the value of dreams and intuition. Elizabeth Frank of Nestlé shared her DesignWorks case and perspectives on collaboration and shared strategic visioning. The Singapore Polytechnic team, along with their sponsoring partner, the Singapore Bakery and Confectionery Trade Association, shared their DesignWorks story as an example of how to re-envision the future and redefine their strategy to set them on a new path. Procter & Gamble and Claudia Kotchka shared their DesignWorks story on enterprise transformation, while Thomas Gosline of Frito-Lay reaffirmed the value of Business Design to an enterprise transformation-in-progress.

Writing a book is a major production. University of Toronto Press's Jennifer DiDomenico provided valuable ongoing support through reviews, design, and management of the project. Editor Penny Tomlin helped bring order and clarity to the manuscript in its early development. Margaret Allen helped to hone the final product, and Anne Laughlin to bring it to press. Designer Natalie Olsen created a distinct typography and layout that enhanced both the style and functionality of the content of this book.

And where would any author be without the support and inspiration of her family? My husband, Neil, is an innovator at heart. He and his team at Medtronic embraced the potential of Business Design through a number of defining student projects early on in DesignWorks' research and development. He has also been an important sounding board and advocate for the relevance and applicability of the principles and practices of Business Design. My philosophically minded designer daughter, Ceilidh, inspires me on an ongoing basis in so many ways. She is a constant source of inspiration with her empathy, mindfulness, originality, and devotion to meaning and the power of intrinsic motivation. She exemplifies the potential for dreams in the making.

My last note of gratitude goes to my late parents. My mom brought inspiration as a humanitarian and inspired artistic thinker, and my analytically minded dad grounded me in the realities of big business as a corporate president who humbly believed that being "smart" is simply a matter of curiosity and hard work. Together, they instilled in me the important mindsets and thinking that underpin the integrated discipline of Business Design.

In the spirit of open source collaboration, I hope that this book opens the doors for new possibilities and brings both inspiration and some pragmatic tips on how to leverage the power of Business Design in unleashing the innate imagination and ingenuity of your enterprise teams. I truly believe that *everyone designs.*

NOTES

1   Roger Martin, correspondence with Heather Fraser, September 2004.

2   Ministry of Finance, Singapore, *Report of the Economic Strategies Committee* (Singapore: Author, 2010).

3   Quotations from enterprise leaders from executive workshops held between 2005 and 2011.

4   Roger Martin, *The Design of Business: Why Design Thinking May Be the Next Competitive Advantage* (Boston: Harvard Business Press, 2009).

5   Deb Powers, eHow, Demand Media Inc., "About Coffee Drinking Trends." Available at: http://www.ehow.com/about_4574027_coffee-drinking-trends. html. Accessed 26 September 2011.

6   Hans-Joachim Richter and Anna Lundstrom, Nestlé Nespresso S.A. Corporate Communications, correspondence with Heather Fraser, August–October 2011.

7   Bruce Nussbaum, Robert Berner, and Diane Brady, "Get Creative! How to Build Innovative Companies," *BusinessWeek*, 1 August 2005. Available at: http://www. businessweek.com/print/magazine/content/05_31/b3945401.htm?chan=gl. Accessed 3 October 2011.

8   Created by Heather Fraser and Roger Martin in collaboration with David Kelley and Patrick Whitney. Developed in October 2005.

9   Participant from a Singapore Polytechnic Management Workshop held at Singapore Polytechnic in Singapore, February 2011.

10   Heather Fraser, "Business Design: Becoming a Bilateral Thinker," *Rotman Magazine* (Winter 2011): 70–6.

11   Roger Martin "Five Questions to Build a Strategy," *HBR Blog Network, Roger Martin* (blog), 26 May 2010. Available at: http://blogs.hbr.org/martin/2010/05/ the-five-questions-of-strategy.html.

12   Isadore Sharp, *Four Seasons: The Story of a Business Philosophy* (New York: Portfolio, 2009).

13   Isadore Sharp, interview by Heather Fraser, 4 May 2011. All quotations from Isadore Sharp in this book are from this interview.

14   For reasons of confidentiality, some details of the project have been omitted.
       Rotman DesignWorks Project: Cardiac Patient Pathways Project Plan, 2007.
       Team members: Jasmin Kwak, Alpesh Mistry, Sandra Ochoa, Rohit Singla.
       Expert Coaches: Heather Fraser, Mark Leung

15   Heart and Stroke Foundation, "Emergency Signs and Actions – for Life." Available at: http://www.heartandstroke.com/atf/cf/{99452D8B-E7F1-4BD6-A57D-B136CE6C95BF}/Emergency-signs-actions-for-life-en.pdf. Accessed 26 September 2011.

16   Dante Morra, MD, correspondence with Heather Fraser, August 2008.

17   Vijay Kumar and Patrick Whitney, "Faster, Cheaper, Deeper User Research," *Design Management Journal* (Spring 2003): 50–7.

18   SPICE framework based on an analysis of a multi-project database of need-finding research outcomes conducted by Heather Fraser in collaboration with Eugene Grichko, 2007–8.

19   Sir Richard Branson and Virgin Management USA Corporate Communications, correspondence with Heather Fraser, March–October, 2011. All quotations from Sir Richard Branson in this book are from this correspondence.

20   *Rotman DesignWorks Project:* Princess Margaret Hospital — Systemic Therapy
      Redesign, 2007.
          Team members
          Princess Margaret Hospital: Sarah Downey, Dr Mark Minden, Janice Stewart,
          Sara Urowitz, Dr David Wiljer
          Rotman DesignWorks: Heather Fraser, Eugene Grichko, Mark Leung
          Rotman School of Management: Brian Golden, Rosemary Hannam
          Donors: Conway Foundation and MDS Inc.: John Rogers, Ron Yamada
21   Brian R. Golden, Rosemary Hannam, Heather Fraser, Mark Leung, Sarah
      Downey, Janice Stewart, and Eugene Grichko, "Improving the Patient
      Experience through Design," *Healthcare Quarterly 14,* 3 (2011): 32–41.
22   Kumar and Whitney, "Faster, Cheaper, Deeper User Research."
23   Earl Bakken, interview by Heather Fraser, 5 June 2011. All quotations from Earl
      Bakken in this book are from this interview.
24   North Hawaii Community Hospital, "NHCH Celebrates 15th Anniversary."
      7 June 2011. Available at: http://www.nhch.com/cms/Static/News.aspx?id=26.
      Accessed 6 October 2011.
25   Earl Bakken, *One Man's Full Life* (Minneapolis: Medtronic Inc., 1999).
26   Singapore Polytechnic WISH Project, 2010–11
          Singapore Polytechnic Team: Keng Hua Chong, Gareth Lai, Kum Yee Lau,
          Lay Leng Low, Phyllis Peter, June Tan Teck
27   Michael E. Porter, "What Is Strategy?" *Harvard Business Review* (November–
      December 1996): 61–78.
28   Hans-Joachim Richter and Anna Lundstrom, Nestlé Nespresso S.A. Corporate
      Communications, correspondence with Heather Fraser, August–October 2011.
29   Roger Martin, *The Opposable Mind: How Successful Leaders Win through
      Integrative Thinking* (Boston: Harvard Business School Press, 2007).
30   Guillaume Le Cunff, correspondence with Heather Fraser, August–September
      2011.
31   Based on a strategic planning initiative led by Sandra Martinez, President,
      Nestlé Confectionery Canada, and Elizabeth Frank, Vice-president, Marketing,
      Nestlé Confectionery Canada, in 2008.
32   Elizabeth Frank, interview by Heather Fraser, 3 August 2011. All quotations from
      Elizabeth Frank in this book are from this interview.
33   Jamshid Gharajed, *Systems Thinking: Managing Chaos and Complexity: A Platform
      for Designing Business Architecture* (Boston: Butterworth-Heinemann, 1999), 25.
34   Claudia Kotchka, interview by Heather Fraser, 22 July 2011. All quotations from
      Claudia Kotchka in this book are from this interview.
35   Thomas Gosline, correspondence with Heather Fraser, September–October
      2011.
36   The Marshmallow Challenge was initially created by Peter Skillman, the former
      VP of Design at Palm, Inc.
37   Peter Schwartz, *The Art of the Long View: Planning for the Future* (New York:
      Currency Doubleday, 1991).
38   Kumar and Whitney, "Faster, Cheaper, Deeper User Research."
39   Ibid.
40   Constantinos Markides and Daniel Oyon, "Changing the Strategy at Nespresso:
      An Interview with Former CEO Jean-Paul Gaillard," *European Management
      Journal 18,* 3 (2000): 296–301.

RECOMMENDED READING

Books

Berger, Warren. *Glimmer: How Design Can Transform Your World*. Toronto: Vintage Canada, 2010.

Brown, Tim. *Change by Design*. New York: Harper Business, 2009.

Buxton, Bill. *Sketching User Experiences: Getting the Design Right and the Right Design*. San Francisco: Morgan Kaufmann, 2007.

Diller, Steve, Nathan Shedroff, and Darrel Rhea. *Making Meaning: How Successful Businesses Deliver Meaningful Customer Experiences*. San Francisco: New Riders Press, 2008.

Govindarajan, Vijay, and Chris Trimble. *Ten Rules for Strategic Innovators: From Idea to Execution*. Boston: Harvard Business Press, 2005.

Kelley, Thomas. *Art of Innovation*. London: Profile Books, 2003.

Kelley, Thomas, and Jonathan Littman. *The Ten Faces of Innovation: IDEO's Strategies for Defeating the Devil's Advocate and Driving Creativity throughout Your Organization*. New York: Currency Doubleday, 2005.

Lafley, A.G., and Ram Charan. *The Game-Changer: How You Can Drive Revenue and Profit Growth with Innovation*. New York: Crown Business, 2008.

Liedtka, Jeanne, and Tim Ogilvie. *Designing for Growth: A Design Thinking Tool Kit for Managers*. New York: Columbia Business School Publishing, 2011.

Lockwood, Thomas. *Design Thinking: Integrating Innovation, Customer Experience and Brand Value*. New York: Allworth Press, 2009.

Martin, Roger. *Design of Business: Why Design Thinking Is the Next Competitive Advantage*. Boston: Harvard Business Press, 2009.

Martin, Roger. *The Opposable Mind: How Successful Leaders Win through Integrative Thinking*. Boston: Harvard Business School Press, 2007.

Mau, Bruce, and Institute without Boundaries. *Massive Change*. New York: Phaidon Press, 2004.

Moggridge, Bill. *Designing Interactions*. Cambridge, MA: MIT Press, 2006.

Osterwalder, Alexander, and Yves Pigneur. *Business Model Generation: A Handbook for Visionaries, Game Changers, and Challengers*. Hoboken, NJ: John Wiley & Sons, Inc., 2010.

Paradis, Zachary Jean, and David McGaw. *Naked Innovation: Uncovering a Shared Approach for Creating Value*. Chicago: Author, 2007.

Patnaik, Dev, and Peter Mortensen. *Wired to Care: How Companies Prosper When They Create Widespread Empathy*. Upper Saddle River, NJ: FT Press, 2009.

Pink, Daniel H. *A Whole New Mind: Why Right-Brainers Will Rule the Future*. New York: Riverhead Books, 2005.

Roam, Dan. *The Back of the Napkin (Expanded Edition): Solving Problems and Selling Ideas with Pictures*. New York: Portfolio, 2010.

Schrage, Michael. *Serious Play: How the World's Best Companies Simulate to Innovate*. Boston: Harvard Business School Press, 1999.

Shedroff, Nathan. *Experience Design*. San Francisco: Waite Group Press, 2001.

Snyder, Carolyn. *Paper Prototyping: The Fast and Easy Way to Design and Refine User Interfaces*. San Francisco: Morgan Kaufmann, 2003.

Suri, Jane Fulton. *Thoughtless Acts? Observations on Intuitive Design*. San Francisco: Chronicle Books, 2005.

Verganti, Roberto. *Design Driven Innovation: Changing the Rules of Competition by Radically Innovating What Things Mean*. Boston: Harvard Business Press, 2009.

Articles

de Waal, Frans B.M. "How Animals Do Business." *Scientific American* (April 2005): 73-9.

Fraser, Heather. "Business Design: Becoming a Bilateral Thinker." *Rotman Magazine* (Winter 2011): 70-6.

Fraser, Heather. "Designing through Dynamic Decision-Making." *Rotman Magazine* (Winter 2010): 80-3.

Fraser, Heather M.A. "The Practice of Breakthrough Strategies by Design." *Journal of Business Strategy 28*. 4 (2007): 66-74.

Fraser, Heather. "Turning Design Thinking into Design Doing." *Rotman Magazine* (Spring/Summer 2006): 24-8.

Houde, Stefanie, and Charles Hill. "What Do Prototypes Prototype?" *Handbook of Human Computer Interaction* (1997): 367-81.

Johnson, Mark W., Clayton M. Christensen, and Henning Kagermann. "Reinventing Your Business Model." *Harvard Business Review 86*, 12 (2008): 50-9.

Kumar, Vijay, and Patrick Whitney. "Faster, Cheaper, Deeper User Research." *Design Management Journal* (Spring 2003): 50-7.

Martin, Roger. "Design and Business: Why Can't We Be Friends?" *Journal of Business Strategy 28*. 4 (2007): 6-12.

Martin, Roger. "The Design of Business." *Rotman Magazine* (Winter 2004): 7-11.

Martin, Roger. "Tough Love: Business Wants to Love Design, But It's an Awkward Romance." *Fast Company* (October 2006): 54-7.

Patnaik, Dev, and Robert Becker. "Needfinding: The Why and How of Uncovering People's Needs." *Design Management Journal (Former Series)* (1999): 37-43.

Porter, Michael. "What Is Strategy?" *Harvard Business Review* (1996): 61-78.

INDEX

listening and recording, 46, 113, 114, 167–9; tips for conducting an interview, 168; visualization of interview roles and note taking, 169

Magimix, 12, 69, 213, 214
management systems, 21, 22, 80, 113, 115, 221, 235–7
mapping: competency, 92, 113, 114, 123–4; competitor activity system, 92, 113, 114, 134–7, 218; current activity system, 74, 92, 113, 114, 129–33, 213; experience, 60, 95, 113, 115, 197–8, 199, 202, 203, 205, 206, 213, 225, 230, 232; "Mapping the Mess," 142; mind, 46, 113, 114, 170–1, 174, 177; motivational, 46, 113, 114, 172–3, 174, 177; stakeholder, 32–3, 38, 41, 46, 104, 113, 114, 142, 143, 144, 155–7, 158, 159, 164, 225
marshmallow prototyping exercise, 120, 121
Martin, Roger, 1, 2, 5, 13, 64, 70, 218; enterprise strategy framework (five choices), 20–1
Martinez, Sandra, 81
Medtronic, 3, 42, 53, 58–9
metaphors, 60, 113, 115, 193, 195–6; and case of early childhood education, 195, 196; and Princess Margaret Hospital (PMH) project, 196
methods/activities, 17–20; activation planning, 80, 115, 121, 219, 220–2; activity system assessment, 80, 113, 115, 218–19, 236; broadening the lens, 32–3; capability requirements, 65, 80, 113, 115, 212–14, 215, 223, 225, 227, 230; co-creation, 18, 23, 55, 60, 66, 95, 101, 108, 113, 115, 199, 200, 201, 202, 203, 205–7; collaboration, 14, 17, 18, 23, 50–1, 52, 57, 58, 64, 84, 85–6, 88, 91, 95, 100, 102, 103–4, 108, 117, 120, 202–4; competency mapping, 92, 113, 114, 123–4; competitor activity system mapping, 92, 113, 114, 134–7, 218; current activity system mapping, 74, 92, 113, 114, 129–33, 213; deep dive, 33, 35, 43, 46, 114, 134, 158; discovery exchange, 46, 113, 114, 172, 176–7, 179, 180; empathy exercises, 46, 113, 114, 153–4; establishing the team, 84, 85–7, 91, 92, 113, 114, 118–19; experience design, 52; experience mapping, 60, 113, 115, 197–8, 199, 202, 203, 205, 206, 213, 225, 230, 232; experimentation, 7, 18, 64, 65, 76, 77, 78, 80, 98, 101, 113, 115, 199, 229, 230, 231–2, 232, 233, 237; facilitation, 92, 113, 114, 125–6, 128, 176; financial sensitivity analysis, 80, 115, 229–30, 231, 232; for Gear 1 (list), 32–3, 113, 114; for Gear 2 (list), 52, 113, 115; for Gear 3 (list), 65–6, 113; ideation, 52, 60, 66, 113, 115, 192–4;

198, 199; iterative prototyping, 18, 22, 52, 60, 64, 65, 66, 73, 95, 100, 113, 115, 132, 136, 199–200, 224; landscape of players, 92, 113, 114, 140–1, 144, 213, 218, 225; listening and recording, 46, 113, 114, 167–9; management systems, 21–2, 80, 115, 221, 235–7; "methods" defined, 6; metaphors, 60, 113, 115, 193, 195–6; mind mapping, 46, 113, 114, 170–1, 174, 177; motivational mapping, 46, 113, 114, 172–3, 174, 177; need-finding research, 15, 18, 33, 34–6, 40, 41, 43, 46, 95, 113, 114, 158–60, 178, 182; need mining and analysis, 46, 114, 172, 178–81; observation, 46, 113, 114, 150–2, 172; photo elicitation, 46, 113, 114, 159, 161, 162, 164–6, 167; for preparing for your quest (list), 84, 113, 114; reciprocity, 80, 113, 115, 215, 223, 224, 225, 227–8; role-playing, 60, 82, 113, 115, 197, 199, 200, 201–2, 205, 206; sense making and synthesis, 33, 92, 113, 114, 142–3; stakeholder mapping, 32–3, 38, 41, 46, 104, 113, 114, 142, 143, 144, 155–7, 158, 159, 164, 225; STEEP analysis, 92, 113, 114, 138–9, 141, 142, 143, 144; storyboarding, 49–50, 60, 113, 115, 199, 200, 203–4, 205, 206, 213; storytelling, 18, 46, 66, 95, 198; subject profiles, 46, 113, 114, 174–5, 177, 183, 185; systems mapping, 18, 64, 66, 95; team-building exercises, 92, 113, 114, 120–2; user journals, 46, 113, 114, 159, 161–3, 167, 171, 177, 183; value exchange, 65, 80, 113, 115, 215, 216, 218, 223 6, 227, 229, 230; visualizing, 18, 22, 64, 66, 95, 103, 146, 188. See also outputs
mind mapping, 46, 113, 114, 170–1, 174, 177; mind map of a patient interview, 171
mindfulness, 19, 43
mindsets, 17–20; courage and vulnerability, 19; embracing constraints, 19; empathy, 19, 24, 26, 43, 52, 57, 72, 84, 168, 172; in Gear 1, 43–4; in Gear 2, 52, 57–8; in Gear 3, 66; intrinsic motivation, 19, 43, 52, 57; mindfulness, 19, 43; openness, 19, 24, 25–6, 43, 52, 58; optimism/positivity, 19, 52, 58, 66; resilience, 19, 66
motivational mapping, 46, 113, 114, 172–3, 174, 177; and Princess Margaret Hospital (PMH) project, 173
multiple prototyping. See iterative prototyping

need articulation, 32, 46, 51, 113, 114, 172, 174, 177, 180, 182–3; and Princess Margaret Hospital (PMH) project, 182

projects: healthy eating project, 139, 140; heart rhythm device project (healthcare company story), 27–32, 34, 36–7, 39, 40, 42, 48, 76, 155, 156, 233; Nestlé Confectionery project, 81–3, 84, 85–6, 87, 91, 100, 202, 207, 220; Princess Margaret Hospital (PMH) project, 2, 47–51, 53, 56, 173, 182, 184, 188–9, 192, 194, 196, 198, 204; Procter & Gamble (P&G) project, 2, 3, 14, 19, 35, 93–4, 109; project brief for the Royal Conservatory, 145; Singapore WISH project, 61–4, 66–8, 71, 72, 76, 211, 223–6

proposition, 21–2, 65, 66, 67, 80, 113, 115, 210–11, 215

prototypes: and design language, 102; iterative prototyping, 18, 22, 52, 55, 60, 64, 65, 66, 73, 95, 100, 113, 115, 132, 136, 199–200, 224; low resolution, 55, 103, 199, 200, 206; marshmallow prototyping exercise, 120, 121; pacemaker prototype, 58–9; prototyping a system for organic waste disposal, 200; rapid, 199

quick wins, 7, 64, 65, 76, 77, 78, 80, 96, 113, 115, 230, 233–4

reciprocity, 80, 113, 115, 215, 223, 224, 225, 227–8; and Nespresso value exchange, 228

resilience, 19, 66

role-playing, 60, 82, 113, 115, 197, 199, 200, 201–2, 205, 206; and Nestlé Confectionery project, 202, 207

Rotman DesignWorks, 2, 4, 5, 14, 15, 17–18, 21, 43–4, 104, 120, 132, 136, 142, 147, 164; heart rhythm device project (healthcare company story), 27–32, 34, 36–7, 39, 42, 48, 76, 155, 156, 233; Nestlé Confectionery project, 81–3, 84, 85–6, 87, 91, 100, 202, 207, 220; Princess Margaret Hospital (PMH) project, 2, 47–51, 53, 54, 56, 173, 182, 184, 188–9, 192, 194, 196, 198, 204; Procter & Gamble (P&G) project, 2, 3, 14, 19, 35, 93–4, 109; as Strategy Innovation Lab, 20. See also Business Design; Singapore Polytechnic/DesignWorks

Royal Conservatory, 145

SAP, 3

scalability, 74

seamlessly integrated experience, 34, 51, 55, 62, 113, 130, 197

seniors, 143, 145, 153, 154

sense making and synthesis, 33, 92, 113, 114, 142–3

Sharp, Isadore, 24–6, 53, 74, 78–9, 88, 101

Singapore Bakery and Confectionery Trade Association (SBCTA), 61–4, 68

Singapore Polytechnic/DesignWorks, 3, 23, 44, 96; Inspiration Corridor, 102; Singapore WISH project, 61–4, 66–8, 71, 72, 76, 211, 223–6. See also Business Design; Rotman DesignWorks

Singapore WISH project, 61–4, 66–7, 71, 72, 77; activity system, 67–8; and POEMS framework, 223; proposition, 211; and value exchange, 223–6

SPICE framework, 37–40, 177, 178, 210

stakeholder mapping, 32–3, 38, 41, 46, 104, 113, 114, 142, 143, 144, 155–7, 158, 159, 164, 225; caring for seniors stakeholder map, 143; healthcare company stakeholder maps, 155, 156, 157. See also stakeholders

stakeholders: 6, 15, 22, 30, 31–2, 33–4; enablers, 41–2, 155; end users, 41, 42, 53, 55–6, 155; engaging, 55–6, 102, 205–6; influencers, 42, 119, 155; and reciprocity, 227–8; stakeholder exchange and sustainability, 72–3; three categories of, 41–2. See also personas; stakeholder mapping

STEEP analysis, 92, 113, 114, 138–9, 141, 142, 143, 144

storyboarding, 60, 113, 115, 199, 200, 203–4, 205, 206, 213; and Princess Margaret Hospital (PMH) project, 49–50, 204

storytelling, 18, 66, 198; contextualizing the opportunity through empathic storytelling, 46, 113, 114, 187–9; listening to consumer stories, 18, 31, 35–7, 40, 43, 82, 167–9; recounting/capturing interview stories, 176, 177; value to market and enterprise of, 95. See also photo elicitation; storyboarding; user journals

Strategic Business Design (Gear 3), 2, 16–17, 20, 22, 61–80, 82–3, 113, 115, 122, 129, 140, 209–37; activation phase, 76–7; activation planning, 80, 113, 115, 121, 219, 220–2; activity system assessment, 80, 113, 115, 218–19, 236; activity system (future), 80, 113, 115, 215–17, 225, 230; capability requirements, 65, 80, 113, 115, 212–14, 215, 223, 225, 225, 227, 230; experiments in, 64, 65, 76, 77, 78, 80, 113, 115, 229, 230, 231–2, 233; financial sensitivity analysis, 80, 113, 115, 229–30, 231, 232; goal in, 65; management systems, 21, 22, 80, 113, 115, 221, 235–7; methods/activities for (list), 65–6, 113, 115; mindsets in, 66; outputs of (list), 65, 113; principles and frameworks of, 66–78; proposition, 21–2, 65, 66, 80, 113, 115,